RETHINKING CANADIAN AID

2015-02-26

To Molly,
It's great to finally meet you!

Stephen Brown

RETHINKING CANADIAN AID

EDITED BY

Stephen Brown, Molly den Heyer
and David R. Black

University of Ottawa Press
2014

u Ottawa

The University of Ottawa Press gratefully acknowledges the support extended to its publishing list by Canadian Heritage through the Canada Book Fund, by the Canada Council for the Arts, by the Federation for the Humanities and Social Sciences through the Awards to Scholarly Publications Program and by the University of Ottawa.

Copy editing: Susan James
Proofreading: Joanne Muzak
Typesetting: Counterpunch Inc.
Cover design: Llama Communications

Library and Archives Canada Cataloguing in Publication

Rethinking Canadian aid / edited by Stephen Brown, Molly den Heyer, David R. Black.

Includes bibliographical references and index.
Issued in print and electronic formats.
ISBN 978-0-7766-2211-8 (pbk.). – ISBN 978-0-7766-2174-6 (pdf). –
ISBN 978-0-7766-2174-6 (epub)

1. Economic assistance, Canadian. 2. Canada – Economic policy.
3. Canada – Foreign economic relations. I. Brown, Stephen, 1967– , editor
II. Den Heyer, Molly, 1972– , editor III. Black, David R. (David Ross), 1960– , editor

HC60.R47 2015   338.91'71   C2014-908036-0
                                            C2014-908037-9

Printed in Canada by Gauvin Press

Table of Contents

Acknowledgments

This book would not have been possible without a Connections Grant from the Social Sciences and Humanities Research Council of Canada, whose generous support allowed us, among other things, to hold an authors' workshop at Dalhousie University in September 2013, organized by Dalhousie's Centre for Foreign Policy Studies and the University of Ottawa's School of Political Studies, and ably coordinated by David Morgan. We are very grateful to all authors for their exceptional efforts to meet the tight timeframes of this project and to the other participants in the workshop who greatly enhanced the quality of the discussion. We also thank others who contributed to the success of the workshop, especially Jill Campbell-Miller, Mary Ruth Machan and Ben O'Bright.

In addition, we would like to thank Taylor & Francis Ltd. for allowing us to publish Chapter 10, which has been adapted from an article that originally appeared in French in the *Canadian Foreign Policy Journal*, as well as the Canadian International Council for publishing excerpts from some of the conference papers on their OpenCanada.org platform (CIC 2013a) and hosting a live video conversation on the theme of Rethinking Canadian Aid, moderated by John McArthur (CIC 2013b). We are also grateful to the University of Ottawa Press staff, especially Lara Mainville, Dominike Thomas and Elizabeth Schwaiger, for their support and assistance; to Dana Hayward, for help with the manuscript preparation; to Susan James for copy-editing, Linda Gustafson for typesetting, Joanne Muzak for proofreading and Heather Ebbs for indexing; and to the University of Ottawa for funding that permitted this book to be available via open access.

Stephen Brown, Molly den Heyer and David R. Black
December 2014

References

Canadian International Council. 2013a. "Rethinking Canadian Aid," September 16. Internet, http://opencanada.org/features/rethinking-canadian-aid/.

Canadian International Council. 2013b. "Starting a New Canadian Aid Conversation: A Live Discussion," September 17. Internet, http://opencanada.org/features/the-think-tank/video/starting-a-new-canadian-aid-conversation-a-live-discussion/.

Abbreviations

AGDM	Age, Gender and Diversity Mainstreaming
AIDS	Acquired Immunodeficiency Syndrome
AusAID	Australian Agency for International Development
BCE	Before Common Era
CBC	Canadian Broadcasting Corporation
CCCI	Conseil canadien de coopération international
CCIC	Canadian Council for International Co-operation
CDFAI	Canadian Defence and Foreign Affairs Institute
CEDAW	Convention on the Elimination of All Forms of Discrimination Against Women
CGD	Center for Global Development (United States)
CIDA	Canadian International Development Agency
CIDP	Canadian International Development Platform
CIFP	Country Indicators for Foreign Policy
CIGI	Centre for International Governance Innovation
CIRDIS	Centre interdisciplinaire de recherche en développement international et société (Interdisciplinary Research Centre in International Development and Society, Université du Québec à Montréal)
CORA	Canadian Opinion Research Archives
CPDF	Country Development Programming Framework (CIDA/DFATD)
CSO	Civil society organization
CSR	Corporate social responsibility
DAC	Development Assistance Committee (OECD)
DANIDA	Danish International Development Agency
DFAIT	Department of Foreign Affairs and International Trade

DFATD	Department of Foreign Affairs, Trade and Development
DFID	Department for International Development (UK)
DND	Department of National Defence
DPG	Development Partners Group (Tanzania)
ECLAC	Economic Commission for Latin America and the Caribbean (UN)
EITI	Extractive Industries Transparency Initiative
EU	European Union
FATDC	Foreign Affairs, Trade and Development Canada
FCAS	Fragile and conflict-affected states
FDI	Foreign direct investment
FEWER	Forum on Early Warning and Early Response
GAD	Gender and development
GDP	Gross Domestic Product
GE	Gender equality
GHA	Global Humanitarian Assistance
GNI	Gross National Income
GOC	Government of Canada
GPSF	Global Peace and Security Fund
HI	Humane Internationalism
HIV	Human Immunodeficiency Virus
ICN	Inter-Council Network
IDPS	International Dialogue on Peacebuilding and Statebuilding
IDRC	International Development Research Centre
IMF	International Monetary Fund
INCAF	International Network on Conflict and Fragility (OECD)
IPS	International Policy Statement

LDC	Least Developed Country
MDG	Millennium Development Goals
MNCH	Maternal, Newborn and Child Health
MP	Member of Parliament
MPH	Make Poverty History
NATO	North Atlantic Treaty Organization
NGDO	Non-governmental development organization
NGO	Non-governmental organization
NORAD	Norwegian Agency for Development Cooperation
NPM	New Public Management
NSI	North–South Institute
OAG	Office of the Auditor General
ODA	Official development assistance
OECD	Organisation for Economic Co-operation and Development
PAGER	Policy and Advocacy Group for Emergency Relief
PCIA	Peace and Conflict Impact Assessment
PD	Paris Declaration
PM	Prime minister
PRSP	Poverty Reduction Strategy Paper
QWIDS	Query Wizard for International Development Statistics (OECD)
RBM	Results-based management
SCEAIT	Standing Committee on External Affairs and International Trade
SCFAID	Standing Committee on Foreign Affairs and International Development
SEMAFO	Société d'exploitation minière–Afrique de l'Ouest
SFU	Simon Fraser University
SIDA	Swedish International Development Cooperation Agency

SOCODEVI	Société de coopération pour le développement international (Canadian Cooperation Society for International Development)
START	Stabilization and Reconstruction Task Force
UBC	University of British Columbia
UNDESA	United Nations Department of Economic and Social Affairs
UNDP	United Nations Development Programme
UNGOMAP	United Nations Good Offices Mission in Afghanistan and Pakistan
UNHCR	Office of the United Nations High Commissioner for Refugees
UNIIMOG	United Nations Iran-Iraq Military Observer Group
UNIKOM	United Nations Iraq-Kuwait Observer Mission
UNOSOM	United Nations Operation in Somalia
UNPD	United Nations Population Division
UNPROFOR	United Nations Protection Force (Yugoslavia)
UNSC	United Nations Security Council
UNTAG	United Nations Transition Assistance Group (Namibia)
USAID	United States Agency for International Development
USD	United States dollars
WAD	Women and development
WGWR	Working Group on Women's Rights
WID	Women in development
WUSC	World University Service of Canada

Introduction:
Why Rethink Canadian Aid?

Stephen Brown, Molly den Heyer and David R. Black

The Need to Rethink Canadian Aid

There has been no shortage of recent calls for "reinventing" or "re-imagining" Canadian foreign aid to respond to the litany of problems that emerged over the forty-five-year lifespan of the Canadian International Development Agency (CIDA), including excessive bureaucracy, slow delivery and frequently shifting priorities (Carin and Smith 2010; Gordon Foundation 2010). Yet there was general surprise in March 2013 when the Canadian government announced its institutional solution: merging CIDA with the Department of Foreign Affairs and International Trade, creating in June 2013 the new Department of Foreign Affairs, Trade and Development (DFATD) – a megalith with no fewer than four Cabinet ministers.

The merger will prove disruptive in the short run and it is unlikely that it will solve the more fundamental issues plaguing Canadian aid (Gulrajani 2012). A more fundamental "rethinking" is required, linked to a national conversation on the topic. Why do Canadians provide foreign aid? What is its role in the international arena? How is Canadian aid delivered and who benefits from it? How does, and should, aid relate to other foreign, security, economic, and commercial policy priorities? Where and how has aid been successful in improving development prospects? Conversely, what persistent weaknesses are associated with aid policy and practice? To what extent can these weaknesses be identified, addressed, and corrected?

Canadian aid requires analytical "rethinking" at four different levels, which this book addresses to varying degrees. First, we undertake a collective rethinking of the foundations of Canadian aid, including both its normative underpinnings – an altruistic desire to reduce poverty and inequality and achieve greater social justice, a means to achieve commercial or strategic self-interest, or a projection of Canadian values and prestige onto the world stage – and its past record. Second, many chapters analyze how the Harper government is itself rethinking Canadian aid, including greater focus on the Americas and specific themes (such as mothers, children and youth, and fragile states) and countries, increased involvement of the private sector (particularly Canadian mining companies), and greater emphasis on deploying aid to advance Canadian self-interest. Third, several contributors rethink where Canadian aid is or should be heading, including recommendations for improved development assistance. Fourth, serious rethinking is required on aid itself: the concept, its relation to non-aid policies that affect development in the global South, and the rise of new providers of development assistance, especially "emerging economies." Each of these novel challenges holds important implications for Canada and other "traditional" Western donors, questioning their development policies and highlighting their declining influence in the morphing global aid regime. The fourth "rethink" is the most difficult and speculative form of rethinking, requiring more concerted and wide-ranging investigation than we were able to accomplish in this volume. We do, however, return to this theme in the conclusion of this volume.

The State of the Debate

At present, the literature that addresses these issues is struggling to keep up with rapidly changing Canadian and international contexts. Over the last decade, the debate on development assistance and its contributions to Canada's role in the world has been re-energized by a series of shifts in the Canadian and international landscapes. Globally, the emergence of a new class of donor countries or "aid providers" (including Brazil, Russia, India, China, and South Korea), the financial crisis of 2007–08 and ongoing economic turbulence have shaken the foundations of North–South relationships. Among other things, these changing global conditions have thrown into question the donor–recipient taxonomy and dynamics that have typically framed research on development assistance. Against this changing backdrop, Western aid donors, orchestrated by the Organisation for Economic Co-operation and Development (OECD), have undertaken significant efforts to restructure the international aid architecture with global initiatives such as the Monterrey Agreement, the Millennium Development Goals, and the Paris Declaration on Aid Effectiveness. Whether or not these efforts are regarded as successful, these trends continue to resonate in the Canadian context.

There is growing uncertainty as to what the goals of Canada's international development assistance policies are and should be, as well as how these goals relate to other Canadian foreign policy objectives. Historically, Canadian scholars have analyzed the intent of aid in terms of a spectrum ranging from altruism to self-interest, whether understood narrowly or in more enlightened terms (see, for example, Freeman 1982; Nossal 1988; Pratt 1994). The latter perspective highlights how policies formally aimed at poverty alleviation are often used to advance Canada's (or the Canadian elite's) security, diplomatic and/or commercial objectives. These debates were brought to the fore once again with the introduction of the "3D" approach in the early 2000s, later expanded and reframed through the "whole-of-government" lens. This post-9/11 approach combined defence, diplomatic, commercial, and development objectives, with particular relevance to Canada's mission in Afghanistan, in ways that organized policy coherence around security objectives and consequently diminished the weight given to development priorities (Brown 2008).

In another example, CIDA's funding and policy relationship with non-governmental organizations (NGOs) and the private sector began to shift in 2008–09 to become more closely aligned with trade and investment objectives, as manifested in the co-funding of projects with Canadian mining companies and the prioritization of middle-income countries in the Americas at the expense of poorer African ones with less promising commercial prospects. The mixed motives and lack of clear vision for Canadian aid undermine clarity of purpose in the design and implementation of projects, and obfuscate appropriate criteria to determine success (Brown 2012a; den Heyer 2012). They also contradict the spirit of the Official Development Assistance Accountability Act of 2008, the purpose of which is "to ensure that all Canadian official development assistance abroad is provided with a central focus on poverty reduction" (Minister of Justice 2013, 1). The persistent uncertainty surrounding the core objectives of Canadian aid, combined with a changing international development landscape, underscores the pressing need for a renewed scholarly dialogue regarding the foundation and rationale for Canadian aid, and how first principles of intervention should be translated in practice.

Brown (2012a) argues that the existing scholarly literature on Canadian aid can be understood in terms of three distinct eras. From the beginning of Canadian aid in the 1960s up until the 1990s, the literature was rooted in distinct ideological approaches that manifested as a radical critique of the intentions of aid, a relatively benign liberal vision of Canadian aid, or a right-wing critique of development inefficiencies. By the 1990s, however, this ideological approach gave way to a more instrumental approach that produced an analysis of the history, motivations, and policies embedded in Canadian aid and in relation to foreign policy. While these works created a strong academic foundation, the end of the Chrétien era and political uncertainty in the new millennium left scholars and practitioners with still more questions regarding the future structure and functioning of the Canadian aid bureaucracy.

In this third and current era of scholarly analysis, there has been an upsurge in institutional grey literature and scholarly publications concerning the structure and functioning of the Canadian aid bureaucracy. For example, the 2007 *Senate Report on Africa* presciently asked whether CIDA should be abolished (Standing Senate Committee on Foreign Affairs and International Trade 2007; see also Brown and Jackson 2009). This conversation was taken up in a series of reports from organizations such as the Canadian International Council, the Walter and Duncan Gordon Foundation, and the Canadian Defence and Foreign Affairs Institute (Greenspon 2010; Carin and Smith 2010; Gulrajani 2010; Johnston 2010; Swiss with Maxwell 2010). These analyses examined the effectiveness of Canadian aid in comparison with the efforts of other OECD countries, highlighting CIDA's own persistent failures and foreshadowing the agency's amalgamation with the Department of Foreign Affairs and International Trade.

Similarly, there has been a renewal of academic analyses, including a special issue of the *Canadian Journal of Development Studies* in 2007 dedicated to "The Canadian International Development

Agency: New Policies, Old Problems" and, more recently, two edited volumes: *L'aide canadienne au développement : bilan, défis et perspectives* (Audet, Desrosiers, and Roussel 2008) and *Struggling for Effectiveness: CIDA and Canadian Foreign Aid* (Brown 2012b). Building on these contributions, a more coordinated and comprehensive effort is required to strengthen the scholarship on Canadian aid, closer links should be forged with policy making and practice, and more foundational questions are needed to undergird this process.

The Contents of this Book

Though a single volume cannot by itself fill all the gaps identified above, this book is an attempt to advance understanding and promote further rethinking of Canadian aid. We kept chapter lengths deliberately short in order to include as many voices as possible. The contributors include twenty-one scholars and practitioners, with several straddling both categories, from all career stages. The resulting sixteen chapters are designed to reach a variety of audiences, including academics, students, policy makers, practitioners in governmental and non-governmental organizations, and members of the general public, in Canada and abroad, who share an interest in Canadian development assistance and foreign policy. The range of topics covered is broad, albeit not exhaustive. For instance, we were unable to include analyses of Canadian aid in relation to the important issues of climate change, food security, or humanitarian assistance. The book also focuses almost exclusively on bilateral aid. These *lacunae* underscore the need for sustained and indeed expanded efforts to study the manifestations and impacts of Canadian development cooperation.

The book's rethinking is divided into three sections: (1) the foundations of ethics, power, and bureaucracy; (2) the Canadian context and motivations; and (3) Canada's role in international development. Each section contains a half-dozen chapters that fall principally under the main theme, though numerous chapters raise issues concerning two or more themes.

The first section examines some of the "first principles" of industrialized countries' involvement in international development. It asks a number of questions, without pretending to answer them fully: What is the logic behind "global social transfers" in relation to other foreign policy priorities and engagements? What is the role of ethics in development practice? Why should Canada provide development assistance? What are (and should be) its purposes and whose interests does it serve? What sorts of themes and approaches should be emphasized in light of Canadian priorities and experiences? How does Canadian aid relate to the imperatives of global citizenship?

David Black opens this section by revisiting the concept of humane internationalism, pioneered in the Canadian context by Cranford Pratt. Black argues that Pratt's influence and this concept in particular have structured the thinking of a generation of analysts on the motivations that should underpin Canadian aid. Pratt's framing of Canadian aid policy has proved insightful, but also limiting in some key ways. His dichotomy between the self-interested motivations of the "dominant class" and the "counter-consensus" emphasis on the primacy of altruistic motives exaggerated the contrast between the "corrupted" government and "ethically pure" non-governmental organizations (NGOs). It overestimated popular support for the latter's perspective, and underplayed the extent to which various actors could be characterized by both sets of motives. The result was to polarize the debate and hinder engagement among politicians, civil servants, and civil society organizations, contributing to the prevalent policy "malaise." Black further argues that the resulting preoccupation with aid alone led to the relative neglect of the ways that other elements of foreign policy can have a positive or negative influence on development.

Adam Chapnick also rethinks the humane internationalist frame, but from a more critical perspective than Black. Like Black, Chapnick recognizes the humane internationalist viewpoint's noble intentions, but believes that it is based on a false dichotomy of good-versus-bad motives and an over-idealized assessment of popular opinion. His chapter argues that it has failed to influence policy makers because it has two fundamental flaws. First, it ignores the extent to which its own objectives can be compatible with national self-interest. Second, it seeks to downplay the stark distinction that realists make between short-term emergency assistance and longer-term development assistance. To help improve Canada's development assistance, Chapnick recommends that humane internationalists work across the humane internationalist–realist divide on common goals, focus more on poverty reduction and less on charity, and collaborate more closely with the government to strengthen its development efforts.

John Cameron's chapter also addresses the normative foundations of foreign aid policy, arguing for the application of cosmopolitan ethics, with its dual imperative of "do good" and "do no harm," to analyze aid along with other foreign policy areas. Cameron suggests that scholars should be inspired by the policy world's "whole-of-government approach" and use the concept of policy coherence for development to assess not just aid policy, but the full range of Canadian policies that have an impact on international development. In doing so, they should rethink not only the extent to which policies seek to "do good," as humane internationalists advocate, but also the extent to which they reflect the more fundamental ethical imperative to "do no harm."

Molly den Heyer's contribution seeks to understand why Canadian aid is stuck in a "policy eddy" of technical and administrative measures that fail to address underlying policy problems. Such rethinking, she argues, requires a closer examination of power, more specifically the "discursive frames" that shape policy. Using the aid effectiveness agenda as a case study, den Heyer demonstrates how understanding policy and policy making requires an examination of not only visible power, but also its hidden and invisible manifestations. Canadian aid, she concludes, can only be reinvigorated if the government stops doing the bureaucratic equivalent of rearranging the deck chairs on the *Titanic* and makes more fundamental modifications to its foreign policy. The latter include recognizing major changes in international politics, adopting a more cosmopolitan approach to global challenges, and engaging in more effective and genuine partnerships.

Like den Heyer's, Ian Smillie's chapter criticizes the Canadian government's overemphasis on technical and administrative concerns. He argues that the excessive focus on effectiveness and results, in particular, has had a counterproductive effect. His chapter demonstrates how various pathologies of the aid world, including self-interested motives, constraining accountability mechanisms, risk avoidance, the lack of learning and local knowledge, short time frames and slow speed, all prevent aid from reaching its full transformative potential. He concludes with a number of recommendations for rethinking, aimed at government and other aid actors, that would help re-inject some common sense into poverty reduction efforts.

Whereas this book's first section analyzes fundamental issues that apply to other donor countries as much as they do to Canada, the second section focuses more closely on the Canadian context. It seeks to address the following questions: How has Canadian aid evolved? What underlying principles and purposes have been espoused and implemented? How have they changed over time? How have foreign policy and development assistance evolved in relation to each other and to broader government structures? What factors have influenced Canadian development assistance policies? How have these factors evolved in relation to the changing global context? What is the public perception of the usefulness of Canadian aid and how has it changed over time?

The second section opens with Liam Swiss's quantitative analysis of Canadian aid distribution patterns in comparison with those of other Western donors from the 1960s to 2010. He finds that Canadian aid resembled most closely the relatively altruistic "like-minded" donors in the 1980s and 1990s, but that after 2000 Canada more closely resembles the more self-interested United States and United Kingdom. While Swiss recognizes that further evidence is required, the numbers suggest a concomitant shift in Canadian motives for foreign aid.

Laura Macdonald and Arne Ruckert's chapter examines the effects on aid of the Harper government's emphasis on the Americas, first signalled in 2007. They focus on three case studies: Peru, site of many Canadian extractive industry investments and of a CIDA-funded partnership between a Canadian mining company and NGO; Haiti, the largest recipient of Canadian aid in the region; and Honduras, site of a controversial *coup d'état*. They analyze the vagaries of Canadian aid to those three countries between 2001 and 2012 and find considerable evidence of mixed motives. Though rapidly rising aid to Peru and Honduras reflects Conservative ideological preferences and especially commercial self-interest, Canadian assistance to Haiti suggests that other, more altruistic, factors are also at play.

Justin Massie and Stéphane Roussel, in their chapter, rethink the relationship between Canadian foreign aid and security. Using the concept of "strategic culture," they trace three successive foreign aid strategies. From 1945 to 1976, the Canadian government used its aid primarily in an effort to prevent conflict and the need for military intervention. From 1977 to 1992, it saw aid mainly as a substitute for security-related involvement. From 1993 onwards, it used aid to complement its military involvement, especially after the September 11, 2001 attacks. Massie and Roussel expect the Canadian government to maintain the latter approach, in large part because it uses it to cement its membership in the Western security alliance.

Whereas other chapters in this volume examine the Canadian government's motivations for providing foreign aid, Dominic Silvio's analyzes Canadian public opinion between 1993 and 2012. He is especially interested in the effect of the 2007–08 financial crisis on Canadians' attitudes towards development assistance. He finds that, despite the economic crisis at home, Canadians still broadly support providing aid abroad, and a slim majority favour increasing the aid budget. Yet Silvio goes on to argue that Canadians' opinions on this topic are not very strongly held and will therefore have little influence on the government's allocation of funds.

Drawing on theoretical frameworks from public administration, François Audet and Olga Navarro-Flores's chapter analyzes the Harper government's development-related decisions between 2010 and 2013. They categorize them according to the underlying rationale provided (economic, efficiency, or other/none) and consider the respective roles of elected officials and the public service. Their analysis reveals a mix of rationales: Some decisions are justifiable under New Public Management's focus on downsizing and efficiency or the desire to promote the private sector. Others, however, point more towards Conservative political ideology and politicians' desire to be re-elected, rather than developmental concerns. The result may have a negative impact on aid effectiveness.

The book's third section addresses key themes concerning Canada's role in international development. It asks: What approach should be taken to put into practice the "first principles of intervention"? What are the different roles that Canadian assistance can play in the world and what are its specific contributions? What is the most appropriate and effective institutional design for the delivery of Canadian foreign assistance? Who are the different constituents in the debate? What are the most promising scenarios for moving forward?

For decades, Canada was a leader on issues related to women/gender and development. Rebecca Tiessen's chapter traces the rise of gender equality concerns at CIDA after 1976, but also its decline, especially after 2009, when the Canadian government apparently rethought its approach. It replaced the globally used term "gender equality" with the more idiosyncratic expression "equality between women and men" and adopted the Muskoka Initiative on maternal health, which conceptualizes women as victims rather than agents of development. In spite of these top-level changes, committed mid-level officials – Tiessen refers to them as a "second CIDA" – still advance gender equality goals, often surreptitiously, but their efforts cannot ensure that gender will remain on the agenda indefinitely.

Christina Clark-Kazak's chapter draws on decades of theories, policies, and practices on women/gender and development to analyze the role of children and youth in Canadian development policies and programming, designated a priority theme in 2009. She argues that current policies adopt a "children-in-development" approach reminiscent of discredited "women-in-development" approaches (described by Tiessen in her chapter), in which children are simply added to the development equation without recognizing the social relevancy or agency of children themselves. Clark-Kazak recommends that the Canadian government adopt instead a "social age mainstreaming" perspective, similar to "gender mainstreaming," and assume a global leadership role in innovative development thinking and practice in relation to this issue area.

The next two chapters examine Canada's aid to fragile states. The first, by David Carment and Yiagadeesen Samy, takes a macrolevel approach. It traces how the Canadian government made important contributions to the analysis of state fragility and the development of networks to respond to the challenges of fragile states, but then "squandered" them. For conceptual, political, and organizational reasons, Canada's significant aid to fragile states has failed to translate into effective programs. According to Carment and Samy, Canadian efforts tend to be "ad hoc, unstructured and unsystematic," lacking in theoretical grounding, common analysis, and coordination among actors.

The second chapter on state fragility, by Stephen Baranyi and Themrise Khan, focuses on Canadian assistance to five specific conflict-affected and fragile states, namely Bangladesh, Ethiopia, Mali, Pakistan, and Palestine (West Bank and Gaza). It analyzes Canadian aid's degree of securitization, its effectiveness, and its relationship to Canadian commercial interests in each of the five countries. It finds wide variations in securitization and effectiveness across the cases and little evidence of problematic commercialization in any of them. The authors therefore argue for greater contextual analysis when considering aid to fragile states and warn against generalizations based solely on the case of Afghanistan. They also outline some options for the Canadian government to rethink its activities in this area.

Canadian trade interests play a central role in the book's last two substantive chapters. In contrast to Baranyi and Khan's analysis, the authors of the next two chapters find clear cause for concern that commercial self-interest increasingly characterizes Canadian aid. Gabriel Goyette's contribution examines the Harper government's growing instrumentalization of Canadian aid for other foreign policy purposes, examining a number of initiatives that together constitute an emerging "new *de facto* Canadian aid policy." He focuses on government support for the Canadian extractive industry, which epitomizes this new approach, analyzing the choice of priority themes and recipient countries, the exaggerated emphasis on results, and the growing role of the private sector. He considers the commercially motivated *de facto* policy highly problematic, as it risks further undermining the effectiveness of aid.

Like Goyette's, Stephen Brown's chapter is critical of the role of commercial self-interest in Canadian foreign aid and its impact on aid effectiveness. He examines the partnerships that CIDA has forged with mining companies and NGOs, starting in 2011, and argues that they epitomize the government's rethinking of aid, specifically its "recommercialization." The partnerships, which heavily subsidize mining companies' corporate social responsibility projects, mainly in mining-affected communities, will help the Canadian extractive industry sustain controversial mining activities and thus constitute indirect subsidies. Rather than hold these companies to account for their controversial practices or seek ways to improve them, these government-funded projects help to recast the companies as humanitarian actors.

The concluding chapter, by the editors, summarizes the main issues raised by the book's various chapters under the rubric of "rethinking Canadian development cooperation," reflecting the insufficiency of rethinking aid alone. It organizes the findings thematically according to four different kinds of partnerships that will be key to the future rethinking: (1) the foundations of development partnerships; (2) partnerships within the international aid regime; (3) partnerships with key Canadian stakeholders; and (4) intra-governmental partnerships. It sums up what we hope will be a useful contribution to the unfolding Canadian aid conversation in an era of unprecedented challenges and uncharted administrative structures.

References

Audet, François, Marie-Eve Desrosiers, and Stéphane Roussel, eds. 2008. *L'aide canadienne au développement: bilan, défis et perspectives*. Montreal: Presses de l'Université de Montréal.

Brown, Chris, and Edward T. Jackson. 2009. "Could the Senate be Right? Should CIDA be Abolished?." In Allan M. Maslove, ed. *How Ottawa Spends, 2009–2010: Economic Upheaval and Political Dysfunction*. Montreal: McGill–Queen's University Press, 2009: 151–74.

Brown, Stephen. 2008. "CIDA under the Gun." In Jean Daudelin and Daniel Schwanen, eds. *Canada Among Nations 2007: What Room to Manoeuvre?* Montreal and Kingston: McGill–Queen's University Press: 91–107.

Brown, Stephen. 2012a. "Canadian Aid Enters the Twenty-First Century." In Stephen Brown, ed. *Struggling for Effectiveness: CIDA and Canadian Foreign Aid*. Montreal and Kingston: McGill–Queen's University Press: 3–23.

Brown, Stephen, ed. 2012b. *Struggling for Effectiveness: CIDA and Canadian Foreign Aid*. Montreal and Kingston: McGill–Queen's University Press.

Carin, Barry, and Gordon Smith. 2010. "Reinventing CIDA." Calgary: Canadian Defence and Foreign Affairs Institute.

den Heyer, Molly. 2012. "Untangling Canadian Aid Policy: International Agreements, CIDA's Policies and Micro-Policy Negotiations in Tanzania." In Stephen Brown, ed. *Struggling for Effectiveness: CIDA and Canadian Foreign Aid*. Montreal and Kingston: McGill–Queen's University Press: 186–216.

Freeman, Linda. 1982. "CIDA, Wheat, and Rural Development in Tanzania." *Canadian Journal of African Studies*, vol. 16, no. 3: 479–504.

Gordon Foundation. 2010. "Re-imagining Foreign Aid." Internet, http://gordonfoundation.ca/programs/other-programs/global-citizenship-program/re-imagining-foreign-aid. Accessed December 1, 2013.

Greenspon, Edward. 2010. *Open Canada: A Global Positioning Strategy for a Networked Age*. Toronto: Canadian International Council.

Gulrajani, Nilima. 2010. "Re-imaging Canadian Development Cooperation: A Comparative Examination of Norway and the UK." Toronto: Walter and Duncan Gordon Foundation.

Gulrajani, Nilima. 2012. "Improving Canada's Performance as a Bilateral Donor: Assessing the Past and Building for the Future." In Stephen Brown, ed. *Struggling for Effectiveness: CIDA and Canadian Foreign Aid*. Montreal and Kingston: McGill-Queen's University Press: 53–78.

Johnston, Patrick. 2010. "Modernizing Canadian Foreign Aid and Development: Challenges Old and New." Toronto: Walter and Duncan Gordon Foundation.

Minister of Justice. 2013. *Official Development Assistance Accountability Act.* Last amended on June 26, 2013. Internet, http://laws-lois.justice.gc.ca/ PDF/O-2.8.pdf. Accessed July 10, 2014.

Nossal, Kim Richard. 1988. "Mixed Motives Revisited: Canada's Interest in Development Assistance." *Canadian Journal of Political Studies,* vol. 21, no. 1: 35–56.

Pratt, Cranford, ed. 1994. *Canadian International Development Assistance Policies: An Appraisal.* Montreal: McGill–Queen's University Press.

Standing Senate Committee on Foreign Affairs and International Trade. 2007. *Overcoming 40 Years of Failure: A New Road Map for Sub-Saharan Africa.* Ottawa: Government of Canada.

Swiss, Liam, with Simon Maxwell. 2010. "A New National Project for Canadian Development Cooperation." Toronto: Walter and Duncan Gordon Foundation.

SECTION I

FOUNDATIONS OF ETHICS, POWER AND BUREAUCRACY

CHAPTER I

Humane Internationalism and the Malaise of Canadian Aid Policy

David R. Black

W hy do national governments provide foreign aid? Why *should* they provide foreign aid? These deceptively simple questions, analytical and normative, are the focus of a voluminous litera-ture within and beyond Canada. Maurits van der Veen (2011) has demonstrated that the way they are answered varies quite widely among donor states and depends substantially on how foreign aid is "framed."

In Canada, the scholarship of, and inspired by, Cranford Pratt has been exceptionally influential in framing analysis of the founda-tions and rationale for the Canadian aid program.[1] With a focus on Canadian aid policy that spanned two decades (e.g., Pratt 1983/84, 1989, 1994, 2001, 2003), Pratt's conceptual and analytical contributions did much to define the terms of debate and shape normative and pre-scriptive discussion of the logic that *should* underpin this important but highly contested policy domain. In particular, Pratt's conceptu-alization of humane internationalism and his related articulations of a "dominant class" account of the limitations of Canadian aid and the role of the "counter-consensus" shaped a pattern of debate that did much to illuminate aid policy and practice in Canada. However, it also in effect framed and limited the debate in ways that have constrained creativity and innovation. By re-examining Pratt's core conceptual contributions and the narrative account of Canadian aid policy they enabled, it becomes possible to understand better the malaise that has settled upon the debate and practice of Canadian aid policy – the sense of insularity, defensiveness, and remove from the real needs of developing countries that has undermined political support for Canadian foreign assistance. Moreover, this analysis allows us to identify some of the ways in which those seeking a renewed and strengthened aid program, properly articulated with other dimensions of development policy and responsive to the imperatives of global poverty and justice, might reinvigorate the debate. These include a more nuanced understanding of the relationship between ethics and interests, a broadening of the constituency for development work in Canadian government and society, and a more grounded and holistic view of the impact of aid and its relationship to other forms of development engagement.

Interpreting Canadian Aid Praxis: Pratt's Enduring Contribution

As noted above, Pratt's analysis of the characteristics and evolution of Canadian aid policy was anchored by three core conceptual constructs. First, he argued that Canadian political culture incorporated a robust and persistent, though eroding, element of "humane internationalism" (HI), defined as "an acceptance by the citizens of the industrialized states that they have ethical obligations towards those beyond their borders and that these in turn impose obligations on their governments" (Pratt 1989, 13). This orientation was, he argued, understood by its adherents to be consistent with the "real long-term interests of the rich countries," but remained at its core ethical and cosmopolitan in orientation (Pratt 1989, 14). It was also widely seen as the logical external corollary of a solidaristic commitment to social equity at home, manifested in the elaboration of the welfare state policies of the post–World War II era. He did not suggest that HI was uniquely Canadian. Indeed, Pratt's fullest articulation of this idea emerged out of a multi-volume collaborative study with scholars from several other "like-minded" Western middle powers (e.g., Pratt 1989; Pratt 1990; Stokke 1989), to which Canada compared relatively unfavourably in terms of generosity. Nevertheless, he considered HI the most widely accepted foundation and justification for Canadian aid, as well as the soundest basis for aid "effectiveness" (to put the point in more contemporary terms).

The evidence for the robustness of the humane internationalist tradition was to be found in several sources: public opinion surveys;

key parliamentary committee reports, and at least some government white papers on aid (e.g., CIDA 1975; 1987; SCEAIT 1987); and most substantially, the proliferating range of internationalist non-state actors that Pratt (1983/84) dubbed the "counter-consensus" – so named because they had increasingly coalesced around a critique of the dominant approach to Canadian foreign policy by the late 1970s. The idea of the counter-consensus was Pratt's second main conceptual contribution to the framing of Canadian foreign policy. It foreshadowed the growing interest in the role and influence of "civil society" and the "democratization" of foreign policy that came to the fore in the 1990s. Pratt regarded this broad coalition of civil society organizations (CSOs), allied in the development domain through the Canadian Council for International Co-operation (CCIC), as the most effective and articulate custodians of HI, and he worked closely with them over the course of his career.

Given what he understood to be HI's public resonance and firm societal roots, the puzzle was why it had not had greater influence on the policy and practice of Canadian aid, which virtually all scholarly commentators saw as bedevilled by "mixed motives," among which ethical considerations were typically (though not unremittingly) subordinated to more narrowly self-interested priorities. To explain this puzzle, Pratt elaborated a "dominant class" approach, combining an emphasis on the relative autonomy of permanent officials within the state with an understanding that their conception of the "national interest" showed a persistent bias towards the interests of "capitalism in Canada." Influenced by structural Marxism, combined in a "non-doctrinaire" manner with international realism and, in later versions, a neo-Gramscian attention to the precepts of neoliberal globalization, Pratt's emphasis on the enduring influence of dominant class interests provided a basis for understanding the policy choices that were made (e.g., regarding tied aid, the choice of recipients, and the use aid funds to promote private sector activity in developing countries) under the ethical cover of the aid program.

Taken together, these three conceptual constructs underpinned an analytical narrative concerning Canada's "limited and eroding internationalism" (Pratt 1989). Pratt argued that due to a "strategic conjuncture" of favourable conditions, both domestic and international, the rapid growth of a more generous and ethically driven aid policy took hold for a ten-year period, from 1966 to 1976. "Because of the strength of social idealism in Canada at that time,"

wrote Pratt, "a major foreign aid policy that was genuinely committed to reaching and helping the poorest peoples and countries
was seen as particularly appropriate" (Pratt 2003, 89). However, a
determined push to win Cabinet acceptance of the 1975 Aid Strategy
that seemed to cement this trend paradoxically led to a systematic
backlash from other quarters of the state and initiated a retreat from
this high-water mark of HI. The story that Pratt tracked over the next
couple of decades featured a CIDA that, for the most part, sought to
protect its core HI mission and the autonomy to pursue it in the face
of repeated efforts to modify its policies to serve better Canadian
material self-interests.

Moreover, CIDA was periodically required to resist efforts to
gain direct control over its policy branch and direction from the
Department of Foreign Affairs and International Trade (DFAIT)
(e.g., Pratt 1998). Depending on the administrative leadership of the
agency, these efforts sometimes took the form of policy shifts to
bring aid policy into closer alignment with the self-interested priorities of Foreign Affairs and Finance – as, for example, during Marcel
Massé's tenure as president when CIDA pre-emptively embraced the
promotion of structural adjustment in recipient countries as a core
priority (Pratt 1994, 354–57). "Humanitarian considerations have
not been obliterated," wrote Pratt "and even periodically resurged
under particular ministers – but they have been required increasingly to yield place to self-interested ... economic and international
political objectives" (Pratt 2001, 67). In the meantime, despite Pratt's
"underlying pessimism about the prospects for the future triumph of
progressive internationalist values" (Matthews 2002, 171), he sought
through his own writing and advocacy, as well as encouragement of
the efforts of others within the "counter-consensus," to make the case
for a more humane and cosmopolitan internationalism and a more
generous aid program flowing from it. Over this period, CIDA was
unable to resist deep cuts to its budget in times of fiscal austerity,
during the 1990s and again after 2010. More recently, with the surprise announcement of its merger with Foreign Affairs in the March
2013 federal budget to form the new Department of Foreign Affairs,
Trade and Development (DFATD), CIDA's resistance to encroachments
on its policy autonomy was finally swept aside.

Where does this leave Pratt's account of Canadian aid policy
and our assessment of it? Much about Pratt's account is both admi-
rable and illuminating. His dominant class approach continues to

highlight enduring biases within the state policy-making apparatus – biases that have tended to fade from view in policy debates on
aid (e.g., regarding the aid "architecture" and particular thematic and
country priorities), but should not. His precise and exacting approach
to the reading of successive parliamentary reports and policy documents, seeking in their formulations clues to the emerging directions
of aid policy and the configuration of forces within government,
showed an attention to detail and to the power of language at a time
when the "discursive turn" was in its infancy, particularly in the
study of Canadian foreign policy. The clarity of his thinking and
reasoning, and not least the persistence and passion with which he
engaged this issue, were inspirational to many.[2]

Nevertheless, Pratt's work was not always on the mark. More
to the point, even (perhaps especially) when it was – that is, much
of the time – his great influence in shaping the debate has had some
unintended consequences that may have forestalled a healthier and
more forward-looking consideration of the foundations upon which
Canadian aid could be renewed. Identifying and critiquing these
tendencies can help us think about ways forward in the current,
dynamic, and uncertain policy environment.

Assumptions and Implications of the Debate

Right Intention

Embedded in both Pratt's analysis and much of the broader debate
concerning Canadian aid policy is the assumption that foreign aid
can and *should* be driven by "sentiments of human solidarity and
… an awakening acceptance of obligations towards those beyond
its borders" (Pratt 2001, 61). This is reflected, for example, in former
Foreign Minister Mitchell Sharp's oft-cited assertion, originally made
in 1961, that, "There is one good and sufficient reason for international aid and that is that there are less fortunate people in the world
who need our help … If the primary purpose of our aid is to help
ourselves, rather than to help others, we shall probably receive in
return what we deserve and a good deal less than we expect" (cited
in Spicer 1966, 6). Yet Pratt and many others have equally shown
that, in practice, Canadian aid policy has rarely attained this clarity
of purpose – this right intention – and has indeed been routinely
corrupted by more selfish and narrowly self-interested motivations.

The result has been a Manichean juxtaposition of "right" versus misguided if not "wrong" intent in the formulation of Canadian aid policy.

Of course, such ideal-typical contrasts have important analytical utility. However, they also have certain risks and ramifications when applied to the "real world" of policy. First, the ethical clarity of purpose associated with the "pure" articulation of HI is virtually impossible to approach in practice. Certainly, all state officials concerned with aid policy must engage in compromises, both internally in relation to their bureaucratic counterparts and externally in the complex terrain of recipients. The ethically defined actors within the counter-consensus have also reflected and faced a range of acute dilemmas as they have been obliged to balance competing interests and motivations. The very political risk is that, in setting a standard for aid practice and practitioners that is impossible to meet, a debate framed by a stark contrast between ethical and self-interested motivations runs the risk of undermining the legitimacy and public acceptance of the aid program as a whole (see Chapnick, this volume). In other words, if aid is persistently failing to fulfil its ostensibly "true" or "right" purpose, its supporters are liable to become disaffected and its opponents emboldened.

On the other hand, a discussion of development that does *not* embed a forthright and sophisticated discussion of ethical purpose will be an impoverished one. A policy domain that is centrally preoccupied with addressing the causes and consequences of global poverty will be infused, inevitably, with conceptions of and arguments about obligation and justice. What is needed, therefore, is a discussion that better captures the dilemmas and ambiguities of ethical purpose, without (implicitly or explicitly) discounting it as somehow "too hard" or too naïve.

The Robustness of the HI Tradition in Canadian Political Culture
With hindsight and the benefit of subsequent research, Pratt's analysis appears to be most off-target in his assessment of the robustness of the HI tradition in Canadian society. To be sure, Pratt always portrayed this tradition as "limited and eroding." He also emphasized that as support for policies dedicated to poverty alleviation and social equity *within* Canada faltered in the neoliberal era, a parallel recession of support in the external domain was to be expected. Nevertheless, he persisted in treating the HI tradition as substantial

and resilient, if embattled, so as to juxtapose this tendency with the more self-interested orientation of much of the Canadian political and economic elite.

Yet the breadth and depth of HI in both the "mass" and "attentive" publics has always been questionable, and is arguably increasingly so. Several insightful analyses have elaborated this point. David Morrison, in his landmark 1998 history of CIDA, noted that "while polls have consistently shown humanitarian sentiment as the leading reason people give for supporting aid, they have also revealed scant general knowledge about the nature or extent of Canadian development assistance – and, except for a small minority, a low ranking in comparison with other public goods" (Morrison 1998, 440). Noël, Thérien, and Dallaire (2004) used publicly available polling data to elaborate on this point, and further noted that there was a deep divide between a soft majority of Canadians who were broadly supportive of aid and a substantial minority who were deeply sceptical or even hostile towards it. They further demonstrated that this division closely aligned with partisan political preferences: Those self-identifying on the party-political "right" were generally more sceptical about aid and suspicious of the agencies responsible for it. This understanding has clearly influenced the Conservative Harper government, whose electoral "base" is considerably less attached to the HI tradition as Pratt conceived it than those of the other two major federal parties.

A related point concerns the depth of parliamentary support for HI as the principal foundation for the aid program. An important theme within Pratt's work was the degree to which key parliamentary committee reports – notably the Winegard Report (SCEAIT 1987), but also the report of the Special Joint Committee reviewing Canadian foreign policy (House of Commons 1994) – consistently supported an HI- and poverty-oriented rationale for Canadian aid policy. The implication was that parliamentarians were more inclined to reflect the orientations of their constituents than relatively autonomous permanent officials of the state and therefore that these reports clearly indicated societal support for HI, whereas the deviations from their recommendations in government responses to them clearly indicated the "dominant class" bias of key state agencies.

I have argued that there is, in fact, a discernible weakening of the erstwhile HI constituency among contemporary parliamentarians, reflecting broader societal trends (Black 2012). Nevertheless, these committee reports, as substantial as they were, are probably better understood as a reflection of the viewpoints of a committed and at least partially self-selected minority of parliamentarians – those inclined towards membership and leadership on foreign affairs committees – rather than the viewpoint of parliamentarians as a whole. In short, without discounting the significance of the HI tradition in Canadian society, it has proved to be a weaker foundation for a stable, informed, and effective aid policy at both mass and elite levels than Pratt anticipated.

The Counter-Consensus as Repository and Champion of Ethical Values

I have noted that the ethically and development-oriented counter-consensus in civil society was regarded as the best-organized and most persistent promoter of an HI approach to aid, both in Pratt's work and in much scholarly and popular commentary. This role and image has been significantly diminished over the past decade, for a number of reasons. Others are far better qualified to elaborate upon this trend than I am (e.g., Plewes and Tomlinson 2013; Smillie 2012), but a few points bear noting in the context of this analysis.

First, and ironically, as the "partnership" between non-governmental development organizations (NGDOs) and CIDA deepened and was institutionalized, these NGDOs became increasingly professionalized and dependent on state funding in ways that compromised their advocacy and policy roles. Second, this same process contributed to the erosion of their local social foundations, as their time and energy was focused on project implementation and upward accountability to CIDA and other funders, especially with the onset of "results-based management." This erosion was also a reflection of broader socio-cultural trends – notably the decline of the organized mainstream Christian institutions that had been such an influential presence within the counter-consensus and such a strong influence on Pratt and many other humane internationalists. Third, roughly the same segment of the Canadian public that has been sceptical of the usefulness of aid, associated with the party-political right, has been deeply suspicious of what are termed "special interest groups." Under the Harper government, therefore, there has been a steadily growing estrangement between the government and traditional pillars of the counter-consensus, as well as a growing instrumentalization of NGDO roles in relation to government policy (see

Smillie 2012). In short, the multiple changes and challenges facing NGDOs and civil society have led veteran analysts to characterize this sector as being at a difficult and uncertain crossroads (Plewes and Tomlinson 2013, 222). Like public opinion more broadly, its role as a bastion of HI has clearly weakened.

CIDA's Relations with Other Government Agencies

Pratt's identification of a widespread, systematic tendency within those departments primarily concerned with Canada's foreign relations (notably DFAIT, Finance, Defence, and the Treasury Board) to conceive of the "national interest" in ways that fundamentally aligned with the preferences of the "dominant class" was a powerful and illuminating insight. His portrayal of CIDA's residual HI orientation and the policies flowing from it as being in tension with, and at times under attack from, officials within these other, more powerful, agencies also held considerable explanatory power. This portrayal, however, reinforced tendencies towards political defensiveness and risk-aversion within CIDA – both in relation to their bureaucratic counterparts and towards the academic and non-governmental development communities.

It is hard to disentangle cause and effect in these tendencies, which I would argue have persisted since at least the early 1990s with the onset of deep budget cuts under the Chrétien Liberals. Regardless of how it began, it produced an unhealthy sense of insecurity and a reluctance among CIDA officials to engage in vigorous policy and intellectual debate about how best to conceive and pursue development objectives, through aid and other related policies and practices.

Conversely, the view that other government agencies – particularly, though not only, DFAIT – were ineluctably "captured" by a dominant class/international realist orientation and were persistently pursuing opportunities to distort aid policy to support their conception of the national interest was a potent, albeit overgeneralized, perspective. If CIDA could *only* seek to defend itself from these narrower objectives and perspectives, pursued by considerably more powerful bureaucratic actors, the struggle was bound to be Sisyphean and deeply demoralizing. It meant, as well, that development analysts and practitioners were less attentive than they might have been to opportunities for forging strategic relationships and alliances with people and branches in other government departments, so as to enlarge and strengthen the constituency for development assistance within government. It would be naïve to think that this could be easily or widely achieved, but it could potentially broaden the range of opportunities and support for development issues within the apparatus of the state.

Aid Policy and the "Political Class"

In line with the theoretical assumptions of both structural Marxism and statism (e.g., Nossal 1988), Pratt emphasized the interests and orientations of permanent officials within a relatively autonomous Canadian state. There are persuasive reasons for this emphasis and it has delivered powerful insights. At the same time, to echo Adam Chapnick (this volume), in a liberal democratic political system (however class-based) it is possible for political elites to impose agendas and/or deliver change if they are determined to do so. Chapnick notes that the key lesson of the UK's remarkable cross-partisan support for a strong and growing aid program, anchored by the Department for International Development (DFID), is the importance of strong and committed political party leadership in making it happen. Similarly, the Harper Conservatives have demonstrated their ability to impose far-reaching policy and institutional changes with remarkably limited consultation and consensus building, as exemplified by the abrupt decision to roll CIDA into the new DFATD. This suggests a need to give closer attention to the macro-political role of political party elites in building the foundation for better aid policies.

An Introverted Debate

The debate concerning the quality and purposes of Canadian aid described above was fundamentally, and paradoxically, focused on the *internal* politics of aid. The fundamental purpose of the HI orientation that Pratt conceptualized and promoted was to foster a more reciprocal, generous, and solidaristic response to the poorest people in the poorest countries, with the ultimate objective of promoting greater global justice. However, the measures of HI and the analysis of whether it was advancing or retreating were largely Ottawa-centric, preoccupied with the balance of forces and decisions taken by Ottawa-based agencies and actors.

There were good and obvious reasons for this focus: These dynamics were important in shaping policy outcomes and there was much to track and analyze in the Ottawa hothouse. It was also (and remains) very difficult to research, analyze, and discern the discrete developmental impacts of Canadian aid efforts in developing countries themselves, given that Canadian aid was typically a small portion of an increasingly diffuse and complex aid regime.

Nevertheless, the increasingly pressing question for many aid sceptics, on both the right and the left, was whether aid was doing any good *at all* for those it ostensibly sought to assist. Would, for example, a more generous aid program translate into better life prospects for poor people and communities? Would the gains made be sustainable, or would they deepen distortions and dependencies? Would the good work undertaken by aid agencies be effectively undermined or even negated by macroeconomic policies or foreign investments (e.g., in the extractive sector) promoted by other arms of the Canadian state? The debate on Canadian aid that unfolded for much of the past few decades provided little insight or reassurance concerning these sorts of questions, either way. What was required was a more systematic and scholarly analysis of substantial Canadian aid programs *in the context of* recipient countries, rather than the anecdotal and sometimes sensational examples highlighted by advocates on both sides of the debate.

Moreover, the analytical emphasis in the HI-influenced scholarly literature on Canadian deviations from these principles and the self-interested distortions that kept encroaching on the aid program raised obvious doubts concerning the *results* that Canadian aid could hope to achieve, given its flawed foundations. Meanwhile, a wounded CIDA, wary of the potential for further damage resulting from negative stories from the field, became less open to these kinds of investigations, or to explorations of the complex lessons they would generate. In short, what has unfolded is a relatively shallow and ill-informed public debate, which the scholarly literature has been unable to raise substantially.

A Preoccupation with Aid as the Means for Poverty Alleviation and Development

A final ramification of the way the debate stimulated by Pratt unfolded was that it ended up being heavily preoccupied with the twists and turns of aid policy in general and CIDA in particular, at the expense of a more holistic emphasis on the full range of policies and practices that bore on poor countries and peoples. This was certainly not Pratt's intention. Indeed, the Middle Powers and Global Poverty project, which essentially launched the idea of HI, was a broadly balanced assessment of North–South policies, including the campaign for a New International Economic Order and the results of various "non-aid" policies towards the developing world (see Helleiner 1989; Pratt 1989). Over time, however, perhaps as a result of the neoliberal reforms affecting all governments that seemed to foreclose a range of alternative policy avenues, this debate became heavily preoccupied with what we might somewhat dramatically characterize as the battle for the soul of CIDA. As broader aspirations towards North–South reforms faded into history, "developmentalists" focused on the policy domain that still seemed accessible and in some sense controllable. This trend was reinforced over the past two decades by the complex and intense politics of "aid effectiveness," including the sustained efforts to achieve consensus around what ultimately crystallized as the Paris Principles and the Millennium Development Goals.

In doing so, however, Canadian development scholars and analysts arguably neglected a series of critical trends in migration, remittances, investment, ecology, and the like. To be sure, they (or rather we) did not *ignore* these important trends. Nevertheless, given the ongoing emphasis on the study of Canadian aid policy and the debate about its underlying motivations and purposes, less attention was given to the *interconnections* between development assistance and these broader trends than their importance warranted.

Conclusion: Ways Forward

In sum, the debate on Canadian aid policy that unfolded over the past generation has tended to be excessively moralistic, Ottawa-centric, and defensive – seeking to protect the "core (HI) mission" of CIDA, while remaining deeply sceptical of CIDA's capacity to advance that mission. It has given insufficient attention to the softness of popular support for HI and the political and institutional weaknesses of the civil society organizations combined under the banner of the counter-consensus. Similarly, it has taken a relatively un-nuanced view of the other bureaucratic actors with which CIDA has been required to interact, and has been relatively inattentive to the importance of the viewpoints held by elected parliamentarians and cabinet ministers. Finally, while recognizing the importance of a range of non-aid factors in shaping Canada's role in the global South, it has tended to study the dynamics and impact of aid policy in isolation from these factors.

The debate concerning the foundations and purpose of Canadian aid policy has now entered a new phase. Whatever the pros and cons of the submersion of CIDA into DFATD, as well as the increasingly tectonic changes unfolding elsewhere in what we used to refer to as North–South relations, it is clear that new questions, approaches and issues will become increasingly prominent. How, in this context, can we foster a more productive, creative, and positive debate concerning Canadian aid policy? The critiques and characteristics of the debate highlighted above provide, if not a coherent agenda, at least some key pointers and parameters:

- Development scholars and analysts must learn to accommodate and interrogate ethical tensions. In the newly integrated era of Canadian aid policy, tensions and contradictions may – indeed, should – be revealed and confronted routinely. The clear and compelling constructs of HI *versus* class-defined self-interest will coexist in various permutations. A more forthright consideration of the difficulties of balancing them needs to be integral to the policy debate.
- The case for an ethical dimension to foreign (aid) policy must be continually refreshed. At the same time, ethical arguments require a robust connection to conceptions of interest. The basis for this already exists, as Pratt noted in his scholarship; it may coalesce around the notion of "self-interest, properly understood" (Smillie, this volume). Complicating this process of ethical argumentation is the degree to which, in an era of "global citizenship," many people's sense of ethical community transcends and/or cross-sects the state. For those (often youthful) Canadians with such a cosmopolitan outlook, the relevance of bilateral aid may seem dubious. Linking the virtual and transnational communities with which they associate to national development cooperation policies will present new challenges.
- The groups associated with the erstwhile counter-consensus have lost much of their presumptive moral authority and must renew both their sense of purpose and their connections to community within Canada, along with their

solidaristic linkages to counterparts in the global South. Some CSOs have chosen to become primarily service providers for government agencies, at some cost to their reputations and advocacy roles. Those that continue to adhere to a more solidaristic ethos must find new ways to connect Canadians in their communities to counterparts in the developing world in order to foster a shared sense of the challenges they confront and their collective interest in addressing these challenges. No one understands this better than the non-state (or civil society) actors themselves.

- Development scholars and analysts need to develop a more complex empirical and strategic analysis of the Canadian state. Besides understanding how political dynamics play out *within* the new DFATD, they must identify *loci* for internationalist thinking and connections in the widening range of departments and agencies with international mandates. They must make the case for poverty-focused and justice-oriented policies across a broader front.

- Like Chapnick (this volume), I think more attention needs to be paid to engaging and educating the "political class," including parliamentarians, cabinet ministers, their staffs, and political party elites. Development analysts and advocates need to challenge the increasingly insular patterns of political debate and articulate the advantages to Canadians of a more expansive vision. We need to foster a political foundation for intelligent development aid policies that are both stable and adaptable.

- This should be grounded in stronger evidence concerning the impact of aid in the field, based on a transnational research effort involving developing-country researchers. Longitudinal studies and longer term, relationship-based policies need to be fostered in recognition of the protracted time frames and imperfect understanding on which more successful development policies are based.

- Students, scholars, and policy analysts need to study the effects and effectiveness of aid in conjunction with the range of other issue areas that bear critically on prospects for poverty reduction. This is now starting to happen, with the growing emphasis on the more holistic idea of development effectiveness, rather than merely aid effectiveness (e.g., Bülles and Kindornay 2013). Again, we need to question the easy assumptions of complementary interests on which main-stream policy has been based and confront their implications. Scholars have a particular opportunity and responsibility in this regard, since the political space and institutional capac-ity for policy analysis by NGDOs has narrowed considerably.

Changing internal and external circumstances require renewed analysis and debate concerning the problems and prospects of devel-opment aid. Ethics and interests in a world of growing inequalities and persistent deprivations demand it.

Notes

1. Cranford Pratt is Professor Emeritus of Political Science at the University of Toronto. In an illustrious career spanning more than four decades, Pratt initially established himself as a leading Africanist and was the first Principal of the University of Dar es Salaam in Tanzania from 1960 to 1965. Later, his work focused principally on foreign aid and human rights in Canadian foreign policy. He was also a deeply respected teacher and mentor. Like many others, I owe a significant intellectual debt to Cran Pratt. In addition to his inspiration of my own thinking on several areas of shared interest (e.g., Black 2012), Pratt was the external examiner for my doctoral dissertation and provided crucial insight and encouragement both prior to and following this personal milestone.
2. For an indication of Pratt's influence and the respect and affection in which he continued to be held by those who knew and worked with him, see the special issue of *International Journal* devoted to his work (vol. 57, no. 2, Spring 2002).

References

Black, David. 2012. "The Harper Government, Africa Policy, and the relative decline of humane internationalism." In Heather Smith and Claire Turenne Sjolander, eds. *Canada in the World: Internationalism in Canadian Foreign Policy.* Don Mills, ON: Oxford University Press: 217–237.

Bülles, Anni-Claudine, and Shannon Kindornay. 2013. *Beyond Aid: A Plan for Canada's International Cooperation.* Ottawa: North–South Institute.

CIDA. 1975. *Strategy for International Development Cooperation 1975–80.* Hull, QC: CIDA.

CIDA. 1987. *Sharing Our Future: Canadian International Development Assistance.* Hull, QC: CIDA.

Helleiner, Gerald K., ed. 1990. *The Other Side of International Development Policy: The Non-Aid Economic Relations with Developing Countries of Canada, Denmark, the Netherlands, Norway, and Sweden.* Toronto: University of Toronto Press.

House of Commons, Special Joint Committee Reviewing Canadian Foreign Policy. 1994. *Canada's Foreign Policy: Principles and Priorities for the Future.* Ottawa: Parliamentary Publications Directorate.

Matthews, Robert O. 2002. "A Tribute to Cranford Pratt." *International Journal,* vol. 57, no. 2: 167–174.

Morrison, David R. 1998. *Aid and Ebb Tide: A History of CIDA and Canadian Development Assistance.* Waterloo, ON: Wilfrid Laurier University Press.

Noël, Alain, Jean-Philippe Thérien, and Sébastien Dallaire. 2004. "Divided over Internationalism: The Canadian Public and Development Assistance." *Canadian Public Policy,* vol. 30, no. 1: 29–46.

Nossal, Kim Richard. 1988. "Mixed Motives Revisited: Canada's Interest in Development Assistance." *Canadian Journal of Political Science,* vol. 21, no. 1: 35–56.

Plewes, Betty, and Brian Tomlinson. 2013. "Canadian CSOs and Africa: the End of an Era?" In Rohinton Medhora and Yiagadeesen Samy, eds. *Canada Among Nations 2013. Canada and Africa: Looking Back, Looking Ahead.* Waterloo, ON: Centre for International Governance Innovation: 213–226.

Pratt, Cranford. 1983/84. "Dominant Class Theory and Canadian Foreign Policy: The case of the counter-consensus." *International Journal,* vol. 9, no. 1: 99–135.

Pratt, Cranford, ed. 1989. *Internationalism Under Strain: The North–South Policies of Canada, the Netherlands, Norway, and Sweden.* Toronto: University of Toronto Press: 24–69.

Pratt, Cranford. 1989. "Canada: A Limited and Eroding Internationalism." In Cranford Pratt, ed. *Internationalism Under Strain: The North–South Policies of Canada, the Netherlands, Norway, and Sweden.* Toronto: University of Toronto Press.

Pratt, Cranford, ed. 1994. *Canadian International Development Assistance Policies: An Appraisal.* Montreal and Kingston: McGill–Queen's University Press.

Pratt, Cranford. 1998. "DFAIT's Takeover Bid of CIDA: The Institutional Future of the Canadian International Development Agency." *Canadian Foreign Policy,* vol. 5, no. 2: 1–13.

Pratt, Cranford. 2003. "Ethical Values and Canadian Foreign Aid Policies." *Canadian Journal of African Studies,* vol. 37, no. 1: 84–101.

SCEAIT [Standing Committee on External Affairs and International Trade, Parliament of Canada]. 1987. *For Whose Benefit? Report of the Standing Committee on External Affairs and International Trade on Canada's Official Development Assistance Policies and Programs.* Ottawa: Supply and Services Canada.

Smillie, Ian. 2012. "Tying up the Cow: CIDA, Advocacy, and Public Engagement." In Stephen Brown, ed. *Struggling for Effectiveness: CIDA and Canadian Foreign Aid.* Montreal and Kingston: McGill–Queen's University Press: 269–286.

Stokke, Olav, ed. 1989. *Western Middle Powers and Global Poverty: The Determinants of the Aid Policies of Canada, Denmark, the Netherlands, Norway, and Sweden.* Uppsala: Scandinavian Institute of African Studies.

van der Veen, A. Maurits. 2011. *Ideas, Interests and Foreign Aid.* Cambridge: Cambridge University Press.

CHAPTER II

Refashioning Humane Internationalism in Twenty-First-Century Canada

Adam Chapnick

The recent merger of the Canadian International Development Agency (CIDA) with the Department of Foreign Affairs and International Trade has been framed by Canada's Conservative government as an effort to better align international development policy with Canadian national interests (Savage 2013). While some within and outside of Ottawa have praised the decision as long overdue, others have criticized it for all but disregarding the moral or ethical obligations that many typically associate with foreign aid (Gulrajani 2013). Indeed, even before the merger, one leading analyst had noted, "Given the Canadian government's growing focus on self-interest, rather than recipient countries' priorities ... it is not surprising that Canada has been slow to implement the more *altruistic* [italics added] elements of the aid effectiveness agenda" (Brown 2012, 8).

Balancing altruism with national self-interest has been a focus of critics of Canada's official development assistance (ODA) policy for decades. The political economist Cranford Pratt is one of many to have depicted the management of these potentially divergent priorities as a conflict between *humane internationalists,* who understand the obligation of developed nations to help the poor help themselves in primarily ethical terms, and *international realists,* who maintain that states have to promote and protect their own interests at all costs regardless of whether their behaviour is consistent with humanitarian norms (Pratt 1989, 1990, 1994, 1999, 2000; see also Black, this volume).

Scholarship about the debate continues to proliferate, but it is dominated by analyses from the humane internationalist perspective. To the international realists, one might infer, there is no real need to argue, since the Canadian government's foreign aid policy has always been framed as more realistic than altruistic. Even *For Whose Benefit? The Report of the Standing Committee on External Affairs and International Trade on Canada's Official Development Assistance Policies and Priorities* (the Winegard Report), a 1987 document heralded by advocates as one of the most progressive assessments of Canadian policy in the post-Vietnam era (Pratt 1994), defined the national interest in political and economic terms as much as it did altruistic ones (Winegard et al. 1987). Since then, the general trajectory of Canadian international policy has hardly changed (Chapnick 2005); nonetheless, as recently as 2010, academics David Black and Molly den Heyer (2010–11, 20) wrote of a Canadian struggle "to reconcile a humane international-ist approach based on an ethical obligation to help alleviate global poverty with a realist approach seeking to deliver aid that supports business and political interests."

There is no question that the humane internationalists are sincere and that their case is emotionally compelling. However, decades of failure to convince Canadian policy practitioners to inject a greater sense of altruism into the national attitude towards official development assistance raises the question of whether their campaign will ever be effective. The answer, it appears, is probably not. For one, the premise of the argument – that a humane internationalist/ international realist dichotomy of views indeed exists – is mislead-ing. Second, by conflating two elements of the Canadian aid agenda that many realists understand as distinct – emergency relief and development assistance – humane internationalists misrepresent the intentions, if not also the views, of their critics.

This chapter examines the gap between the humane inter-nationalists, who generally stand on the outside of the strategic decision-making process, and the international realists, who at times make political decisions without the necessary policy expertise. In the hope of beginning to bridge this gap, this chapter begins by reviewing the debate in greater detail. It then considers four plau-sible motivations for framing the divergences in Canadian attitudes towards foreign aid in binary terms: Proponents of the idea could believe that the dichotomy is real; the strategic infrastructure of the humane internationalists' advocacy programs could encourage such thinking; personal gain could be at stake; or the Canadian political atmosphere could condition such a black-and-white approach. This chapter suggests that, however credible or reasonable, not one of these explanations alters the basic truth: the Canadian public continues to demonstrate a poor understanding of foreign aid and therefore remains incapable of appreciating the importance of investing in poverty reduction abroad; its support for development assistance is particularly fickle and shallow (see Silvio, this volume), leaving popular thinking more inclined to the realist framework; and the broader national commitment to poverty reduction efforts continues to rise and fall based on the strength of the Canadian economy rather than the needs of recipient countries, once again running counter to best international practices. While making no claim to having the perfect solution to the humane internationalists' challenge, this essay concludes with three actions that might better integrate the spirit of altruism into Canada's international policy.

Framing the Debate

The most significant problem with the humane internationalist/international realist construct is its conflation of what policy makers in Ottawa — most of whom appear to be sympathetic to realist thinking — typically understand as two separate forms of support: emergency (or humanitarian) relief and development assistance. Duke University's Tim Büthe and his colleagues (2012, 572–73) have explained the distinction by differentiating between a *humanitarian* discourse, which is preoccupied with "a normative commitment to serving underdeveloped or neglected populations ... and provid[ing] services to those in need," and a *development* discourse, committed to tackling the "'root causes' of poverty" and to promoting "sustainable, long-term improvements" to the quality of life in developing societies. In policy terms, although the humanitarian imperative *could* serve to promote long-term poverty reduction goals, it might also translate into funding short-term relief operations in states that suffer natural and human-induced disasters. In the latter case, it can easily be interpreted as altruistic, and thereby equated with the concept of charity (Winegard et al. 1987). By contrast, development assistance policy is grounded in more, even if not entirely, traditional conceptions of the national interest. As the Winegard Report (1987, 8) makes clear, its purpose is *not* "to demonstrate our moral sensibilities but to provide timely and effective assistance to those who need it most." "Investments in the well-being of the poor," the document goes on to explain, "are very much in the long-term interests of Canada and other industrialized countries" (Winegard et al. 1987, 9).

There is no debate in Canada over the merits of limited humanitarian relief operations. As one poll demonstrated, at least 70 percent of Canadians agree that their country has a moral obligation to assist others in need (CDFAI 2007). Even the realists, then, embrace the spirit of altruism in times of crisis, although some might still emphasize the anticipated diplomatic benefits arising from so-called humanitarian initiatives. The real public and political differences exist over whether Ottawa has an obligation to invest in developing states' long-term futures; whether it is in Canada's best interests to do so; and whether there are motivations other than altruism that might legitimately drive official development assistance policy. Practically, Canadians did not dispute the moral imperative faced by their government to respond generously to the 2010 earthquake in Haiti. The public was and remains divided, however, over whether Ottawa has a duty to pursue a longer-term partnership through, for example, investments in good governance initiatives, social services, and economic development that might help Haitians rebuild their society (Canadian Press 2010).

At the conceptual level, where realists ultimately differ from humane internationalists is over whether specific development goals such as gender equality should be considered, as they are by scholar Liam Swiss (2012), altruistic. To realists, if gender equality leads to economic growth and orderly, sustainable social development, then it is good policy, period. And if it does not, then it should not be a primary concern of any donor country. Certainly, some might, as the Canadian government has in past policy pronouncements, attempt to combine altruism with realism through "an integrated view of humanity" (Government of Canada 1987, 6). Alternatively, however, one might simply accept that, in spite of the impression left by the humane internationalist/international realist dichotomy, both groups will often agree on development assistance policy; they will merely do so for different reasons.[1] It is therefore hardly in the interests of government critics to paint the realists as an impediment to long-term social progress. Cooperating with them in the pursuit of common ends should be more productive.

The Dichotomy Explained

Why would members of the humane internationalist movement reject the realists' differentiation between emergency relief and development assistance when doing so – and thereby positioning themselves outside of the strategic decision-making process – could compromise their capacity to effect global change? Here are four possible explanations:

> 1. *The commitment to a rigid approach to humane internationalism is a product of sincere, strongly held normative beliefs.*

Advocates such as Tony Vaux maintain that one should never differentiate between disaster relief and sustainable poverty reduction strategies; furthermore, he and others hazard, it cannot be done. "Humanitarian aid should play a role not only in saving lives today but also saving lives tomorrow," Vaux (2007, 15) has argued, "and this means contributing to a just society. Issues such as participation, consultation, gender equity, and respect for minorities are not just 'quality' aspects of a humanitarian response. They may be its essence, if they contribute to peace." Vaux explicitly rejects what he identifies as the minimalist approach to humanitarian assistance, popularized since 1997 by the Sphere Project (2013), and promotes instead the more holistic, developmentalist position first formally articulated in the Red Cross Code of Conduct in 1994 (Vaux 2007). In Vaux's defence, the latter position makes sense from a practitioner's perspective: Refugees who have lost everything during a natural or human-induced disaster and are then forced to return, post-disaster, to a country that lacks a functioning governance mechanism or sustainable infrastructure are hardly better off than they were before. If one does not, therefore, invest in that country's development, another disaster is almost inevitable. Strategic decision makers, however, often view the disaster and its long-term implications as distinct tactical challenges. One requires an immediate response to mollify a concerned (domestic) public; the second lacks the same political urgency.

2. *Structural realities prevent humane internationalists from recognizing why government decision makers see fundamental differences between emergency relief initiatives and policies explicitly designed to promote sustainable poverty reduction.*

The structural explanation is straightforward. Some non-governmental organizations (NGOs) – particularly those committed to the "disaster-development continuum" (Anderson 1994) – are mandated to pursue a combination of humanitarian and developmental assistance goals (Büthe et al. 2012). Their staff's responsibilities can spread over both challenges, and advocates among their workers might be split between Sphere minimalists and Red Cross developmentalists. The lack of cohesion within NGOs themselves might therefore prevent a more coherent approach to, and understanding of, foreign aid advocacy at the political level.

3. *Notions of personal self-interest prevent humane international-ists from adapting their tactics to accommodate political realities.*

Aid organizations and their workers cannot help but look out for themselves and their interests. While Büthe and his colleagues (2012) have convincingly rejected what for years was a commonly held view that NGOs behave like money-hungry institutions in competition for scarce resources and therefore focus on rallying support for media-intensive international tragedies as opposed to longer-term social and economic challenges, research by development consultant Ian Smillie and others has demonstrated that a significant percentage of northern NGOs continue to rely on programs like child sponsorship to raise money for what they nonetheless frame as development assistance initiatives (Smillie 1998; Vaux 2007). That such ventures are generally successful as short-term fundraisers is undeniable, and Büthe's suggestion that activists who use these strategies remain motivated by altruism is plausible. Still, in making the welfare of individual children the face of so-called development assistance initiatives, these organizations miscast ODA as a series of quick-impact projects rather than a long-term investment in sustainable development. In other words, they condition the public to believe – incorrectly – that paying for a single child to eat a healthy breakfast and attend school will have a lasting impact on the overall ability of that child's larger community to grow economically and provide a sustainable, prosperous environment for future generations.

At the individual level, recent research into the motivations of international aid volunteers rejects the standard assumption that altruism and selfishness are mutually exclusionary (de Jong 2011; Fechter 2012). Optimistic analysts, such as development assistance scholar Sara de Jong (2011, 30), suggest that the reality is more complex and that "it is possible for an act to be altruistic when the consequences of the act benefit both the person who performs the act and the person the act is done for." Others are more critical, suggesting that "the idea of 'wanting to help' is an expression of ... young ... men and women's privileged position; helping is structurally associated with a position of power and freedom of action" (Mangold 2012, 1495). In both cases, the ethical/practical divide is hardly clear-cut, leading one to question how it could possibly be helpful to frame development assistance discourse in binary terms.[2]

4. *The politics of gaining and maintaining public support for development assistance initiatives has caused humane internationalists to frame their cause in an overly simplistic and ultimately misleading manner.*

A fourth motivation to differentiate between altruism and pragmatism could be politics. The development assistance community functions under the (reasonable) assumption that the general public is most willing to support foreign aid when it is framed in altruistic terms and focused on results (Brown 2012; Büthe 2012; Lindstrom and Henson 2011; Mc Donnell et al. 2002; Pratt 2000). Presumably, then, some NGOs might court the popular humanitarian impulse as a means of initiating a relationship with the broader community. The thinking, it would follow, is that once the public is interested in global or individual hardship and even moderately committed to doing something about it, it will become easier for advocates to expand that support to include long-term development assistance priorities. As for the focus on results, citizens simply like to know how their tax dollars are being used, and it is easier to observe and measure immediate outcomes in responses to disasters. Again, however, the challenge in both cases is that focusing on either grave emergencies or individual stories skews popular understandings of foreign aid, making it more difficult for the general public to recognize the value and importance of long-term poverty reduction programs. Moreover, as Brown (2012, 6) has made clear, short-term results, as positive as they might be, "do not guarantee a concomitant positive impact on broader development outcomes" (see also Smillie, this volume). The effect the public tends to see in the aftermath of a disaster often cannot be sustained without a long-term commitment to development (hence, the disaster-development continuum), nor will improvements to the life of a single child necessarily benefit an entire community.

The Results of the Humane Internationalist Campaign Thus Far

Regardless of whether the humane internationalist movement is driven by a rigid commitment to a disaster-development continuum, the joint mandates of NGOs, the self-interest of such groups and their workers, or the political realities of contemporary Canada, Ottawa's inconsistent, if not simply disappointing, effort to support poverty reduction programs around the world makes it clear that attempts to frame development assistance policy as a moral imperative have been largely unsuccessful. The long-lasting problems are threefold: (1) after more than half a century of advocacy and education, the Canadian public – much like publics across the Western world – maintains a limited understanding of ODA; (2) popular support for foreign aid is fickle and shallow, and significant numbers of Canadians believe that aid is failing; and (3) the national commitment to development assistance rises and falls based on the strength of the domestic economy, with official contributions to emergency relief consistently finding greater favour among voters than long-term investments in sustainable partnerships. This section examines these three problems in turn.

Lack of Public Understanding

Over the last two decades, studies by reputable organizations like the Organisation for Economic Co-operation and Development (OECD) and the United Kingdom's Institute for Public Policy and Research have demonstrated that, in the words of the former OECD president, Jean Bovin, "people in most countries lack adequate knowledge about development co-operation and about the difference that aid can actually make in the lives of people in developing countries. While there is a stable level of 'compassion' for the poor, most people find it difficult to arrive at a sophisticated judgment about the develop-ment efforts of their governments and NGOs" (Bovin and Martinez 1998, 7; see also Glennie et al. 2012; Mc Donnell et al. 2002). Put less generously, most Westerners "believe that ODA *is* humanitarian assistance" (Mc Donnell et al. 2002, 12) and therefore question its long-term strategic impact.

Domestic research suggests that Canadians are no exception to these observations. In the early 1990s, a series of surveys by CIDA found that Canadians identified aid primarily as a means to relieve human suffering. Moreover, as citizens of a generous country, the data showed, Canadians felt a moral obligation to do their part to help the less fortunate during their times of greatest need (Pratt 1994). Two decades later, the feelings of generosity persisted, as did the belief in providing assistance to those "in need of [immediate] support" (Environics Institute 2011). Consistently missing from these findings, however, is any sense that a strategic investment in sustain-able poverty reduction is an international obligation of the Canadian government in either a moral or a political sense.

Since both Ottawa and development-focused NGOs have tradi-tionally spent little money or energy on information campaigns that might correct this skewed understanding of foreign aid (Smillie 1998), the role of educating the public has been left largely to the media. In Canada, popular journalism appears to have only reinforced the common ignorance. As one analyst has shown, when the Canadian Broadcast Corporation covered the Haitian earthquake in early 2010, its stories consistently emphasized the words "help" and "generous," and paid significantly less attention to the long-term needs of Haitian society that were exacerbated by the disaster (Mason 2011; see also Smillie 1998). There is nothing inherently wrong with being gener-ous, of course, but it is not the *primary* ingredient in any strategically meaningful, effective, long-term international development assistance strategy. So long as Canadians fail to understand the difference, there is no reason to believe that their altruistic inclinations will translate into a sustained commitment to poverty reduction around the world.

Fickle and Shallow Public Attitudes

The Canadian public's support for development assistance has been described at various times over the last fifty years as "fickle" (Spicer 1966, 38), "fragile," and "profoundly ambivalent, if not incoherent" (Noël et al. 2004, 33, 37). Consistent with these findings are polls that note that, in times of financial difficulty at home, support for foreign aid declines significantly (Environics Institute 2010). Such attitudes mirror the results of similar international surveys, reinforcing the idea that the worldwide approach to promoting development assistance as humane public policy is failing (Lindstrom and Henson 2011; Mc Donnell et al. 2002). The common attitude, to paraphrase a former Canadian prime minister, seems to be "generosity if necessary, but not necessarily generosity."

In the current context, there is reason to believe that humane internationalists are more than just failing; some of them have become part of the problem. Some analysts accuse NGOs of oversimplifying the complex challenges of long-term aid and of mixing messages (Glennie et al. 2012; Smillie 1997, 1998). Others argue that ongoing advocacy that emphasizes desolation can result in disengagement, if not disbelief. In other words, when developing states are framed as places where disasters happen and children suffer, and if the crises seem to be ever-present, some Canadians will eventually give up on aid's efficacy (Glennie et al. 2012; Lindstrom and Henson 2011; Mc Donnell et al. 2002; Noël et al. 2004; Pratt 2000; Smillie 1998; Spicer 1966).

Consistency with the Donor's Agenda, Not the Recipient's

The combination of the lack of strategic importance ascribed to development assistance by the Canadian government and the absence of real public understanding and commitment has enabled poorly conceived, tactically focused official policies to persist.[3] As would any liberal democratic regime, Ottawa has traditionally responded to the basic demand to demonstrate generosity towards the poor through actions that privilege domestic support over causes abroad.[4] Successive Canadian governments of every political inclination have done so for two understandable reasons: First, because that is what the public wants. Charity, it is often said, should begin at home. In difficult times, limited government resources should be used to support Canadian taxpayers (Lindstrom et al. 2011; Mc Donnell et al. 2002; Pratt 1994). Second, as international realists would expect, the federal government has been true to its responsibility to promote and protect the interests of the state. As one of the first analyses of Canadian development assistance policy argued in 1966:

Philanthropy is plainly no more than a fickle and confused policy stimulant, derived exclusively from personal conscience. It is not an objective of government. Love for mankind is a virtue of the human heart, an emotion which can stir only individuals – never bureaucracies or institutions. Governments exist only to promote the public good; and, as a result, they must act purely in the selfish interest of the state they serve. Altruism as foreign policy is a misnomer, even if sometimes the fruits of policy are incidentally beneficial to foreigners. To talk of humanitarian "aims" in Canadian foreign policy is, in fact, to confuse policy with the ethics of individuals moulding it, to mix government objectives with personal motives. (Spicer 1966, 11)

Or, as the political scientist Kim Richard Nossal maintained,

Organized groups of humans have mandates that are ruthlessly exclusive, and their members generally have a well-developed sense of their obligations to the group. In particular, they are able and prone to distinguish between their personal sentiments and their positions as officials of organizations. More importantly, their positions *oblige* them to limit the organization's altruism ... Because of these limits, a fundamental lack of concrete, or real, concern for those who lie outside the scope of the organization's mandate naturally follows. (Nossal 1988, 35–56)

To be sure, the "organizational altruism" of the state, and therefore its officials, is wider than that of most individuals, who tend to be truly altruistic only towards kin. But it is limited, nonetheless. Having never defined its mandate in imperial terms, the Canadian government has no authority over, and thus no real responsibility for, the condition or behaviour of those living outside Canada's borders. A lack of the kind of ethical obligation to other peoples that leads to meaningful and altruistic concrete action follows inexorably (Nossal 1988, 49–50).

The Way Ahead?

It would be arrogant for any analyst to suggest a simple solution to the challenges identified in this essay, but it would be equally inappropriate to engage in such extensive criticism of the humane internationalist approach without offering at least some thoughts on how to improve its effectiveness. Here are three:

1. *Rather than criticizing the international realists' thought process, emphasize a shared desire for common outcomes.*

So long as international realists advocate a stable, liberal world order, humane internationalists must learn to manage their antagonism towards them. Put another way, if humane internationalists simply accept that international realists will never be convinced that altruism should drive public policy, they will soon recognize opportunities for cooperation and collaboration to support shared goals that have been neglected for much too long.

2. *Avoid reinforcing the common perception that development assistance is no different than common charity.*

The humane internationalist campaign might also focus its public awareness and fundraising campaigns on issues and events that are less likely to reinforce standard popular misconceptions about official development assistance and its implications. Admittedly, doing so might temporarily hurt the ability of certain organizations to raise much-needed money. In the long run, however, a more strategic approach to public education that aims to break the links that so many Canadians make between charity and development assistance will enable the humane internationalist movement to cultivate more sustainable popular support for causes that it holds dear. In other words, rather than using, if not exploiting, an earthquake in Haiti by framing it as an effort to "save" individual Haitians, advocates might treat such a crisis as an opportunity to promote development assistance efforts in other states that share similar vulnerabilities.

3. *Build public support from the top down.*

Finally, the recent merger of CIDA and the Department of Foreign Affairs and International Trade presents a significant opportunity to effect real political change. While the tendency within the humane internationalist movement has been to try to build support from the ground up, and steady public sympathy will be necessary to ensure a long-term government commitment to an effective, sustainable poverty reduction program (Otter 2003), for now, it might be prudent to focus advocacy and education efforts on the political elite. It is worth recalling that the United Kingdom's early twenty-first-century transition from development assistance laggard to global leader was accomplished without significant popular involvement, let alone support; rather, a meeting of the minds among the leaders of the country's most significant political parties enabled the government to exercise leadership (Glennie et al. 2012). In that spirit, rather than merely criticizing the decision to merge, humane internationalists might focus on practical proposals to help shape the new Department of Foreign Affairs, Trade and Development in a manner that preserves and protects the poverty reduction mandate of the old development agency.

Conclusion

Humane internationalists have been pursuing a noble, yet perennially unsuccessful, campaign to effect a change in Ottawa's and the Canadian public's understanding of the purpose and impact of foreign aid for more than half a century. Rather than persisting in an effort that seems doomed to disappoint, it is time to refashion the campaign to reflect better the contemporary challenges and opportunities of promoting sustainable poverty reduction and emergency relief programs around the world. The solution is not to abandon altruism in its entirety. Rather, it is to concede that as an advocacy strategy, humane internationalism has never succeeded in altering realist thinking. Finding common ground with the realists, thinking more carefully about the negative impact of drawing disproportionate public attention to crises that conflate assistance with charity, and focusing on the policy-making elite as opposed to everyday Canadians might not be strategies that will excite Cranford Pratt's many followers, but they are more likely to advance the cause of sustainable poverty reduction around the world than the current approach.

Notes

1. Others, such as Morrison (2000) and Nossal (1988), have criticized the humanitarian internationalist/international realist dichotomy for additional reasons.

2. Unless one is using such a framework to relieve the guilt associated with profiting personally from work in the development field.
3. For a helpful summary of public and government thinking, see Otter (2003).
4. Canada's history of tied aid is a prime example.

References

Anderson, Mary B. 1994. "Understanding the Disaster–Development Continuum." *Gender and Development*, vol. 2, no. 1: 7–10.

Black, David, and Molly den Heyer. 2010–11. "A Crisis of Conscience?" *The Broker*, no. 23: 20–23.

Bovin, Jean, and Miguel Angel Martinez. 1998. "Preface." In Ian Smillie and Henry Helmich, eds. *Public Attitudes and International Development Co-operation*. Paris: OECD: 7.

Brown, Stephen. 2012. "Canadian Aid Enters the Twenty-First Century." In Stephen Brown, ed. *Struggling for Effectiveness: CIDA and Canadian Foreign Aid*. Montreal and Kingston: McGill–Queen's University Press: 3–23.

Büthe, Tim, Solomon Major, and André de Mello e Souza. 2012. "The Politics of Private Foreign Aid: Humanitarian Principles, Economic Development Objectives, and Organizational Interests in NGO Private Aid Allocation." *International Organization*, vol. 66, no. 4: 571–607.

Canadian Press. 2010. "Canadians See Bigger Role for Charities." *Toronto Star*. February 18.

CDFAI. 2007. "Canadian Views on Foreign Aid." Innovative Research Group Poll. Internet, http://www.cdfai.org/PDF/Poll%20on%20Foreign%20Aid.pdf. Accessed February 15, 2013.

Chapnick, Adam. 2005. "Peace, Order and Good Government: The 'conservative' Tradition in Canadian Foreign Policy." *International Journal*, vol. 60, no. 3: 635–50.

De Jong, Sara. 2011. "False Binaries: Altruism and Selfishness in NGO Work." In Anne-Meike Fechter and Heather Hindman, eds. *Inside the Everyday Lives of Development Workers: The Challenges and Futures of Aidland*. Sterling, VA: Kumarian Press: 21–40.

Environics Institute. 2010. *Focus Canada 2010*. Internet, http://www.queensu.ca/cora/_files/fc2010report.pdf. Accessed May 29, 2013.

Environics Institute. 2011. *Focus Canada 2011*. Internet, http://www.queensu.ca/cora/_files/Environics%20Institute%20-%20Focus%20Canada%202011%20FINAL%20REPORT.pdf. Accessed May 28, 2013.

Fechter, Anne-Meike. 2012. "The Personal and the Professional: Aid Workers' Relationships in the Development Process." *Third World Quarterly*, vol. 33, no. 8: 1387–1404.

Glennie, Alex, Will Straw, and Leni Wild. 2012. *Understanding Public Attitudes to Aid and Development*. London, UK: Institute for Public Policy and Overseas Development Institute.

Government of Canada. 1987. *Canadian Development Assistance: To Benefit a Better World*. Ottawa: Minister of Supply and Services.

Gulrajani, Nilima. 2012. "Improving Canada's Aid Performance as a Bilateral Donor: Assessing the Past and Building for the Future." In Stephen Brown, ed. *Struggling for Effectiveness: CIDA and Canadian Foreign Aid*. Montreal and Kingston, ON: McGill–Queen's University Press: 53–78.

Gulrajani, Nilima. 2013. "Global Evidence Suggests Merging CIDA and DFAIT Will Be a Mistake." *Toronto Star*. March 28. http://www.thestar.com/opinion/commentary/2013/03/28/global_evidence_suggests_merging_cida_and_dfait_will_be_a_mistake.html. Accessed May 28, 2013.

Lindstrom, Johanna, and Spencer Henson. 2011. *What Does the Public Think, Know, and Do about Aid and Development? Results and Analysis from the UK Public Opinion Monitor*. Brighton: Institute of Development Studies.

Mangold, Katharine. 2012. "'Struggling to do the Right Thing': Challenges during International Volunteering." *Third World Quarterly*, vol. 33, no. 8: 1493–1509.

Mason, Corinne Lysandra. 2011. "Foreign Aid as Gift: The Canadian Broadcasting Corporation's Response to the Haiti Earthquake." *Critical Studies in Media Communications*, vol. 28, no. 2: 94–112.

Mc Donnell, Ida, Henri-Bernard Solignac, and Liam Wegimont. 2002. *Public Opinion Research, Global Education, and Development Co-operation Reform: In Search of a Virtuous Circle*. Paris: OECD.

Morrison, David R. 2000. "Canadian Aid: A Mixed Record and an Uncertain Future." In Jim Freedman, ed. *Transforming Development: Foreign Aid for a Changing World*. Toronto: University of Toronto Press: 15–36.

Noël, Alain, Jean-Philippe Thérien, and Sébastien Dallaire. 2004. "Divided Over Internationalism: The Canadian Public and Development Assistance." *Canadian Public Policy*, vol. 30, no. 1: 29–46.

Nossal, Kim Richard. 1988. "Mixed Motives Revisited: Canada's Interest in Development Assistance." *Canadian Journal of Political Science*, vol. 31, no. 1: 35–56.

Otter, Mark. 2003. "Domestic Public Support for Foreign Aid: Does it Matter?" *Third World Quarterly*, vol. 24, no. 1: 115–25.

Pratt, Cranford. 1989. "Humane Internationalism: Its Significance and its Variants." In Cranford Pratt, ed. *Internationalism Under Strain: The North–South Policies of Canada, the Netherlands, Norway, and Sweden*. Toronto: University of Toronto Press: 3–23.

Pratt, Cranford. 1990. "Middle Power Internationalism and Global Poverty." In Cranford Pratt, ed. *Middle Power Internationalism: The North–South Dimension*. Montreal: McGill–Queen's University Press: 3–24.

Pratt, Cranford. 1994. "Humane Internationalism and Canadian Development Assistance Policies." In Cranford Pratt, ed. *Canadian International Development Assistance Policies: An Appraisal*. Montreal: McGill–Queen's University Press: 334–70.

Pratt, Cranford. 1999. "Competing Rationales for Canadian Development Assistance." *International Journal*, vol. 54, no. 2: 306–23.

Pratt, Cranford. 2000. "Alleviating Global Poverty or Enhancing Security: Competing Rationales for Canadian Development Assistance." In Jim Freedman, ed. *Transforming Development: Foreign Aid for a Changing World*. Toronto: University of Toronto Press: 37–59.

Savage, Luiza Ch. 2013. "On Canada's Changing Aid to Haiti, the Merger of CIDA and DFAIT, and the Role of the Private Sector in Development." *Macleans.ca*. May 10. http://www2.macleans.ca/2013/05/10/on-canadas-changing-aid-to-haiti-the-merger-of-cida-and-dfait-and-the-role-of-the-private-sector-in-development/. Accessed May 28, 2013.

Smillie, Ian. 1997. "NGOs and Development Assistance: A Change in Mindset?" *Third World Quarterly*, vol. 18, no. 3: 563–77.

Smillie, Ian. 1998. "Optical and Other Illusions: Trends and Issues in Public Thinking about Development Co-operation." In Ian Smillie and Henry Helmich, eds. *Public Attitudes and International Development Co-operation*. Paris: OECD: 21–39.

Sphere Project. 2013. *Humanitarian Charter and Minimum Standards in Humanitarian Response*. Internet, http://www.sphereproject.org/. Accessed October 18, 2013.

Spicer, Keith. 1966. *A Samaritan State? External Aid in Canada's Foreign Policy*. Toronto: University of Toronto Press.

Swiss, Liam. 2012. "Gender, Security, and Instrumentalism: Canada's Foreign Aid in Support of National Interest?" In Stephen Brown, ed. *Struggling for Effectiveness: CIDA and Canadian Foreign Aid*. Montreal and Kingston, ON: McGill–Queen's University Press: 135–58.

Vaux, Tony. 2007. "Humanitarian Trends and Dilemmas." In Deborah Eade and Tony Vaux, eds. *Development and Humanitarianism: Practical Issues*. Bloomfield, CT: Kumarian Press: 1–23.

Winegard, William et al. 1987. *For Whose Benefit? Report of the Standing Committee on External Affairs and International Trade on Canada's Official Development Assistance Policies and Programs*. Ottawa: Queen's Printer for Canada.

CHAPTER III

Revisiting the Ethical Foundations of Aid and Development Policy from a Cosmopolitan Perspective

John D. Cameron

Debates about normative ethics and Canadian aid policy are long-standing but surprisingly thin. In spite of the normative values that underlie public support for aid, and indeed the motivations of many scholars who write about it, the actual ethical underpinnings of aid have rarely been seriously examined in the Canadian context. Many scholars have discussed the relative importance of humanitarian and realist considerations in the making of aid policy, but few have sought to examine aid itself in the context of broader normative ethical frameworks. Recent changes in the institutional framework for Canadian aid following the merger of the Canadian International Development Agency (CIDA) into the Department of Foreign Affairs, Trade and Development (DFATD) and the increasingly explicit role of domestic political and economic interests in the design of aid policy make it more important now than ever before to revisit and deepen the debate about the role of ethical considerations in the analysis of Canadian aid policy and practice.

The absorption of CIDA into DFATD and explicit subordination of aid policy to broader foreign policy suggests two possibilities for how we analyze aid and development policy. The first is to abandon any expectation that aid is connected to or inspired by moral concerns for the well-being of other people and to employ realist methodological perspectives that analyze aid purely as an instrument of foreign policy. Indeed, numerous scholars have suggested that although moral concerns may be an important source of public support for aid, they do not seriously affect aid policy (Chapnick, this volume; Silvio, this volume).

The alternative, for which I make the case here, is to re-examine the ethical basis for aid and to analyze aid in the context of a more theoretically consistent and coherent normative framework that draws attention to the broader range of government policies that affect developing countries. To the extent that aid has been analyzed in the light of ethical considerations, scholars have generally, if often only implicitly, emphasized positive ethical obligations to provide assistance to people in need, overlooking equally important but often neglected negative obligations to not cause harm in the first place through other non-aid policies. If scholars and activists are to make the case for reconnecting Canadian aid to its ethical foundations, the understanding of those foundations needs to be much broader – and include both positive and negative ethical duties, which cannot be hived off from one another. From this perspective, arguments for aid as an expression of ethical obligations generally overlook half of the normative framework on which they draw – negative duties to not cause harm. The practical application of a normative ethical framework concerned with both positive and negative moral duties would shift attention beyond aid policy to all of the policy areas in which the Canadian government affects the lives of people in other parts of the world, particularly people who are vulnerable or marginalized.

This chapter makes a normative argument directed not at policy makers, but rather at analysts of Canadian aid, including students. It argues that analysis of aid policy needs to be more explicitly informed by cosmopolitan political theory, which would expand the object of analysis from aid to development policy. At its core, cosmopolitanism asserts that all humans have moral obligations to all other humans, regardless of their location in the world and national citizenship. Those obligations include positive moral duties to provide assistance to others in need as well as negative moral duties to not cause harm to others in the first place, either directly or indirectly, intentionally or unintentionally. A growing number of political theorists assert that cosmopolitan normative perspectives have become particularly urgent in the context of contemporary globalization, which forces human beings everywhere into much closer connections than they ever experienced in the past (Brown and Held 2010; Kymlicka and Walker 2012).

Although cosmopolitanism is not without its critics (discussed below), the need for some sort of cosmopolitan ethics in an era of intensifying globalization means that it no longer makes sense from either a practical or an ethical perspective to analyze Canadian aid in isolation from the rest of Canadian foreign policy. With the merger of CIDA into DFATD – indicating the thorough incorporation of aid policy into Canada's broader foreign policy framework – the time has come to likewise shift analysis of aid policy and practice into a broader normative framework that takes into consideration not just aid policy, but other non-aid aspects of Canadian development policy from the perspective of both positive and negative moral obligations. It seems the Harper government does not distinguish aid policy from the rest of Canadian foreign policy; this shift should also lead analysts beyond the confines of analyzing aid in isolation from other government policies to ground their analysis in a holistic understanding of ethical principles.

In the terms of contemporary policy discourse, I make an argument for analyzing Canadian aid and development policy from a "policy coherence for development" approach that is grounded in "ethical coherence." Various scholars and organizations have put forward pragmatic, policy-oriented arguments for greater attention to "policy coherence for development" in aid and development policy, but little attention has been paid to the underlying normative ethical arguments for analyzing aid and development policy using this approach.

To make this argument, the chapter is organized into three sections. The first reviews debates about ethics and aid policy in Canada. The second section connects the policy-oriented debates about "policy coherence for development" to ethical considerations grounded in cosmopolitan political theory, seeking to explain how cosmopolitan ethics provide substantive normative support for the analysis of aid and development policy. The third section then outlines the implications of a cosmopolitan approach to the analysis of aid and development policy for research methodology and teaching.

Ethics and Contemporary Aid Policy in Canada

This is perhaps a strange time to make an argument for renewed emphasis on normative ethics in the analysis of Canadian aid. Although it has been widely recognized that aid policy reflects a mix of ethically driven humanitarian motives and self-interest, there is a growing consensus that over the past two decades self-interest has increasingly displaced humanitarian considerations in the crafting of aid policy (Black, this volume; Brown 2012; Pratt 1994, 2000). Indeed, following the merger of CIDA into DFATD and recent policy decisions from CIDA and statements by then Minister of International Cooperation Julian Fantino in 2012 that explicitly articulated domestic self-interest as a legitimate motive for aid, it appears that the space for moral considerations in Canadian aid policy making has shrunk considerably.[1] In short, *realpolitik* seems to be the order of the day, suggesting that realist perspectives are much more appropriate for understanding Canadian aid policy than approaches grounded in normative ethics.

However, my argument here is not so much about what Canadian aid policy should look like, as about how analysts should examine and evaluate it. From this perspective, choices about the issues we choose to research and the analytical methods we use can be understood as ethical decisions. It is probably safe to argue that most scholars who study aid policy do so out of a moral concern for the well-being of people in other parts of the world. As Brown and Raddatz note in the conclusion to a 2012 volume on Canadian aid, "All [sixteen] contributors to this volume share a normative concern about poverty in the global South and want to see the Canadian government deliver better aid" (2012, 338).

Nevertheless, the normative foundations for studying aid are rarely examined in depth. A full review of the literature on Canadian aid is beyond the scope of this short chapter, but it is useful to examine how the work of one particular scholar, Cranford Pratt, has shaped scholarly thinking in Canada about the moral foundations for aid (Pratt 1989, 1994, 2000). As David Black argues in this volume, "the scholarship of, and inspired by, Cranford Pratt has been exceptionally influential in framing analysis of the foundations and rationale for the Canadian aid program." However, as Black goes on to explain, Pratt's understanding of the relationship between Canadian aid and what he called "humane internationalism" also "limited the debate in ways that have constrained creativity and innovation." One important limitation was an excessive emphasis on aid as an expression of positive moral duties to do good, at the expense of attention to negative moral duties to not cause harm through other policy areas. Indeed, Pratt's conception of "humane internationalism" focused almost exclusively on the provision of aid. As Black notes, Pratt defined humane internationalism as "an acceptance by the citizens of the industrialized states that they have ethical obligations towards those beyond their borders and that these in turn impose obligations on their governments" (Pratt 1989, 13, quoted in Black, this volume). Nonetheless, although potentially cosmopolitan in scope, the ethical obligations that Pratt emphasized focused predominantly on aid. Given Pratt's influence, it is perhaps not surprising that discussions about the ethical foundations of Canadian aid have similarly focused on positive duties to provide assistance. Unfortunately, that focus appears to have come at the expense of attention to the linkages to other policy areas, such as immigration and finance, which might be more appropriately analyzed from a "do no harm" perspective – for example, considering how the impacts of CIDA-funded projects to promote child and maternal health might be undermined by immigration practices that effectively poach medical professionals from developing countries.[2]

Some recent works have examined Canadian foreign and development policy from a perspective that highlights the harm and potential harm done by Canada in other parts of the world (Engler 2009; Gordon 2010). A growing body of work focuses specifically on government support for Canadian extractive industries overseas, including the use of aid to support extractive activities and the negative consequences for the well-being of people who live in mining-affected communities (e.g., Blackwood and Stewart 2012; Brown, this volume). However, this body of work remains marginal to the larger body of research that focuses more narrowly on aid policy itself, often criticizing the extent to which it fails to fulfil positive duties to provide assistance to those in need (although not always framed in those terms). A separate body of work focuses specifically on ethical issues in development policy (Gaspar and St. Clair 2010; Goulet 1995; Irwin 2001; Quarles Van Ufford and Giri 2003). Many of the works within these volumes focus on moral problems with how the idea of development itself has been operationalized and often imposed, while a smaller number (Giri 2003; Penz 2001) highlight the importance of cosmopolitan perspectives in the analysis of development policy. These debates need to be rekindled and revisited.

Quite separate from discussions of ethics and development policy, other analysts and organizations, including the OECD's Development Assistance Committee (OECD/DAC) and the Centre for

Global Development (CGD) have expanded analysis of aid policy to also include non-aid development policies, highlighting the importance of "policy coherence for development" (Brown 2012; McGill 2012). Although it makes no mention of ethical considerations, this analysis represents an important step towards a more ethically coherent approach that analyzes aid policy and practice as part of a broader array of development policies and explicitly considers how those policies may do both good and harm. Both the OECD/DAC and the CGD assert the importance of a "policy coherence for development" approach from a completely pragmatic, policy-oriented perspective. In this chapter I try to link the "policy coherence for development" approach to deeper considerations of normative ethics, and in particular to cosmopolitan political philosophy, with the goal of demonstrating that there are both pragmatic and ethical reasons for devoting greater attention to policy coherence for development.

It is important to make the distinction between the analysis of development policy and practice from a "policy coherence" approach, on the one hand, and the actual implementation of "policy coherence" in government policy, on the other. The failure to make this distinction has clouded recent debate. As Brown explains, "At its best, policy coherence *for development* recognizes that more than just aid is required for development, including reforms to the global trading system" (2012a, 9). The difficulty comes with analysis of actual experience with policy coherence, in which the *"for development"* elements tend to disappear as other foreign policy and domestic political and economic considerations take precedence. Nevertheless, even though the actual practice of "policy coherence" may "undermine development rather than promote it" (Brown 2012, 10), a very strong case remains for *analyzing* aid from a "policy coherence for development" approach. The next section examines the ethical basis for such an analytical perspective in cosmopolitan political theory.

From Policy Coherence for Development to Cosmopolitanism

Most scholars of aid acknowledge that public support for development assistance is largely grounded in ethical principles – even if aid policies and practices are largely shaped by strategic, partisan, economic, and bureaucratic factors. Moreover, many, if not most, scholars of aid are themselves motivated by ethical concerns. However, in spite of these normative motivations, the actual ethical underpinning of aid has rarely been seriously examined in the Canadian context. In the context of the 2013 merger of CIDA into DFATD, it is extremely important to revisit the ethical considerations that underlie the provision of development assistance and that, as I argue here, should also inform analysis of both aid and non-aid aspects of development policy, and particularly the linkages between them.

Questions about ethical obligations to other humans who live beyond state boundaries – which clearly inform the moral basis for aid – have been actively debated since the fourth century BCE in the context of what is widely understood as cosmopolitan political theory. The term cosmopolitanism is typically attributed to the Greek philosopher Diogenes, who, when asked where he was from, became famous for answering "I am a *kosmou politês*" (citizen of the world), implying that he understood his ethical and civic commitments as applying to all of humanity and not only to the fellow citizens of his city-state (Brown and Held 2010, 4). The question of what ethical obligations humans owe to other humans has been hotly debated by cosmopolitan philosophers since the time of Diogenes (Brown and Held 2010). The basic principle that those moral duties exist is widely agreed upon, even if their specific content and the mechanisms for putting them into practice are not. Indeed, as the political philosopher David Miller asserted, "'cosmopolitan' is probably now the preferred self-description of most political philosophers who write about global justice" (2007, 23).

The central questions addressed in cosmopolitan theory concern the substance of the ethical obligations that all humans hold to all other humans by virtue of their shared humanity. Cosmopolitan philosophers do not agree on what those obligations are or what specific actions they require, but they do agree that our ethical obligations involve both *positive* duties to provide assistance to others in need and *negative* duties to not cause harm in the first place. Most cosmopolitan theorists are quick to point out that negative duties involve not only an obligation to not cause direct harm to others, but also to not cause or contribute to *indirect* and *unintended* harm, including harms that result only from the cumulative actions of many people (Brown and Held 2010; Held 2010).

The relative importance of *positive* and *negative* moral duties is debated by proponents of different frameworks of normative ethics. In particular, consequentialist or utilitarian ethical frameworks assert that moral questions should be assessed on the basis of an action's outcome or result and so do not privilege positive or negative ethical duties over one another. By contrast, deontological ethical frameworks, widely associated with eighteenth-century German scholar Immanuel Kant, make considerations about human dignity the reference point for ethical questions, and so prioritize negative duties. From a deontological or Kantian perspective, the failure to respect negative duties to not cause harm (that is, to cause harm to others) causes greater damage to human dignity than the failure to provide assistance to others in need. The contemporary human rights scholar, Thomas Pogge, makes a similar argument that the greatest causes of human suffering in the world are caused by failures to act on *negative* duties to not cause harm, in particular through the global trade system. Consequently, Pogge argues that negative duties should be prioritized (2007, 16–17). Paehlke (2012) makes a similar argument about the failures to prevent harm through climate change. However, the crucial point here for analysis of Canadian aid and development policy is that cosmopolitanism, along with virtually all of the prevailing normative ethical frameworks, including most of the world's religions, includes both positive and negative moral obligations.

Scholars have raised legitimate concerns with cosmopolitanism that need to be carefully considered. First, various postcolonial critics have highlighted the Western roots of cosmopolitan theory and have argued that it cannot possibly represent a global ethical framework for all of humanity. In response, other scholars have highlighted the many non-Western expressions of cosmopolitanism and have argued that if these articulations are given the attention they deserve, cosmopolitanism can indeed be understood as a global ethic (see Gaspar 2006; Gidwani 2006; Giri 2006; Pieterse 2006).

Second, some political scientists (e.g., Miller 2007; Nagel 2005) have argued that global moral obligations cannot be effectively realized without some sort of global state and that such a state is both unfeasible and undesirable (because it could not be democratic). In response, growing numbers of scholars have abandoned discussions of *legal* and *political* cosmopolitanism that focus on global political institutions, moving to place more attention on civic and moral cosmopolitanism – that is, the cultivation of cosmopolitan attitudes and practices (Brown and Held 2010, 11–13).

Finally, research in psychology suggests that the moral focus of cosmopolitanism on all of humanity is not tenable, that the actual exercise of cosmopolitan attitudes requires that individual humans be grounded in particular communities to which they feel and exercise greater obligations than they do to the rest of humanity. Emerging from these critiques, the idea of "rooted cosmopolitanism" asserts that "rootedness" in local communities is not just inevitable but necessary for the exercise of cosmopolitanism (Kymlicka and Walker 2012). In short, the versions of cosmopolitanism articulated by contemporary political theorists are quite different from those of Ancient Greece, the Enlightenment, or even the 1980s and 1990s. As Kymlicka and Walker point out,

> If current realities have made some form of cosmopolitanism inevitable, these realities have also made clear that we need to revise our inherited ideas of cosmopolitanism … Enlightenment images of cosmopolitanism seem paradoxically both utopian and dystopian. They are utopian in their expectations of a democratic world state, but dystopian in their suppression of cultural and linguistic diversity. Indeed, European colonialism was often justified as a means of spreading a cosmopolitan order and ethos … Any defensible conception of cosmopolitanism for today's world must avoid these connotations. It must be a postcolonial cosmopolitanism. (Kymlicka and Walter 2012, 2–3)

The difficulty with most discussions of the moral basis for Canadian aid is that they prioritize – often only implicitly – positive ethical obligations but leave negative obligations unaddressed. To discuss moral obligations towards the rest of humanity only in terms of development assistance, while ignoring negative duties to not cause harm is not only theoretically inconsistent, but borders on political irresponsibility – at least to the extent that the scholarly analysis of aid has any influence on public understanding of it. Ethical consistency and political responsibility suggest that scholars of aid should give equal consideration to positive and negative ethical duties. In practical methodological terms, this would require the expansion of our analytical frameworks beyond aid as an expression of positive duties to also include greater examination of the potential harms caused by both aid and non-aid aspects of development policy, in particular the ways in which other policies might undermine the impacts of aid. Of course, there is a real danger that concerns to "do no harm" could be twisted into a justification to not provide aid at all, especially in the context of the loud chorus of aid critics. A pragmatic cosmopolitan response to this danger would be to focus attention first on the policy areas that present the greatest risk of harm, which might include trade, finance, defence, and the promotion of extractive industries; in comparison, the risks of doing harm through aid would be much less significant and justify less concern.

Significantly, growing numbers of analysts of aid have also come to the conclusion that aid should be examined within the broader context of other policy areas, albeit for reasons that are primarily pragmatic rather than ethical. In 2009, Clare Short, then British Minister for International Development, asserted, "Development is more than aid. If we really mean to establish a more equitable and sustainable world order, then all areas of policy must be re-examined. It is a mistake to confine thinking on development to how aid budgets are managed" (quoted in McGill 2012, 40). McGill (2012) highlights the ways that the governments of both the UK and Ireland – in contrast to Canada – have incorporated analysis of non-aid policies into their development policy frameworks. In so doing, he emphasizes the importance of analyzing both the aid and non-aid policies of donor countries from the perspective of "policy coherence for development" and draws on data collected since 2002 by both the OECD/DAC and the CGD's Commitment to Development Index. The OECD 2008 Ministerial Declaration on Policy Coherence for Development – to which Canada is a signatory – requires the Canadian cabinet to "ensure that information is gathered on the development impact of [non-aid] policies so that it can influence Canadian policy and its interactions with the developing world. This in turn requires cabinet to inform the various departments dealing with policy decisions that might affect development" (OECD 2012, 37). While the OECD/DAC emphasizes policy processes to enhance policy coherence for development, the Commitment to Development Index focuses explicitly on six non-aid policy areas (as well as aid itself) in its analysis of rich country development policies. Those six policy areas are trade, investment, migration, environment, security, and technology transfer (CGD 2013).

While academic debate has focused on whether the idea of "policy coherence for development" actually improves or undermines development when it is implemented, the key point here concerns the need to *analyze* Canadian foreign policy from a "policy coherence for development" perspective. The central questions are:

How and to what extent does the Government of Canada promote or undermine the well-being of people in other parts of the world through its foreign and domestic policies? How do decisions in one policy area support or undermine development efforts in other policy areas? The adoption of a "policy coherence for development" approach among analysts is important not just for practical reasons of aid effectiveness, but as a methodological expression of ethical considerations as well.

The Practical Implications of Cosmopolitan Ethics for Aid and Development Research

While most scholars of development policy aim for objectivity in their analysis, the choice of what questions to ask and what research methods to employ are ultimately normative decisions. Making research on development policy more "ethically coherent" would require a number of shifts to expand the scope of analysis of Canadian development policy well beyond aid. The Center for Global Development's Commitment to Development Index already provides systematic longitudinal data since 2002 on six non-aid components of rich country development policy (trade, investment, migration, environment, security, and technology transfer), but there remains significant scope for research in other government policy areas that have important implications for development – in particular the connections between aid and non-aid policies and how they complement or undermine one another.

In the current Canadian context, research on the development impacts of government support for Canadian extractive businesses operating overseas is particularly important (Brown, this volume), but so too are other less-examined policy areas, such as Canada Pension Plan investment policies and practices (Blackwood and Stewart 2012). There are simply no good reasons for scholarly research to continue to place such disproportionate emphasis on aid as an expression of humanitarian concerns about doing good, without at least simultaneously expanding analysis of other aspects of Canadian government policy that may undermine the good done through aid.

Conclusion

The argument presented in this chapter for greater emphasis on negative ethical duties in the crafting of our research agendas on Canadian development policy is fairly simple and is certainly not new. However, the argument still needs to be made – at the risk of sounding like a broken record – as, time and time again, when scholars and analysts discuss development policy, it is aid policy that receives disproportionate attention, perhaps because of inflated hopes that aid can resolve problems of injustice, inequality, and poverty, and perhaps because of desires to highlight doing good rather than doing harm. If the primary underlying motivation for studying, writing about, and advocating aid in Canada is ultimately humanitarian, then we – as a scholarly community – also need to be more coherent and rigorous in choosing research questions and research methods that reflect these normative concerns. Cosmopolitan ethics call for consideration and analysis of both positive and negative moral obligations. As various scholars have argued (Held 2010; Pogge 2007), in the context of contemporary globalization, the negative ethical duties to not cause harm – or not benefit from the suffering of others – are increasingly more relevant to global well-being and justice than the positive duties to provide assistance.

In this context, it makes little sense to analyze Canadian aid as if it were separate from the broader framework of Canadian foreign policy and as if positive and negative duties can be isolated from one another. If the broader context of globalization was not sufficient incentive to adopt a cosmopolitan-inspired framework for government policy analysis in Canada, the merger of CIDA into DFATD should make the urgency of such a perspective clear. The time has come to merge consideration of positive ethical obligations – or "humane internationalism" in the words of Pratt – with attention to negative moral duties, thus creating a methodological perspective that analyzes Canadian government policy and practice both in terms of relative success and failure in providing humanitarian and development assistance and in terms of relative success and failure in not causing harm or benefiting from it. Indeed, we may need to think of a kind of Hippocratic oath for scholars of development policy, that in our analysis we focus first on the duty to do no harm (*primum non nocere*).

Notes

1. For example, in a 2012 interview with the *Globe and Mail*, Fantino explicitly argued that CIDA initiatives should benefit Canadians: "This is Canadian money ... And Canadians are entitled to derive a benefit" (Mackrael 2012). CIDA's partnerships with Canadian mining companies operating in developing countries also clearly indicate an explicit emphasis on the promotion of domestic self-interest as a valid goal for aid (Brown, this volume).

2. For more on Canadian immigration policies targeting medical professionals from the global South, see Shuchman (2008).

References

Blackwood, Elizabeth, and Veronika Stewart. 2012. "CIDA and the Mining Sector: Extractive Industries as an Overseas Development Strategy." In Stephen Brown, ed. *Struggling for Effectiveness: CIDA and Canadian Foreign Aid*. Montreal and Kingston: McGill–Queen's University Press: 217–45.

Brown, Garrett, and David Held, eds. 2010. "Editors' Introduction." In *The Cosmopolitan Reader*. Cambridge, UK: Polity Press: 1–13.

Brown, Stephen. 2012. "Canadian Aid Enters the Twenty-First Century." In Stephen Brown, ed. *Struggling for Effectiveness: CIDA and Canadian Foreign Aid*. Montreal and Kingston: McGill–Queen's University Press: 3–23.

Brown, Stephen, and Rosalind Raddatz. 2012. "Taking Stock, Looking Ahead." In Stephen Brown, ed. *Struggling for Effectiveness: CIDA and Canadian Foreign Aid*. Montreal and Kingston: McGill–Queen's University Press: 327–44.

Center for Global Development. 2013. The commitment to development index. Internet, http://www.cgdev.org/initiative/commitment-development-index/index. Accessed November 6, 2013.

Engler, Yves. 2009. *The Black Book of Canadian Foreign Policy*. Winnipeg and Black Point, NS: Fernwood Publishing.

Gaspar, Des. 2006. "Cosmopolitan Presumptions? On Martha Nussbaum and her Commentators." *Development and Change*, vol. 37, no. 6: 1227–46.

Gasper, Des, and Asunción Lera St. Clair, eds. 2010. *Development Ethics*. Burlington, VT and Surrey, UK: Ashgate.

Gidwani, Vinay. 2006. "Subaltern Cosmopolitanism as Politics." *Antipode*, vo. 38, no. 1: 7–21.

Giri, Ananta. 2003. "Afterword: The calling of global responsibilities." In Philip Quarles Van Ufford and Ananta Kumar Giri, eds. *A Moral*

Critique of Development: In Search of Global Responsibilities. London and New York: Routledge: 279–301.

Giri, Ananta. 2006. "Cosmopolitanism and Beyond: Towards a Multiverse of Transformations." *Development and Change*, vol. 37, no. 6: 1277–92.

Gordon, Todd. 2010. *Imperialist Canada.* Winnipeg: Arbeiter Ring.

Goulet, Denis. 1995. *Development Ethics: A Guide to Theory and Practice.* London: Zed Books.

Irwin, Rosalind, ed. 2001. *Ethics and Security in Canadian Foreign Policy.* Vancouver: UBC Press.

Kymlicka, Will, and Kathryn Walker, eds. 2012. *Rooted Cosmopolitanism: Canada and the World.* Vancouver: UBC Press.

Mackrael, Kim. 2012. "Fantino defends CIDA's corporate shift." *Globe and Mail.* December 3. Internet, http://www.theglobeandmail.com/news/politics/fantino-defends-cidas-corporate-shift/article5950443/. Accessed October 29, 2013.

McGill, Hunter. 2012. "Canada Among Donors: How Does Canadian Aid Compare." In Stephen Brown, ed. *Struggling for Effectiveness: CIDA and Canadian Foreign Aid.* Montreal and Kingston: McGill–Queen's University Press: 24–52.

Miller, David. 2007. "Cosmopolitanism." In *National Responsibilities and Global Justice.* New York: Oxford University Press: 23–50.

Nagel, Thomas. 2005. "The Problem of Global Justice." *Philosophy and Public Affairs Journal*, vol. 33, no. 2: 114–47.

OECD. 2012. "DAC Peer Review of Canada." Paris: OECD. Internet, http://www.oecd.org/dac/peer-reviews/canadapeerreview2012.pdf. Accessed October 29, 2013.

Paehlke, Robert. 2012. "Climate Change and the Challenge of Canadian Global Citizenship." In Will Kymlicka and Kathryn Walker, eds. *Rooted Cosmopolitanism: Canada and the World.* Vancouver: UBC Press: 206–26.

Penz, Peter. 2001. "The Ethics of Development Assistance and Human Security: From Realism and Sovereigntism to Cosmopolitanism." In Rosalind Irwin, ed. *Ethics and Security in Canadian Foreign Policy.* Vancouver: UBC Press 38–55.

Pieterse, Jan Nederveen. 2006. "Emancipatory Cosmopolitanism: Towards an Agenda." *Development and Change* vol. 37, no. 6: 1247–57.

Pogge, Thomas. 2007. "Severe Poverty as a Human Rights Violation." In *Freedom from Poverty as a Human Right: Who Owes What to the Very Poor.* New York: Oxford University Press: 11–53.

Pratt, Cranford, ed. 1989. *Internationalism Under Strain: The North–South Policies of Canada, the Netherlands, Norway, and Sweden.* Toronto: University of Toronto Press.

Pratt, Cranford. 1994. "Humane Internationalism and Canadian Development Assistance Policies." In Cranford Pratt, ed. *Canadian International*

Development Assistance Policies: An Appraisal. Montreal and Kingston: McGill–Queen's University Press: 334–70.

Pratt, Cranford. 2000. "Alleviating Global Poverty or Enhancing Security: Competing Rationales for Canadian Development Assistance." In Jim Freeman, ed. *Transforming Development: Foreign Aid in a Changing World.* Toronto: University of Toronto Press: 37–59.

Quarles Van Ufford, Philip, and Ananta Kumar Giri, eds. 2003. *A Moral Critique of Development: In Search of Global Responsibilities.* London and New York: Routledge.

Shuchman, Miriam. 2008. "Searching for docs on foreign shores." *Canadian Medical Association Journal,* vol. 178, no. 4: 379–80.

CHAPTER IV

Power and Policy: Lessons from Aid Effectiveness

Molly den Heyer

Introduction

When the federal government's plan to fold the Canadian International Development Agency (CIDA) into the Department of Foreign Affairs and International Trade (DFAIT) leaked from the back pages of the omnibus budget in March 2013, it sparked yet another round of cries for renewing the Canadian aid conversation. This is a familiar theme, dating back over a decade. The cycle begins with a new aid policy that bypasses questions of overarching vision in favour of administrative and technical solutions, followed by the aid watchers' chorus of policy critiques and calls to reinvigorate debates, often in keeping with international trends. While these debates are interesting, the real challenge is to understand why we are stuck in this policy eddy and how we can escape from it.

Breaking free from this pattern requires more than just a critique or new set of policies; it requires a shift in perspective and reconfiguration of power. Cameron (this volume) argues that development scholars should ground their analysis in cosmopolitan ethics emphasizing the principles of assistance, as well as "do no harm." The latter requires development scholars and practitioners to move beyond the myopic focus on aid policy to understanding how we, as a country, interact and engage with others on the international stage and in the backrooms of far-off nations. It also requires a deeper, more thorough conceptualization of how power infuses policy and everyday development practices.

This chapter uses power as an analytical tool and subject. As an analytical tool, the chapter examines the multifaceted environment of development policy and the series of complex interactions and influences that shape its outcomes. The effects can be divided into three forms: how policy is put into practice; how the various actors interpret and negotiate policy; and the underlying narratives or discursive frames. I pay particular attention to the latter, in which narratives (including conceptualization of first principles and ethics) can have a significant influence on policy, either as a source of resistance or as the driving force behind innovation.

I apply the analytical frame to Canadian aid effectiveness policies as it relates to international and country-specific partnerships. One of the stated goals of aid effectiveness polices is to forge a new development partnership in which recipient countries have ownership of their development processes. While this attempt to reconfigure power relations between donor and recipients has failed to come to full fruition, the analysis reveals the subtle and varied forms of contestation, norm-setting, and compromises embedded in everyday development practices.

This discussion is based on current debates and my doctoral research on aid effectiveness policies in the international, Canadian, and Tanzanian contexts. The research included a policy and literature review and thirty-eight interviews, as well as focus groups and participant observation (den Heyer 2012a). Drawing on this study, I argue that development scholars and practitioners should embrace a broader and more complex understanding of policy. This will allow us to move past the hubris that accompanies policies such as aid effectiveness and identify more strategic and effective ways to advocate transformative change.

Understanding Policy through Power

This chapter traces the various ways power acts on and within aid effectiveness policy by using VeneKlassen and Miller's (2002) elegant analytical framework of visible, hidden, and invisible forms of power. Visible forms of power are expressed through formal negotiations between officials in the policy process. Hidden forms of power, such as control over invitation lists, timing, and agenda, are used to shape policy spaces and outcomes. Lastly, invisible forms of power are exercised through subconscious filters and categorizations that all members of society accumulate through processes of socialization. These include negotiations concerning the different roles that individuals and organizations can legitimately play within the policy process, and what types of knowledge are valued or not. Below, I examine each of these forms of power as applied to the contours of Canadian aid effectiveness policies. In doing so, I point to areas of contestation and the different ways the policies are modified.

Visible Power

Most policy research (including my own) starts with the mapping of finite objects and events, such as descriptions of publicly recognized authorities and formal institutions, as well as policies and procedures that comprise the aid industry. These objects and events represent the visible exercise of power. National laws grant authority to societal institutions, reaffirmed through public transcripts and exercised along formal decision-making lines. Power analysis focuses on the technical aspects of decision making captured in public discussions and official documents, including policy statements, press releases, planning documents, and reports.

Using the aid effectiveness policy framework as an example, the formal institutions, events, policies, and procedures involved are easily mapped. The current policy configuration began to flourish in the 1990s with the Organisation for Economic Co-operation and Development/Development Assistance Committee's (OECD/DAC) report *Shaping the 21st Century: The Contribution toward Development Co-operation* (OECD 1996), and in the early 2000s with Goal 8 of the UN Millennium Development Goals (MDGs), which aims to "develop a global partnership for development to increase effectiveness" (UNDP 2013). Since then, the OECD/DAC has blazed a trail of agreements from Rome (2002) to Paris (2005), Accra (2008) and Busan (2011). The Declarations, High Level Forums, Working Parties, Advisory Groups, and so forth created a formal structure within which plans unfolded, policies were implemented, and activities were monitored and evaluated.

As a supranational policy framework, aid effectiveness rests on the principles of ownership, alignment, harmonization, managing for results, and mutual accountability (see box below). More specifically, donor partners committed to harmonizing their administrative procedures and aligning their programming objectives with the recipient government's priorities, as well as to coordinating activities among themselves. Simultaneously, recipient countries committed to strengthening good governance and fiscal management in order to assume full ownership of their development. As a set, aid effectiveness policies were supposed to make aid distribution more efficient by streamlining administration and more effective by transferring ownership of the development process from donor partners to recipient countries.

The Aid Effectiveness Principles

1. Ownership: Partner countries exercise effective leadership over their development policies and strategies, and coordinate development actors.

2. Alignment: Donors base their support on partner countries' national development strategies, institutions, and procedures.

3. Harmonization: Donors' actions are more harmonized, transparent, and collectively effective.

4. Managing for Results: Donors and partners manage resources and improve decision making.

5. Mutual Accountability: Donors and partners are accountable for development results.

Source: OECD (2005, 3)

As a member of OECD/DAC, Canada participated in the design of the aid effectiveness framework and officially committed to implementing it. The Canadian government used the global policy framework as the basis of numerous policy documents, starting with *Canada Making a Difference in the World: Policy Statement on Strengthening Aid Effectiveness* (CIDA 2002). The policy emphasizes some of the key concepts embodied in aid effectiveness, including ownership, donor coordination, policy coherence, and managing for results. Over the subsequent decade, aid effectiveness language and concepts appeared frequently in the Canadian government's policy statements, strategies, press releases, speeches, action plans, and procedural documents. CIDA implemented the aid effectiveness policies through program-based approaches,[1] a slow and reluctant crawl towards untying aid, another disappointing attempt at decentralization, and efforts to improve aid predictability (den Heyer 2012a; Lalonde 2009). Despite the promises, the policy framework failed to reform Canada's beleaguered aid bureaucracy, let alone transform its partnership with recipient countries.

Canadian aid policy exists within a complex institutional setting. In many cases, other policies, procedures, and formal decision-making processes conflict with, if not subvert, the stated aims of the aid effectiveness policies. In an earlier publication (den Heyer 2012b), I showed there was particular tension between CIDA's efforts to pool funds with other donors and align policies with the recipient government, and the fiduciary requirements outlined in the Accountability Act and by the Treasury Board of Canada. The Treasury Board sets the rules and regulations around departmental spending and reviews any item over $20 million. Its reluctance to provide general budget support and use recipient government systems to administer aid hampered CIDA's effort to transfer ownership. These competing policy frameworks (aid effectiveness and accountability) and associated formal institutions illustrate how other forms of visible power often stand as obstacles to or diversions from the implementation of aid policy and its intended change.

CIDA is not alone in its struggles to apply aid effectiveness policies in practice. The central message of the Paris Declaration evaluation was diplomatic, but tough:

> The global Paris Declaration campaign to make international aid programs more effective is showing results. But the improvements are slow and uneven in most developing countries and even more so among most donor agencies, although the changes expected of them are less demanding. (Wood and Betts 2013, 5)

These words echoed loudly in the corridors of CIDA, known as a laggard in aid effectiveness (Bülles and Kindornay 2013).

These visible forms of power are easy to identify and track, but they only describe the tip of the policy iceberg. A wider analytical approach should also explore how hidden power and invisible power act on policy.

Hidden Power

Hidden power describes the influential processes that operate behind the scenes and determine who sets the political agenda. In the case of aid effectiveness policies in Canada, there are two distinct but interwoven applications of hidden power. First, development actors exercise hidden power by frequently modifying aid effectiveness policies in order to make them work within particular contexts. Second, they do so as an inclusionary/exclusionary process that includes agenda-driven influence over invitation lists, meeting agendas, media coverage, or the structure of the decision-making process. While the intentions behind these exercises of power are very different (practical implementation and/or persuasion), the combined influence creates significant drift in the articulations of policy, especially as the policy is implemented in the international, Canadian, and recipient country contexts.

Lewis and Mosse (2006) describe how development practitioners act as brokers, interpreting and translating policy as it moves through the international development bureaucracy. The result is a sophisticated version of "whisper down the lane" or long chains of meanings. Development practitioners fuel policy drift by wrestling with implementation, applying their own interpretation of the policy, and negotiating with others' interpretations. In this regard, several studies have shown that development actors modified aid effectiveness policy as it was applied in the national context, resulting in a uniquely "made-in-Canada" version (Brown 2011; Bülles and Kindornay 2013; den Heyer 2012ab; Lalonde 2009).

Policy implementation often involves practical compromise with other policy frameworks (such as the Accountability Act), individual judgment calls in terms of lived experiences of what works or does not, and the fit with organizational culture. While Wood and Betts do not directly mention CIDA in their paper, the following observation is quite applicable to its highly centralized and risk-averse culture:

> It is clear from the evidence gathered by the Evaluation that some donors have been too uncoordinated and risk-averse to play their expected proactive part in the relationship. Most donors have set high levels of partner country compliance as preconditions for their own reforms rather than moving together reciprocally and managing and sharing risk realistically. (Wood and Betts 2013, 11; see also Smillie, this volume)

The phrase "partner country compliance as preconditions" highlights one of the key issues in donor implementation of commitments under the principle of alignment, and consequently the principle of ownership. The Paris Declaration calls for partner countries to strengthen their government systems and for donors to use these systems to distribute aid. Yet, within the aid corridors, donors are reluctant to relinquish control of aid dollars over concerns around accountability to taxpayers, corruption in recipient countries, and general lack of capacity. As a result, some donors (including CIDA) set demanding preconditions and effectively stall policy implementation under the rubric of feasibility.

The vague terms and inherent contradictions embedded in the aid effectiveness framework create ample space for practitioners to interpret and reinterpret key terms. As McNeil and St. Claire observe,

> [C]oncepts used by the UN System agencies act as intellectual "boundary objects," trying to bridge policy and research, agendas and goals and linking diverse (and often) contradictory communities. The broader the range of meanings of an intellectual boundary object, the more the possibility for common ground among partners, communities and interests. However, the manifold range of meanings of intellectual boundary objects may also be a way for the prevalence of dominant interpretations under the pretension of consensus. (McNeil and St. Claire 2005, 4)

Terms such as aid effectiveness, coherence, accountability, and ownership carry a number of definitions and interpretations that often coexist and are used interchangeably in the same policy spaces. For example, the research on ownership shows two distinct meanings within the aid effectiveness framework. One version of ownership calls for an end to Western influence over Southern nations. This perspective emphasizes the recipient government's exertion of control over its own economic and social policies, including the ability to critique and design them. The second version also defines ownership as control over the development process, but then limits it through secondary terms and conditions. The limitations ensure recipient countries' commitment to mainstream development and economic policies, making ownership essentially something recipients must earn by meeting Western standards. This version emerges from an expert-centric, managerial approach that focuses on visible institutions, documents, processes, and events (Castel-Branco 2008).

These competing definitions also lead to two different assessments of aid effectiveness policies. The OECD indicator for country ownership is that by 2012 "at least 75 percent of partner countries have operational development strategies" (OECD 2005, 9). However, even in such cases, there are many subtle ways in which donors still exercise hidden power and influence national development strategies or Poverty Reduction Strategy Papers (PRSPs). Numerous authors have documented the World Bank's veto power over PRSPs, the extensive consultation with Donor Partners Groups, and the minimal participation of domestic non-governmental organizations (NGOs) and constituents (Gould 2005; Harrison et al. 2009; Hayman 2009; Holtom 2005; Hyden 2008; Whitfield 2009).[2]

Development practitioners are continuously negotiating these two coexisting definitions of ownership among themselves and with others in various policy spaces. This interactive meaning-making process is further influenced by the context and location of the policy space. In Canada, trends towards more fiscal conservatism and a general distrust of public officials led to an increased emphasis on accountability in the 2000s. The context accentuated CIDA's already risk-averse and highly centralized organizational culture (see Smillie, this volume), leading to a version of aid effectiveness that emphasized fiscal accountability, results-based management, and donor coordination, while effectively de-emphasizing harmonization, alignment, and ownership (Brown 2011; den Heyer 2012ab; Lalonde 2009). However, this version of aid effectiveness only partially influenced the policy in country offices, such as in Dar es Salaam, Tanzania.

In Tanzania, the aid effectiveness discussions took on a more international flair. The five-block radius surrounding the Ministry of Finance and Economic Affairs in Dar es Salaam hosts numerous government buildings, embassies, and aid offices. Here, the CIDA and DFAIT officials interact with the government of Tanzania and non-governmental actors, including private businesses, international NGOs, local civil society, and the University of Dar es Salaam. Given the diverse participation, the official discussions around aid effectiveness policies often reflected international agreements. CIDA representatives in the field are constantly negotiating their own procedures, with intense peer pressure from other donors and the government of Tanzania. The need to balance CIDA's policies and procedures with in-country demands led CIDA officials to emphasize strengthening recipient government processes as an expression of ownership and future promises of donor alignment. Further, CIDA has joined the club of donors working diligently towards harmonization, often defined as their own coordination.

While many development actors negotiate and interpret policy as part of their everyday struggles of applying abstract concepts in practice, others clearly represent vested interests. As part of the negotiations embedded in the various policy spaces, development actors make amendments, compromises, and adjustments to accommodate different interests or positions. Those with money, as well as the right education and cultural background, gain access to these venues in order to influence the outcomes through activities such as lobbying, producing knowledge, or currying favours. These exercises of power often result in the privileging of some development actors and consequently the marginalization of groups and issues with fewer resources.

While the exercise of visible and hidden power provides a wider view of how power acts on and within aid policy, it still only represents the top two layers of the iceberg. Underneath the practical compromises and backroom lobbying for policy change, are our own deep-rooted, subconscious narratives. This invisible power often sets the parameters for what is acceptable or not acceptable to say, do, and see.

Invisible Power

Invisible forms of power often play on the subtle and sometimes subconscious ways in which meaning and subsequently behaviour is shaped. Power operates in a multi-variant way that infuses every interaction, from state to familial relationships. Regimes of discourse and discipline interact to create a web of power relations. Processes of socialization and surveillance entrench identities, traditions, habits, and expected behaviours. These ways of being in the world eventually become internalized and are subsequently expressed by development actors in official venues (VeneKlassen and Miller 2002). They reflect who has and who does not have the legitimacy to convey expert knowledge, provide commentary, and make decisions.

The exploration of the metaphors, narratives, and rationales embedded in the discourse can render invisible power visible. In this vein, Mosse (2004) argues the new aid architecture has four largely unquestioned characteristics. First, the architecture is built on a foundation of neoliberalism and institutionalism. Second, Western managerial standards extend to all facets of development. Third, all countries and development organizations are striving towards the 2015 MDGs. Finally, development actors have shifted away from risky and intensive on-the-ground projects towards scaled-up programs and policy dialogue. As a set, they present the very narrow and highly technical definition of poverty reduction, based on common development archetypes embedded in a neoliberal context.

These grand narratives contain many smaller, more fluid pieces of discourse that compete, combine, and coexist with each other. Terms such as "corruption" and "capacity building" embody particular meanings or are associated with certain storylines that resonate within the aid debates. For example, the phrase "lack of capacity" is linked to underlying assumptions regarding Western expertise and Southern incompetence. Development actors from the North and the South frequently use the expression to frame issues and exert their influence. The research found that the word "capacity" was used in a number of ways, including genuine assessments, diplomatic insults, excuses to gain and retain authority, excuses not to do work, and subtle strategies of resistance, as well as a reason to extend contracts, design training workshops, and charge sitting fees. The deep-seated assumptions and subconscious power dynamics around capacity feed into hidden strategies (i.e., the donors' conditions for government reform programs and the recipient government's reasons for delays and slippage) and are expressed in visible terms and conditions. In this manner, the three levels of power are not discrete but play upon each other.

In keeping with these international trends, the underlying narratives in Canadian aid assume a neoliberal, managerial-styled development, as described by Mosse (2004). However, two particular sub-stories frame current debates. First, Canadian aid policy draws on charity archetypes that often conflate international development with humanitarian assistance. The focus on topics such as earthquake relief in Haiti and childhood and maternal health is important, but the way in which media and development actors convey the story often perpetuates the underlying narrative of a saviour–victim relationship. This relationship resonates in the second, distinctly Canadian story of Lester B. Pearson and middle-power status. Whether myth or reality, it evokes an image of do-good, earnest Canadian diplomats "sticking up for the little guy" in international politics (Jefferess 2009). These storylines stand in direct contrast with a transformative definition of ownership as control over the development process.

The aid effectiveness example illustrates how underlying power dynamics influence policy. While promoted as reform, aid effectiveness policies are firmly rooted in mainstream development discourse, essentially reflecting prevailing power dynamics within the Canadian and international development bureaucracy. However, this is not a black-or-white issue. Policy spaces embody a great deal of complexity and are sites of much contestation, norm-setting, and value judgment. As the next section argues, substantive change does not come from a policy framework alone, but from strategic and persistent pressure towards a tipping point.

Navigating the Crosscurrents

The above discussion of visible, hidden, and invisible forms of power illustrates how policy is pushed and pulled in the crosscurrents of development assistance. The pressures occur within and among the different forms of power. First, the trappings of aid effectiveness policies (declarations, events, policy papers, committees) provide development actors with the visible and legitimate authority to implement the policies. However, these visible forms of power compete with, and are often mitigated by, other forms of visible powers, such as those exercised under the Accountability Act. Second, there is also a great deal of negotiating in the corridors of aid, leading to constant reinterpretations, compromises, and amendments. These hidden forms of power generate significant policy drift. Third, development actors (as all human beings) exist within set parameters or discursive regimes, which subconsciously frame debates and privilege some forms of thinking over others. In the case of aid effectiveness, the invisible forms of power create an undertow or constant pull towards mainstream norms, limiting the possibility of transformation.

It is important to note that this analysis does not imply that significant policy change is impossible. Instead, it suggests that new policy language and technical solutions are not enough to reform the aid bureaucracy. It is in the labyrinth of development actors, who contest, influence, and implement policies and practices, where the smaller battles are won and lost. Any effort to transform the donor–recipient relationship should operate on multiple fronts, broadly corresponding with the three forms of power:

1. Despite the inherent hubris, it is still important to work with official policy. Good policy provides overarching direction and, most important, legitimacy for development actors to carry out their work.
2. Scholars and practitioners should also follow the policy process during implementation and in the backrooms. This involves strategies that either expose hidden forms of power and/or engage in lobbying.
3. Efforts to uproot discursive power should involve strategies that change narratives or provide alternative storylines. As Mills (2003, 55) suggests, "discourse transmits and produces power; it reinforces it, but also undermines it and exposes it, renders it fragile, and makes it possible to thwart it."

Efforts on all three fronts are essential for generating enough momentum to initiate substantive reform or a rethinking of Canadian aid.

Rethinking Canadian Aid

Returning to the problem presented in this chapter's introduction, Canadian aid seems stuck in a policy eddy that focuses on technical and bureaucratic solutions and critiques. Current policy debates address the visible and hidden forms of power behind the priority setting, countries of focus, private/public partnerships, and the process of folding CIDA into DFAIT, now the Department of Foreign Affairs, Trade and Development (DFATD). While these issues are important, rethinking Canadian aid will require the aid conversations to go farther in terms of substance and context. First, efforts to address invisible power should expose underlying narratives and generate discussions of alternative storylines and rationales. This requires a long-term and wider public dialogue involving awareness campaigns, media coverage, political debates, academic critiques, education, and so forth. Second, the discussions must reflect on and engage with our global partners in a changing international landscape.

In this regard, Michael Edwards (2013) identifies four significant changes in the international development context worth considering. First, the complexity of international politics continues to grow with multipolar international politics and the emerging economies of Brazil, Russia, India, and China (BRICs). The BRICs, along with many recipient countries, are questioning the traditional postcolonial approach to aid. Second, global poverty can no longer be described neatly by a North–South distinction. Instead, extreme wealth and poverty reside side-by-side within the same countries – or in Michael Edwards's (2013, 3) words – there are now "pockets of extreme poverty and conflict." Third, there is an increase in the number of complex global and regional issues that require cooperation. Fourth, in some circles the 2008 global financial crisis and ongoing economic problems in Europe have shaken faith in linear growth-based development models that promote the notion that developing nations should strive to become just like developed nations.

For aid watchers, it is becoming increasingly apparent that Canada needs to cast off old storylines and rethink its approach to development. This means shedding the longstanding North–South charity model laden with false generosity and top-down bureaucratic processes. It requires us to reconceive Canada's place in the world, not as a leader or middle power, but as a nation grappling with common issues stemming from an imperfect global economic system, regional conflicts, climate change, and so forth. This transition is rooted in cosmopolitan concepts of development cooperation that emphasize partnership and shared global responsibilities.

Notes

1. Program-based approaches are funding mechanisms that coordinate with other donor partners, civil society organizations, and recipient governments. They include general budget support, thematic and sector programing, and pooled and basket funding. General budget support is a transfer of funds from one government to another without conditions. The recipient government includes this money in its budget and it is spent through government systems.
2. Membership in Development Partners Group (DPG) includes bilateral and multilateral donors operating in a specific recipient country. In Tanzania, the DPG comprised seventeen bilateral and five multilateral donor organizations in 2013.

References

Brown, Stephen. 2011. "Aid Effectiveness and the Framing of New Canadian Aid Initiatives." In Duane Bratt and Christopher J. Kukucha, eds. *Readings in Canadian Foreign Policy: Classic debates and New Ideas* (2nd ed.). Toronto: Oxford University Press: 469–86.

Bülles, Anni-Claudine, and Shannon Kindornay. 2013. *Beyond Aid: A Plan for Canada's International Cooperation*. Ottawa: North–South Institute.

Canadian International Development Agency. 2002. *Canada Making a Difference in the World: A Policy Statement on Strengthening Aid Effectiveness*. Ottawa: Government of Canada.

Castel-Branco, Carlos Nuno. 2008. "Aid Dependency and Development: A Question of Ownership? A Critical Review." Working paper No. 1. Maputo, Mozambique: Instituto de Estudos Sociais e Económicos.

den Heyer, Molly. 2012a. "The Reshaping of Aid Effectiveness Policies in the International, Canadian, and Tanzanian Context." PhD diss., Dalhousie University, Halifax, NS.

den Heyer, Molly. 2012b. "Untangling Canadian Aid Policy: International Agreements, CIDA's Policies and Micro-policy Negotiations in Tanzania." In Stephen Brown, ed. *Struggling for Effectiveness: CIDA and Canadian Foreign Aid*. Montreal and Kingston: McGill–Queen's University Press: 186–216.

Edwards, Michael. 2013. "Thinking Ahead: Four Questions for NGOs to Ponder." Internet, http://www.ccic.ca/_files/en/what_we_do/2013_05_14_Thinking_ahead_ME.pdf. Accessed November 3, 2013.

Gould, Jeremy. 2005. "Timing, Scale, and Style: Capacity as Governmentality in Tanzania." In David Mosse and David Lewis, eds. *The Aid Effect*. London: Pluto Press: 61–84.

Hayman, Rachel. 2009. "From Rome to Accra via Kigali: 'Aid Effectiveness' in Rwanda." *Development Policy Review*, vol. 27, no. 5: 581–99.

Harrison, Graham, Sarah Mulley, and Duncan Holtom. 2009. "Tanzania: A Genuine Case of Recipient Leadership in the Aid System?" In Lindsay Whitfield, ed. *The Politics of Aid: African Strategies for Dealing with Donors*. Oxford: Oxford University Press: 271–98.

Holtom, Duncan. 2005. "The Challenge of Consensus Building: Tanzania's PRSP 1998–2001." *Journal of Modern African Studies*, vol. 45, no. 2: 233–51.

Hyden, Goran. 2008. "After the Paris Declaration: Taking on the Issues of Power." *Development Policy Review*, vol. 26, no. 3: 259–74.

Jefferess, David. 2009. "Responsibility, Nostalgia, and the Mythology of Canada as a Peacekeeper." *University of Toronto Press Quarterly*, vol. 78, no. 2: 709–27.

Lalonde, Jennifer. 2009. "Harmony and Discord: International Aid Harmonization and Donor State Influence: The Case of Canada and the Canadian International Development Agency." PhD diss., Johns Hopkins University, Baltimore.

Lewis, David, and David Mosse. 2006. "Theoretical Approaches to Brokerage and Translation in Development." In David Lewis and David Mosse, eds. *Development Brokers and Translators: The Ethnography of Aid and Agencies*. West Hartford, CT: Kumarian Press: 1–26.

McNeill, Desmond, and Asunción Lera St. Clair. 2005. "Development Ethics and Human Rights as the Basis for Global Poverty Reduction: The Case of the World Bank." Budapest: Workshop for Researchers on the World Bank.

Mosse, David. 2004. "Is Good Policy Unimplementable? Reflections on the Ethnography of Aid Policy and Practice." *Development and Change*, vol. 35, no. 4: 639–71.

Mills, Sara. 2003. *Michel Foucault*. London: Routledge.

OECD. 1996. *Shaping the 21st Century: The Contribution of Development Co-operation*. Paris: OECD. Internet, http://www.oecd.org/dac/2508761.pdf. Accessed November 3, 2013.

OECD. 2005. *Paris Declaration on Aid Effectiveness*. Internet, http://www.oecd.org/dac/effectiveness/parisdeclarationandaccraagendaforaction.htm#Paris. Accessed November 3, 2013.

United Nations Development Programme. 2013. *Eight Goals for 2015*. Internet, http://www.undp.org/content/undp/en/home/mdgoverview/. Accessed November 3, 2013.

VeneKlassen, Lisa, and Valerie Miller. 2002. "Power and Empowerment." *PLA Notes*, no. 43: 39–41.

Whitfield, Lindsay. 2009. "Aid and Power: A Comparative Analysis of the Country Study." In Lindsay Whitfield, ed. *The Politics of Aid: African Strategies for Dealing with Donors*. Oxford: Oxford University Press: 329–60.

Wood, Bernard, and Julia Betts. 2013. "Results of the Paris Declaration Evaluation." *Canadian Journal of Program Evaluation*, vol. 27, no. 3: 103–28.

CHAPTER V

Results, Risk, Rhetoric and Reality: The Need for Common Sense in Canada's Development Assistance

Ian Smillie

Introduction

A n outsider studying the websites of the world's most prominent international development organizations – DFID, USAID, the World Bank, UNDP – could not fail to notice that the words "effectiveness" and "results" appear so frequently that they hint at some sort of problem. The same is true of SIDA, NORAD, DANIDA, and AusAID. The phenomenon was even more prominent on the CIDA website and it still exists on the "Development" pages of the new DFATD, located by clicking a tab on that site between "Trade" and "Assistance to Travellers."

Why the enormous emphasis on effectiveness and results? The international development community has always emphasized effectiveness, and before "results" the operative concept was "impact." Even the "results" vocabulary is not new. It dates from the US Government Performance and Results Act of 1993, a bipartisan effort to change the way the US government was doing business (Brass 2012). The act requires that departments set performance goals and measure their success in meeting them, as opposed to budgeting solely in terms of inputs and outputs. A teaching *result* would be measured, not in terms of teachers employed or children taught, but in the *results* of that education: improved cognitive skills, better pass rates, graduation to higher levels of education, higher rates of employment, and so on.

This seems like common sense, but in 1993 this was new to a development business that *assumed* impact, but often failed to make the necessary link between input (teaching), output (children taught), and a more meaningful and measurable result. There was an additional problem: Many aid programs did not actually have the sort of impact – localized or generic – that was advertised. That, in turn, made aid programs an easy target for critics with sharp pens – Peter Bauer, Michael Marren, Graham Hancock, Dambisa Moyo, all bestselling authors of anti-aid screeds.

Many aid critics approach the topic from a shake-and-bake perspective that puts development, poverty reduction, and growth into the same pan in the same oven at the same temperature, predicting the same "results" in places as varied as China, Taiwan, and South Korea. Scott Gilmore, chief executive officer of an organization called Building Markets, provides an example of this: While aid programs "wallow" in ineffectual indolence, he says, "the most powerful force for poverty reduction is not development assistance – it's local entrepreneurs. When they are given an opportunity to compete, they can transform even the poorest country ... Entrepreneurs, not aid spending, are driving this growth" (Gilmore 2012).

Like others, Gilmore equates economic growth with development, and development with poverty reduction. That sequence is possible, and in some places perhaps even likely. However, the words and the concepts are not synonymous, and in too many poor countries the economy has grown on little more than the coattails of an extractive industry. Gross domestic product growth and averages often mask a reality in which real improvement to the lives of those at the bottom has simply not occurred, while in many cases the disparity between rich and poor has grown.

Markets are certainly a partial solution to development problems, but left to their own devices, they are not enough. This is a lesson Canadians learned a long time ago when federal and provincial governments created education and health care systems, social safety nets, transfer payments, and regulatory systems for investment, money, and banking. These, along with good and transparent governments that are answerable to the electorate, were and remain essential parts of our development.

The answer to development is not one thing; it is many. The question is not whether the market is an alternative to aid, but whether aid can deliver on its part of the promise. The answer to that question seems not to be all that clear.

Lying with Statistics[1]

The Economist, using World Bank data, recently stated that the number of people living in absolute poverty has fallen in the past two decades by "almost a billion" (*Economist* 2013). We are now down to 1.1 billion people living in destitution. This sounds like good news, but it is not – at least not the part about a reduction.

The problem is that the figures used by the World Bank a decade or so afterwards for 1980, 1985, and 1990 are not the same figures it used at the time. In its 1980 *World Development Report,* the World Bank said, "The number of people living in absolute poverty in developing countries (excluding China and other centrally planned economies) is estimated at around 780 million" (World Bank 1981). At the time, China had an estimated 360 million destitute people, so the global total was probably about 1.1 billion – the same as today.[2] The fudging changed the definition of absolute poverty from an income of $1.00 a day to $1.25.

In other words, hoopla, braggadocio, and revisionism aside, poverty has *not* been reduced by a billion. That is not to say there has been no progress. If that 1.1 billion number can be taken seriously, it represented 25 percent of the world's population in 1980, and today it represents 16 percent. The world's population grew, but the absolute number of destitute did not. That is encouraging. In fact, we know that absolute numbers have declined in some countries – conspicuously in Asia. That probably means, however, that absolute numbers have actually increased elsewhere, notably in Africa.

So here is a second problem: Despite billions of dollars spent on development assistance, we seem not to have made much progress in reducing poverty. Where there *has* been progress – in places like China and other East Asian economies – it can be ascribed much less to aid and more to the phenomenon so beloved of aid critics like Gilmore and Moyo: the market. It is perhaps no wonder, then, that politicians attempting to make sense of their country's aid budgets are demanding better and more evident *results.*

Before we get to the issue of how the concept of *results* affects an aid program, a detour is required into a discussion about the purpose of aid. Go back to those websites for DFID, USAID, NORAD, and SIDA, and look at Canada's ODA Accountability Act. All speak first and foremost in terms of poverty reduction. They always have. It was the basis for the 1969 Pearson Commission's inquiry into why development assistance had failed to deliver on its promise up to then, and it was the basis of the subsequent Brandt and Brundtland reports, the 1990 Children's Summit, the Millennium Development Goals, and a dozen other well-known and well-publicized commissions, panels, and targets.

Heading in the Wrong Direction

The challenge in reducing poverty is often framed in terms of *technique*: the "how" of aid. That leads in due course to a discussion about results. However, the issue is not just one of technique. A bigger problem has to do with the diversion of aid away from its stated purpose into byways where no amount of technique will make it more effective. For more than half of the modern aid era, development assistance was as much about the Cold War as it was about anything else. Huge amounts of aid money were fed into the maw of governments led by – not to put too fine a point on it – criminals. These criminals did not misspend the money; the donors did by giving it to them. They did so knowingly, year after year.

The phenomenon did not end with the Cold War. The largest aid recipient by far in recent years has been Afghanistan, where donors' strategic concerns overshadow everything else. Lashings of aid money still flow to countries with bad governments whose friendship or minerals a donor may want. Other kinds of politics play a role as well. Until it was removed from the DAC list of eligible countries, Mayotte (a French colony by another name off the coast of Mozambique) received more French aid than any other place on earth except the Republic of Congo – more in real terms, and infinitely more in per capita terms; more money, in fact, than Switzerland and Australia combined spent in Sub-Saharan Africa.[3] Most donors have their own version of Mayotte, a favourite where largesse outpaces common sense.

After security and politics, and sometimes before them, commercial interests loom large. Only a few years ago, China was

Canada's second-largest aid recipient, and it is still on the recipient list of several donor countries. A degree in rocket science is not required to figure out why. Canada recently shifted its aid priorities from Africa to Latin America, notably to Peru and Colombia, both middle-income countries where the Harper government was negotiating free trade agreements and where Canadian mining companies play an active role.

If donors are serious about poverty reduction, one might think that a preponderance of aid would go to the poorest countries. Not so. In fact, only one-third of all ODA goes to the least developed countries and, if one takes Afghanistan out of that mix, the percentage drops to about one-quarter (OECD 2012).

Much has been made in recent years of Canada's generous untying of aid. Tied aid, of course, was a perennial problem in projects tied to inappropriate and expensive goods and services. The problem is that while Canadian aid is no longer *formally* tied, much of the connection to Canada remains unchanged, with a clear umbilical link to Canadian goods and services. Part of the tying has to do with the use of consultants and other forms of personnel, known in development speak as "technical assistance." In 1969 the Pearson Report bemoaned the fact that some 20 percent of all ODA was being swallowed up by salaries and fees for external advisors (Pearson 1969, 182). Today the amount is closer to 13 percent globally, but for Canada in 2011 it was 21 percent (OECD 2012). Most of the 118 contracts over $10,000 signed by CIDA between January 1 and March 31, 2013 went to Canadian companies, consultants, and NGOs (CIDA 2013a). Much, if not most of it, by its very nature, never reached a developing country.

Humanitarian spending should also be discounted or removed entirely from the effort to reduce poverty. Humanitarian response is essential in complex emergencies and natural disasters, but it is only tangential to long-term development. As a share of global ODA, humanitarian assistance has hovered in recent years around 10 percent of the total (GHA 2013). At 9 percent of ODA in 2011, Canada's contribution was more or less typical (CIDA 2013b). Another amount should be removed from a calculation of Canada's financial commitment to poverty reduction as well: the ODA-eligible imputed costs to the federal and provincial governments of supporting refugees during their first year in Canada. In 2011–12, Canada calculated this at $299.8 million (CIDA 2013b) or about 5.5 percent of ODA.

So before we get to the question of results in terms of the stated aim for development assistance – poverty reduction – we need to think about how much money is actually available for the effort. To do this, we should heavily discount or even remove

- ODA spent in pursuit of political, strategic, and security interests;
- ODA spent in pursuit of commercial interests;
- ODA spent on technical assistance;
- ODA tied (directly or indirectly) to Canadian goods and services;
- ODA spent on humanitarian assistance;
- ODA spent on refugees during their first year in Canada;
- the cost of administering the aid program, probably understated at $244 million in 2010–11 (CIDA 2013b); and
- the cost of foreign student subsidies, estimated at $168 million in 2010–11 (CIDA 2013b).

The point of all this is to say that if one wants *results* in terms of poverty reduction, one has to spend money in ways that demonstrate a contribution to the effort. A great deal of Canada's ODA – perhaps half or even two-thirds – does not.[4]

Now we can begin to talk about how an emphasis on results might affect the balance in terms of its impact on poverty reduction. Three major themes dominate the issue: planning, risk, and timing.

Planning for Results: An Obsessive Measurement Disorder

In Canada's aid program, planning for results has been elevated to an almost religious fervour: It has become highly complex, full of ritual, mystery, arcane language, and – despite all its scientific pretensions – a reliance on faith and a belief system that is passionately intolerant of dissent.

Before it disappeared, CIDA created a series of agency-wide systems that remain in place.[5] The volume of paperwork on planning and managing for results has become enormous since 1993, with rules and forms and guidelines changing and piling up like snow on the Queensway during an Ottawa blizzard. Despite the herculean effort, CIDA still had a hard time explaining its results. The government's report, *Development for Results 2010–11*, is almost exclusively about what CIDA *did* during the year: activities rather than results (CIDA 2011). Here is an example:

> Today, with support from CIDA, Oxfam Canada, Oxfam Great Britain, and their local partners in South Sulawesi, coastal women and men are learning that restoring mangrove ecosystems – and their sustainable use – can generate long-term economic benefits. An important habitat for many fish species, restored mangroves will increase the output of fisheries and resilience to natural hazards. The forests will boost the local economy by increasing the production of raw materials, such as food, firewood, charcoal, medicinal plants, fibres, and dyes. CIDA's support to the restoration, conservation, and improved management of mangroves will benefit more than 18,000 households in South Sulawesi between 2010 and 2015. (CIDA 2011, 4)

This is not about *results*: it is about activities and what the plan *hopes* to achieve. The entire report is like that, although mostly with less precision.

Behind this pretty but rather vague picture are a myriad additional forms, guidelines, and checklists. There is a "logic model template," a "performance measurement framework template," an "investment risk management template" a "How-To Guide" for results management at CIDA, and no doubt much more. The application guidelines for funding from the branch of DFATD that deals with Canadian "partners" (NGOs, universities, etc.) is forty-five pages long. That is worth repeating: *the guidelines* on how to apply for a grant consume forty-five pages.

Andrew Natsios, former head of USAID, could be speaking about Canadian aid when he says that bureaucracies have "become infected with a very bad case of Obsessive Measurement Disorder (OMD), an intellectual dysfunction rooted in the notion that counting everything in government programs … will produce better policy choices and improved management" (Natsios 2010, 4). Some years ago, Henry Mintzberg, one of North America's most prominent management gurus, wrote a book called *The Rise and Fall of Strategic Planning*, in which he examined the success and failure of large corporations and found – in what he called the "fallacy of predetermination," the "fallacy of detachment," and the "fallacy of formalization" – that a lot of the received wisdom about planning was simply wrong. He spoke of the need to "loosen up the process of strategy formation rather than try to seal it off through arbitrary formalization" (Mintzberg 1994, 416).

Centralized, top-down, rigid, paper-bound, and mostly conceived, prepared, and managed five or ten thousand miles from where the activity is supposed to take place, results-based management in Canada's development assistance resembles nothing so much as a product of the Soviet Gosplan: an ideologically hidebound institution turning out good-looking but impossible plans, and results that bear no resemblance to their objective. In the Soviet case, pressure to meet Gosplan targets led to widespread falsification of data, which in turn led to new planning that was even more detached from reality. The same is evident in much of what passes for development assistance in Canada today.

Risk Avoidance

Risk is a major consideration in the *results* world, one the aid establishment treats with almost unalloyed paranoia. The fear of failure – and of public discovery of failure – is in part what has driven the results agenda into its current planning pathologies. Better planning, it is assumed, will lead to fewer failures, even if "better" is only a euphemism for "more."

Three things happen in organizations seeking to avoid risk. The first is to put the money on safe bets. That is why so many aid agencies pile into countries that are "better performers." This is not to suggest that countries like Ghana, Ethiopia, and Mozambique – where development results are more observable than elsewhere – should be ignored. Far from it. It *is* to say, however, that donor avoidance of the poorest and most fragile states hardly makes sense in terms of the stated overall objective of development assistance. The poorest and most fragile are precisely where the greatest effort in poverty reduction is required. These countries have the most difficulty in attracting sound, long-term foreign investment, and the most to gain from well-managed, targeted development assistance.

Where Africa is concerned, not only has Canada assiduously ignored some of the poorest countries, it compounded the problem in 2009 when it shut down longstanding bilateral efforts in eight very poor African nations. It did this in the name of *focus*, a subject worthy of a separate rant, but even accepting that the concept of focus is legitimate and real, CIDA could have protected one or two its poorest partner countries and left a couple of the overcrowded "aid darlings" to others.

A second type of risk avoidance has to do with the kinds of projects that are selected – invariably the safer and more measurable the better. This, Natsios says, "ignores a central principle of development theory – that those development programs that are most precisely and easily measured are the least transformational, and those programs that are most transformational are the least measurable" (Natsios 2010, 4). In other words, they are "least measurable" in part because they are about people rather than things.

A third problem with risk avoidance in a business that is inherently risky, comes straight out of Gosplan central casting. Having planned a project to the top of the snowdrift, having filled out the "investment risk management template," having written down all the operational, financial, development, and reputational risks, and having presumably either minimized these or shown how they will be thwarted, the project manager is left holding a can of worms. If something unexpected goes wrong – pretty likely in most development projects – and if there is no room for timely manoeuvring, the black cloud of failure looms just over the horizon. Things *do* go awry. However, in a rigid, results-based system, they are not supposed to, and if they do, it is often much more expedient to cover up the problem than to fix it. I defy anyone to go to the development website of DFATD, AusAID, the World Bank, or any other development organization or NGO – with the exception of Engineers without Borders – and find an admission of failure. Failure is endemic in the development business. This should not be a surprise. If we knew how to end poverty or create jobs for young Kenyans, or better governance in Congo, we would have done it a long time ago. Yet the aid establishment is incapable of saying this or of admitting to a failure.

Some years ago, Dennis Rondinelli wrote a book called *Development Projects as Policy Experiments: An Adaptive Approach to Development Administration* (Rondinelli 1993). It should be compulsory reading for anyone who works in the field of development assistance. The title more or less explains Rondinelli's thesis. Development projects are, by nature, experimental. If they work, they are no longer projects *per se* because they can be scaled up. Development projects are about learning, and one learns from mistakes as well as success. An essential point about learning, of course, is that if it is to be useful, a lesson has to be *remembered*, so mistakes are not repeated. Learning, however, especially *adaptive learning*, is a concept that is alien to the way results-based management is applied in the Orwellian world of aid "experts." There, the only allowable outcomes are positive, and The Plan is the basis for everything, regardless of reality. The failure to learn from failure (because there *is* no failure) becomes endemic and, in the few cases where failure is either admitted or discovered, punishment – in the form of no-funding-next-time or career U-turns – is meted out accordingly. This is Gosplan in spades.

Time and Timing

There is an important paper, perhaps a book, to be written about time and timing in international development assistance. The essence would run like this: Development does not happen on the basis of a development agency's calendar. Farmers cannot wait an additional month to plant; sick people cannot be put on hold while Phase II is being planned. To paraphrase an expression from the judicial system, development delayed is development denied.

That is about timing. The second part of the time problem has to do with the project cycle and a growing demand to see quantifiable results during the life of a project. That makes sense in bricks-and-mortar projects where hospitals, wells, and schools can be counted and photographed. However, in many projects dealing with health, education, agriculture, or governance, the real results – the *development* results – may not be at all evident in the short run. Even in hospital, well-drilling, and school projects, the result is not the *thing*; it is what the thing contributes to change. The real result is what takes place inside the school; it is about whether the well and the hospital result in healthier people. These will not be measurable the day the ribbon is cut. Demanding results within a project's lifetime pushes the discussion away from transformational projects and true results, and back into the realm of outputs – like the self-congratulatory South Sulawesi Project described above, where the real results, if they occur, are still several years down the road.

The third *time* issue is about how long it takes to get anything done. Because the aid community is so besotted with its planning mechanisms, so paralyzed by its risk avoidance and its fear of failure, it has added more and more steps to the planning and approval process, and these take ever-increasing amounts of time. CIDA/ DFATD, known for years to many recipient countries as one of the slowest of the bilateral donors, has in recent years become even slower. It can actually take as much as four years to get a bilateral project up and running (OAG 2009, 68–72). The underspending of its 2012–13 budget by almost \$300 million is further evidence of the problem (Berthiaume 2013). It is not that there was nothing in the pipeline. The pipeline was jammed by the fear of failure, the demand for advance guarantees of results, the sheer bureaucratic weight of the results-based management system, and a perverse culture of micromanagement at the very top of the government's Everest-like decision-making pyramid.

Conclusion

Nobody should be surprised that foreign aid has not done a great deal to reduce deeply entrenched poverty. Most of the money has not been spent on that. Andrew Natsios could have been referring to Canada's aid program when he wrote, "The command and control system for foreign aid programs is out of control … it is uncoordinated and undisciplined; driven by a set of dysfunctional regulatory incentives that focus oversight on the wrong issues; done in a highly politicized setting; and has become a major impediment to aligning good development practice with the best research on good development theory" (Natsios 2010).

There is plenty of evidence, however, from projects where poverty reduction is front and centre that aid can and does work. The answer to change will not be found in submitting development planning to ever more draconian torture devices. Some of what needs doing is simple common sense:

For government

- Observe the ODA Accountability Act. If the objective of the aid program is to reduce poverty, ODA must focus on poor people in poor countries and on things that will make a difference in their lives. If private sector development is deemed a solution, then whatever plan is developed should include verifiable indicators that will show it is delivering the intended results. If a project is about restoring mangrove

ecosystems, do not report what might happen; say what really happened or leave it out until something has. If Canadian companies need help abroad, use trade promotion budgets, not ODA.
- Decentralize. When he was President of CIDA, Marcel Massé tried decentralization, but it was costly; many senior managers at headquarters would not go to the field, and they would not *let go* either. When she was CIDA minister, Bev Oda promised to decentralize, but then she tightened the hatches until the pips squeaked. If one cannot put decision makers close to the shop floor, the product will always look like it came from Gosplan.
- Cut the paperwork. Even the Auditor General – responsible for many of the problems inherent in the passion for results – has criticized CIDA for the incredible weight of its bureaucracy (OAG 2009).
- Speed it up.

For all development practitioners, including contractors, NGOs, and government

- Deal with risk, embrace failure, and learn from it. The problem here lies not so much in developing countries as it does with the media, politicians, and the voting Canadian public. Many Canadians no longer believe the hype, the endless success stories, and the revisionist data. Far too many think that "aid does not work" or "the money never gets there." It is time to start treating the media, politicians, and the public like adults, finding ways to explain how inherently difficult development is, and letting them in on the importance of and the difficulty in ending poverty.
- Get off the tarmac. This is an old Robert Chambers admonition (Chambers 1983). If decision makers want to understand something about development – and especially about poverty – they have to get away from cities and paved highways; they have to get out to where the problem is; they have to *understand*; and they have to *empathize*. It is a bit like decentralization, but it is the necessary extra mile.
- Build knowledge. Some of this will come from getting people into the field and off the tarmac; reward people who can

think; encourage discussion and debate; make development the priority rather than the command-and-control audit culture.

- Remember. Knowledge is only useful if it is remembered and applied. Far too many people in the development business think the world began the day they arrived. Aid administrators have an obligation to learn from experience and to build on it.
- Expand the time horizon. Serious development efforts take time. Do more *ex post facto* evaluations; re-evaluate some "successful" projects a few years *after* completion; think five years instead of two; ten years instead of five.

Most of this is simple common sense, but in a world of development assistance where so little common sense is available, even some would go a long way.

Notes

1. *How to Lie with Statistics* (Huff 1954) is a terrific book on this subject, used in many university courses over the years.
2. The Bank confirmed that figure in its 1990 WDR, saying, "In 1985 more than one billion people, or almost one third of the total population of the developing world, were living on less than $370 a year." Ten years later in its 2000-01 WDR, it was still reporting that "Of the world's 6 billion people, 2.8 billion – almost half – live on less than $2 a day, and 1.2 billion – a fifth – live on less than $1 a day." Over the past decade, however, the Bank began to tinker with the 1980-2001 base. For example, "The Bank's annual statistical report, *World Development Indicators 2004* (WDI) … shows a drop in the absolute number of people living on less than $1 a day in all developing countries *from 1.5 billion in 1981*, to 1.1 billion in 2001" (emphasis added). In other words, the 1981 base had increased to 1.5 billion – and it kept rising thereafter to its current level of 1.9 billion. What remains constant is the 1.1 or 1.2 billion people living in poverty "today" (whether that "today" is 2013, 2004, 2000, 1985, or 1980).
3. French aid to Mayotte in 2010 totalled US$603 million. Swiss aid to Sub-Saharan Africa that year totalled $342 million and Australian aid totalled $190 million (OECD 2012).
4. Moreover, if one thinks of the aid effort in global terms, the volumes are relatively small in relation to the task. Global ODA in 2011 was

$95 billion, with no discounts for emergency assistance or any of the political, commercial, and strategic alarums and excursions that are so endemic to the system. To put this apparently large number – aimed at reducing poverty in more than 150 developing countries – into perspective, one might compare it with the cost of the London Olympics ($13.7 billion) or the amount of money spent globally in a year on pet food ($55 billion), or the 2014 budget for the City of New York ($70 billion).

5. Although CIDA no longer exists, it lives on in its systems and policy documents now found on the DFATD website. I debated whether to use DFATD as the working acronym for this paper, but none of what I write about was created by DFATD, so I continue to use the CIDA acronym where common sense seems to apply.

References

Berthiaume, Lee. 2013. "Hundreds of Millions in Foreign Aid Unspent Last Year, Federal Records Confirm." *Ottawa Citizen*, November 1. Internet, http://www.ottawacitizen.com/business/Hundreds+millions+foreign+unspent+last+year+federal+records+confirm/9114155/story.html. Accessed November 8, 2013.

Brass, Clinton. 2012. *Changes to the Government Performance and Results Act (GPRA): Overview of the New Framework of Products and Processes.* Washington, DC: Congressional Research Service.

CIDA. 2011. *Development for Results 2010–2011*. Internet, http://www.acdi-cida.gc.ca/results2010–2011. Accessed November 8, 2013.

CIDA. 2013a. *Contracts over $10,000; 2012–2013 - 4th quarter (January 1st, 2013 to March 31st, 2013).* Internet, http://www.acdi-cida.gc.ca/acdi-cida/contrats-contracts.nsf/vQuarter-Eng?OpenView&RestrictToCategory=2012–2013-Q4. Accessed November 8, 2013.

CIDA. 2013b. *Statistical Report on International Assistance 2011–2012 – Table A.* Internet, http://www.acdi-cida.gc.ca/acdi-cida/acdi-cida.nsf/eng/NAT-319142528-PLZ. Accessed November 8, 2013.

Chambers, Robert. 1983. *Rural Development: Putting the Last First*. Burnt Mill, UK: Longman.

Economist. 2013. "Towards the End of Poverty." *The Economist*, June 1. Internet, http://www.economist.com/news/leaders/21578665-nearly-1-billion-people-have-been-taken-out-extreme-poverty-20-years-world-should-aim. Accessed November 8, 2013.

Global Humanitarian Assistance. 2013. *Global Humanitarian Assistance Report 2013*. Internet, http://www.globalhumanitarianassistance.org/wp-content/uploads/2013/07/GHA-Report-20131.pdfhttp://www.globalhumanitarianassistance.org/report/4216. Accessed November 8, 2013.

Gilmore, Scott. 2012. "Poverty Reduction Depends on Entrepreneurs, Not Aid." *Globe and Mail,* January 26. Internet, http://www.theglobeand-mail.com/commentary/poverty-reduction-depends-on-entrepreneurs-not-aid/article4202336/. Accessed November 8, 2013.

Huff, Darrell. 1954. *How to Lie with Statistics.* New York: Norton.

Mintzberg, Henry. 1994. *The Rise and Fall of Strategic Planning.* New York: Free Press.

Natsios, Andrew. 2010. "The Clash of the Counter-Bureaucracy and Development." Washington, DC: Center for Global Development.

OECD. 2012. *Statistics on Resource Flows to Developing Countries.* Internet, http://www.oecd.org/dac/stats/statisticsonresourceflowstodeveloping countries.htm. Accessed November 8, 2013.

Office of the Auditor General of Canada. 2009. *Report of the Auditor General of Canada to the House of Commons.* Ottawa: Government of Canada.

Pearson, Lester. 1969. *Partners in Development: Report of the Commission on International Development.* New York: Praeger.

Rondinelli, Dennis. 1993. *Development Projects as Policy Experiments: An Adaptive Approach to Development Administration.* New York: Routledge.

World Bank. 1981. *World Development Report: 1980.* Washington, DC: World Bank and Oxford University Press.

SECTION II

THE CANADIAN CONTEXT AND MOTIVATIONS

CHAPTER VI

Mimicry and Motives: Canadian Aid Allocation in Longitudinal Perspective

Liam Swiss

Introduction

There is no consensus over the first principles of Canadian foreign aid. If anything, ideas about the principles of Canadian aid have become more fragmented since 2006. Does Canada provide aid to help the neediest? Is Canada simply trying to ensure access for its multinational firms abroad? Is Canadian aid little more than a blunt tool of foreign policy? These questions are at the heart of our understanding of the first principles of Canadian aid. Indeed, the motives that underpin Canadian foreign aid have garnered significant attention in the media and the research literature since 2010. Gone are the days when Canada would be counted as one of the states operating its aid program primarily on a "moral vision" (Lumsdaine 1993). Running the gamut from humanitarian solidarity to the most capricious forms of national self-interest, Canada has been lumped into every category of donor, depending on the perspective of the critic or author and the various incidents or cases studied (Brown 2007; Morrison 1998; Pratt 1994b; Sumner 2012; Swiss 2011, 2012ab). A common feature of these sorts of studies has been their use of comparative cases to situate Canada among other donors (Action Aid 2010; Gulrajani 2010). By examining how Canada compares to other donor countries—often to the perceived "leading" donors—analysts and critics alike point to positive behaviours or "best practices" for Canada to emulate

(Gulrajani 2010; McGill 2012; Pronk 2001). These comparisons tend to be qualitative, small-N, and cross-sectional (stationary in time) research, yielding recommendations for Canada based on a limited set of comparators and a short period of time. From the perspective of trying to shape policy, these approaches are often warranted, but they overlook lessons that can be drawn from a larger-scale comparison of Canada to other donors over a longer period.

This chapter, by way of contrast, uses a novel quantitative approach with a large-N sample of bilateral aid flows over a fifty-year time period. By examining patterns of aid allocation over time, I uncover new information about where best to situate Canada among other donors and discuss the implications of these findings for our understanding of the motives underpinning Canadian aid. Where Canada more closely resembles humanitarian-inspired donors, one might infer more humanitarian motives, while instances where Canada falls in line with more self-interested donors suggest more realist motives behind Canada's aid. My findings suggest that although Canada's mimicry of other donors has shifted significantly over time from a more humanitarian set of donors to those motivated by self-interest, the evidence of these realist motives shaping aid flows at the recipient country level are less clear.

Aid Allocation: A Matter of Principle?

Examining the allocation of Canadian aid reveals important evidence about the motives and first principles that support it. By following the flow of money, and not just the press releases, policy statements, or country strategies developed by donors, a macro perspective shows how a donor allocates funds on the global level and what this indicates about its aid. In the case of Canada, this chapter uses aid allocation patterns to do two things: (1) discern which other donor countries Canada's aid allocation most closely resembles over time to identify which countries and, in turn, motives Canada may be emulating in its aid practices; and (2) examine several key factors underpinning the provision of aid to recipient countries on a dyadic basis to highlight the motives that drive Canadian aid relationships over time.

Using aid allocation to examine what motivates the foreign aid process has been one of the major threads of foreign aid research since 1990 (Tierney et al. 2011). In an oft-cited example, Alesina and Dollar (2000) use cross-national statistical analysis to argue that patterns of aid allocation highlight a realist motive for aid: Donors provide aid based on self-interest. More recent research on aid allocation has also used large-N statistical analysis to examine how aid is allocated and the motives behind various donors' aid programs (Clist 2011; Dreher et al. 2011; Neumayer 2003). Likewise, other research has used small-N comparative case studies to arrive at similar conclusions (Schraeder et al. 1998; Woods 2005). Similar analysis has also examined the Canadian context, concluding most often that the Canadian aid program reflects a tension between realist and humanitarian motives (Macdonald and Hoddinott 2004; Morrison 1994; Noël et al. 2004; Pratt 1994ab; Thérien and Noël 1994).

For the purposes of this chapter, I will examine aid allocation patterns using network techniques and cross-national statistical models to identify which donors Canada most closely emulates and whether Canada considers similar or differing criteria when providing aid to developing countries when compared with other donors. These features of Canadian aid allocation provide valuable evidence regarding the motives behind Canada's aid and how they have changed over time.

Mimicry is a technique used by many organizations to attempt to gain greater certainty within the context of their organizational field (DiMaggio and Powell 1983). My earlier research has indicated the role mimicry plays in shaping bilateral donor policies in the cases of security sector reform (Swiss 2011) and gender equality (Swiss 2012). In this chapter, I investigate the extent to which Canada's aid allocation is marching in lock step with other donors and mimicking factors used by a wide range of other donors to determine such allocation. Looking at what other donors Canada is emulating at various points in time provides a better understanding of how mimicry reflects aid motives at a given point in time. Asking these questions using longitudinal analysis will help explain how both mimicry and motives shift over the longer term.

Keeping Up with the Joneses

To examine Canadian aid allocation over time at the macro level, I compiled a network dataset of all bilateral aid flows included in the Organisation for Economic Co-operation and Development's (OECD) QWIDS database from 1960 through 2010 (OECD 2013). This dataset captures the bilateral aid ties of all members of the OECD's

Figure 1. Canadian Aid Recipient Network, 1960

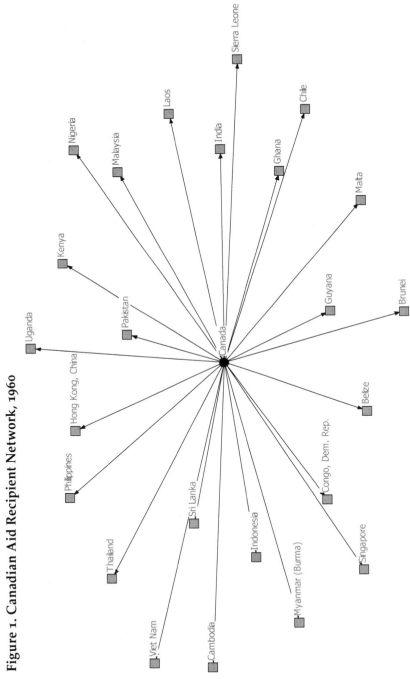

Figure 2. Canadian Aid Recipient Network, 1985

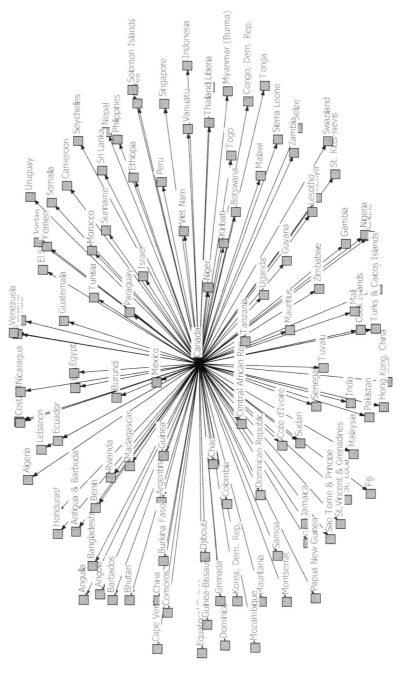

Figure 3. Canadian Aid Recipient Network, 2010

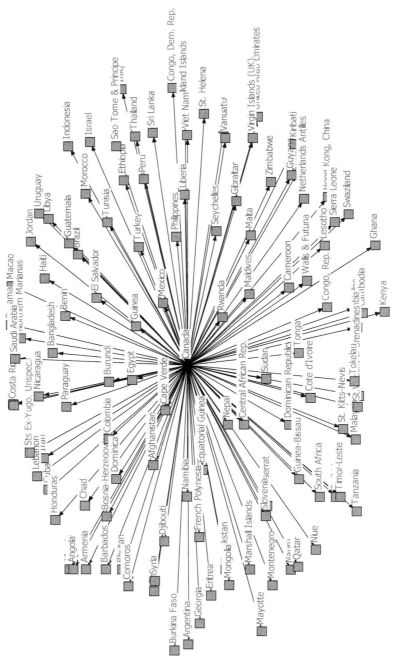

Development Assistance Committee (DAC) and a select few other donors with all recipient countries in each year over the fifty-year period. Examining the data using UCINet social network analysis software reveals patterns of the overall aid network at the global level, as well as for individual donors' networks. The first part of my analysis relies on this full dataset to examine the Canadian bilateral aid network and how it compares to other DAC donors over time.

Figures 1 through 3 depict the scope of Canada's bilateral aid ties in 1960, 1985, and 2010, respectively. Every recipient country noted in the network diagram in a given year is a net positive recipient of Canadian bilateral ODA. Examining these network diagrams in isolation, one can simply conclude that the scope of Canadian aid widens significantly over the time period of my analysis. More detailed analysis of this sort of network data is possible, but for the purposes of this analysis, it is sufficient to note that every other bilateral donor in the world in a given year has a potentially similar network of aid ties that can be depicted in the same fashion.

Using social network analysis tools, it is possible to take a single country's network in a given year and compare it to every other donor's network in the same year. Rather than examining every network diagram individually, one can quantify the aid ties of each donor and mathematically compare the similarity of each donor's network. Many such measures of similarity exist, but in this analysis I opt to use the Jaccard coefficient as a measure of similarity. This coefficient reflects the percentage of all possible aid network ties that a pair of donors have in common in a given year. This measure incorporates both similar positive ties (both donors give) and similar negative ties (neither donor gives). An index ranging from 0 to 1 permits the comparison of any country's network to every other donor, with values nearer to 1 reflecting the greatest similarity.

By calculating Jaccard coefficients to measure the similarity of the Canadian aid network to all other DAC donors every five years over the period from 1960 to 2010, I map out which donor countries Canada most closely resembles in terms of aid allocation. Figure 4 depicts these coefficients in a heat map table: those countries most similar to Canada have a coefficient closer to 1 and are depicted in a darker shade of grey; countries most dissimilar to Canada have index scores closer to zero and are in lighter shades of grey. These measures indicate not only similarities in terms of countries Canada provides ODA to, but also those it does not.

Figure 4. Similarity of Canadian Aid Networks to Networks of Other Donors, 1960–2010 (Jaccard Coefficients)

Country	1960	1965	1970	1975	1980	1985	1990	1995	2000	2005	2010
Australia	0.000	0.453	0.378	0.382	0.348	0.597	0.475	0.432	0.545	0.459	0.708
Austria	0.000	0.225	0.191	0.286	0.509	0.544	0.656	0.734	0.770	0.736	0.679
Belgium	0.038	0.095	0.571	0.629	0.614	0.685	0.748	0.783	0.677	0.702	0.622
Czech Republic	0.000	0.000	0.000	0.000	0.000	0.000	0.000	0.000	0.198	0.599	0.618
Denmark	0.120	0.200	0.468	0.426	0.486	0.409	0.508	0.566	0.557	0.528	0.630
Finland	0.000	0.000	0.000	0.340	0.462	0.471	0.591	0.519	0.629	0.730	0.788
France	0.071	0.292	0.408	0.389	0.595	0.728	0.777	0.768	0.788	0.811	0.759
Germany	0.240	0.521	0.677	0.624	0.594	0.791	0.866	0.788	0.800	0.833	0.775
Greece	0.000	0.000	0.000	0.000	0.000	0.000	0.000	0.000	0.393	0.599	0.586
Hungary	0.000	0.000	0.000	0.000	0.000	0.000	0.000	0.000	0.000	0.101	0.328
Iceland	0.000	0.000	0.000	0.000	0.000	0.000	0.000	0.000	0.031	0.071	0.136
Ireland	0.000	0.000	0.000	0.111	0.225	0.248	0.328	0.620	0.607	0.617	0.650
Italy	0.173	0.267	0.455	0.519	0.500	0.721	0.701	0.689	0.622	0.559	0.643
Japan	0.342	0.364	0.394	0.540	0.570	0.748	0.782	0.742	0.811	0.837	0.732
Korea	0.000	0.000	0.000	0.000	0.000	0.000	0.256	0.713	0.693	0.803	0.793
Luxembourg	0.000	0.000	0.000	0.000	0.000	0.000	0.437	0.614	0.450	0.621	0.661

Figure 4. (continued)

Country	1960	1965	1970	1975	1980	1985	1990	1995	2000	2005	2010
Netherlands	0.077	0.138	0.494	0.646	0.610	0.794	0.805	0.809	0.799	0.797	0.625
New Zealand	0.000	0.000	0.000	0.280	0.245	0.294	0.321	0.399	0.514	0.596	0.457
Norway	0.040	0.219	0.347	0.413	0.586	0.636	0.675	0.740	0.809	0.771	0.733
Poland	0.000	0.000	0.000	0.082	0.022	0.035	0.008	0.000	0.459	0.420	0.492
Portugal	0.040	0.000	0.000	0.000	0.000	0.000	0.042	0.183	0.165	0.369	0.315
Slovak Republic	0.000	0.000	0.000	0.000	0.000	0.000	0.000	0.000	0.000	0.122	0.115
Spain	0.000	0.000	0.000	0.000	0.000	0.000	0.537	0.595	0.615	0.706	0.737
Sweden	0.115	0.254	0.288	0.230	0.379	0.387	0.633	0.831	0.791	0.746	0.700
Switzerland	0.000	0.377	0.511	0.640	0.593	0.707	0.782	0.771	0.778	0.732	0.723
Turkey	0.000	0.000	0.000	0.000	0.000	0.000	0.000	0.116	0.233	0.410	0.692
UK	0.255	0.553	0.523	0.607	0.629	0.758	0.809	0.715	0.888	0.732	0.721
US	0.258	0.545	0.570	0.674	0.633	0.686	0.650	0.657	0.763	0.841	0.820

In the earlier period of my analysis, Canada clearly has a network of aid recipient countries that stood apart from those of many
other donors, with only the UK and the US sharing more than half
of network ties in common in 1965 and no countries sharing more
than 80 percent of ties until 1990. The most similar comparator in
the sample is seen in the year 2000, when Canada and the United
Kingdom mirrored more than 88 percent of ties in their respective
aid networks. In the most recent panel year, 2010, Canada's network
most closely resembles that of the United States. In earlier years,
however, Canada's pattern of aid allocation more closely resembled
that of countries such as West Germany (1970), the Netherlands (1985),
and Sweden (1995).

What does it mean that, in its aid allocations, Canada resembles
countries such as the UK, the US, Sweden, and the Netherlands
more closely than countries such as France or Australia? One might
expect Canada's aid provision to parallel closely the UK and the US,
given our past colonial and geographic ties. It would not be surprising, for instance, to see Canada and the UK providing aid to all the
same countries in the Commonwealth. More curious, however, is the
fact that in the 1980s and 1990s Canada's aid network most closely
resembled donors such as Sweden and the Netherlands. This speaks
to an alignment of interests between Canada and these smaller donor
countries—something commonly referred to as the "like-minded"
group of donors, including Canada, Denmark, the Netherlands,
Norway, and Sweden (Neumayer 2003). These donors have traditionally been seen to allocate aid based on recipient need and merit rather
than in terms of donor political or commercial interests (Dreher
et al. 2011). By emulating these like-minded donors in this period,
Canadian aid motivations would more closely align with principles
of humane internationalism.

From 2000 onwards, the similarity of Canada's aid network to
those of this like-minded group diminishes. Instead, Canada's aid
appears to become more generic—more like that of a larger number of
donors—as well as falling much more closely in line with American
aid patterns. This might result from an overall intensification of the
international aid regime in this period, or from pressures to stan-
dardize and harmonize aid practices (witness the Paris Declaration),
but it might also speak more simply to shifting Canadian aid motivations. Reasons for this might be found in Canada's shift in focus
(at least rhetorically, see chapter by Macdonald and Ruckert in this

volume) in the latter part of the 2000s to a greater focus on the Americas, but also may speak to a shift in attitude or first principles from those indicated by the like-minded group of donors in the 1980s and 1990s to a more self-interested form of aid by Canada in the 2000s. One need only look at Canada's list of "countries of focus" to see how ties such as trade and political interest are informing our aid allocation in this period.

Examining the similarity of the Canadian aid network over the fifty-year period shows that Canada has experienced a shift in which countries it most resembles in terms of aid allocation. Indeed, Canada has emulated several other donors in different periods. This is not surprising – the use of mimicry as an organizational tool has long been understood to play a role in bureaucracies and other institutions globally (DiMaggio and Powell 1983). Having the most in common with the UK and the US in its early years as a donor, Canada then began to more closely parallel the like-minded group of donors, before again following a path where its aid allocation matched most closely the US and the UK. This preliminary analysis suggests that, rather than strike a maverick path of its own and allocate aid along a uniquely Canadian set of criteria, Canada has been a mimic over the years. To examine this further, I turn in the next section to a comparison of which recipient country factors serve as criteria to provide aid to a country and how Canada's criteria compare to the criteria of the rest of the major Western donors.

Breadcrumbs and Yardsticks

In this section, I use a subset of the larger dataset, encompassing the quantity of aid flows between Canada and all its recipient partner countries from 1960 to 2010, to determine which criteria are most closely associated with receiving Canadian aid over time and how these vary by period. A sample of 6,324 dyad years reflect all bilateral ODA flows between Canada and a recipient country partner in this period, illustrating the flow of Canadian aid to 148 different recipient countries. I then compare the same criteria to a sample of all other donor ties, as well as to four individual donors (Norway, Sweden, UK, and the US) in the same period, drawing from a sample of 68,775 dyad years. To assess the factors contributing to the presence of any aid ties, I employ a longitudinal analysis using random effects panel regression. This technique allows me to analyze the change in relationships between certain country factors and the level of ODA Canada or another donor provides to a given country in a given year, and how the effect of these factors on aid flows change over time.

Along with the network data above on the presence or absence of Canadian and other bilateral ODA, I compiled additional variables used to measure the criteria/factors that contribute to the provision of aid. These variables were derived from extant data sources, including the World Bank's World Development Indicators database, the Polity IV database and the Correlates of War dataset (Marshall et al. 2009; Pevehouse et al. 2004; World Bank 2012). Measures incorporated into the models below include: the distance between Ottawa and recipient country capital cities; recipient country population; total trade between Canada and the recipient country; recipient country GDP per capita; total ODA received by a country; the Polity IV measure of autocracy/democracy; whether a recipient country was affected by disaster; and whether a recipient country was affected by intrastate conflict.

Using a sub-sample of 3,587 country-years for which all data was available for Canada, I first model the effect of the above factors

Table 1. Random Effects Models of Determinants of Canadian Bilateral ODA Flows, 1965–2010

	Model 1 Full Sample	Model 2 1970s	Model 3 1980s	Model 4 1990s	Model 5 2000s
Lagged Dyadic ODA Flow	0.51***	0.32***	0.36***	0.35***	0.19**
Logged Distance between Dyad Capital Cities	-2.25	4.01	0.03	-1.55	-4.67
Polity IV Recipient Score	0.04	0.61***	-0.17	-0.10	-0.19
Country Affected by Disaster	0.52	-0.36	-1.03	0.63	2.96
Presence of Intrastate Conflict	1.05	1.67	0.63	-2.96**	-2.58
Logged Total Trade	-0.42	0.28	-0.41	0.09	1.80
Recipient GDP per capita	-2.14**	-4.46***	-0.88	-0.74	-6.34**
Logged Total Recipient ODA Volumes	1.19**	1.61	1.69**	0.75	2.00
Logged Total Recipient Population	1.87**	2.79*	3.26***	0.57	0.91
Constant	-11.23	-69.93*	-70.29**	-1.60	35.59
Observations	3,587	677	812	1,019	631
R^2 Overall	0.46	0.62	0.62	0.26	0.19

* $p < 0.05$, ** $p < 0.01$, *** $p < 0.001$

on the continuous measure of net dyadic ODA flows (millions of constant 2000 USD). I lag all independent variables five years to account for temporal priority and the time needed to plan and implement new aid programming. Table 1 shows the results of these models for the full sample (Model 1) and then for each decade from the 1970s onward (Models 2–5). The results show the effect of each covariate on dyadic aid flows between Canada and each recipient country.

Model 1 shows that in the full sample, several criteria are associated with an increased amount of aid flow between Canada and a recipient country. These include higher levels of existing ODA provided to the country by all donors, and a greater recipient country population.[1] In contrast, only one factor decreases the odds of a country receiving Canadian aid: higher levels of economic development as measured by recipient country GDP per capita. Throughout the full fifty-year period of my study, Canada is likely to provide more aid to poorer, more populous countries, with a preference for donor darlings that receive more aid from other donors, all else being equal.

Models 2 through 5 show how these criteria vary over the decades. A few interesting patterns emerge when the various time periods are taken into account. No criterion is statistically significant in its association with aid provision in all decades. In the 1970s, more democratic states were likely to receive more aid, while wealthier countries received less. In the 1980s, only larger population and total aid received are associated with higher levels of aid from Canada. The 1990s model shows only the effect of conflict on Canada's aid: those countries in conflict would receive on average $3 million less in aid than those at peace. Finally, in the 2000s, the only factor significantly associated with dyadic aid flows is the level of a country's economic development. Overall, these results show little consistency over time for the factors determining Canadian aid, but raise the question of how these factors compare to other donors overall and over time.

Does Canada employ the same aid allocation criteria as the rest of the donor community? Figure 5 compares Canada's results on five measures from Table 1 to identical analyses for Norway, Sweden, the UK, and the US for the same period of time.[2] Figure 5 shows the calculated coefficients and 95 percent confidence intervals for each factor when all other variables are held constant. Coefficients significant at the $p<0.05$ level are labelled. Comparing Canada's results in this manner reveals which donors Canada resembles in a given

Figure 5. Comparison of Determinants of Foreign Aid Flows, Five Donors

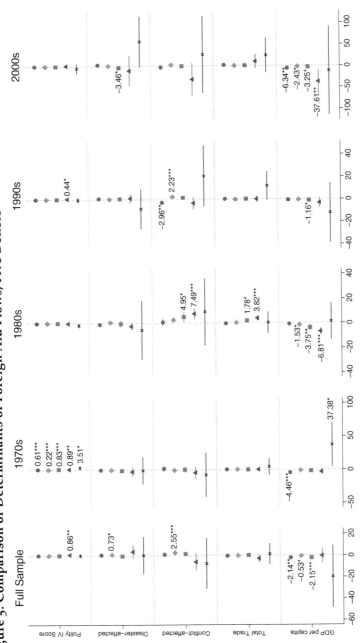

Millions of dyadic aid flows (constant 2000 USD)

● Canada   ◆ Norway   ■ Sweden   ▲ UK   × USA

* p < 0.05, ** p < 0.01, *** p < 0.001

period in terms of the factors shaping Canada's aid allocation and volumes. The figure illustrates the statistically significant factors Canada shares in common with other donors, and the factors that are not significantly associated with aid allocation. In the 1970s, for several donors, including Canada, the only factor increasing aid flows is the Polity IV score, which measures levels of democracy and autocracy. All five donors in this period provided more aid to more democratic recipient countries. Several other factors increase other donors' aid flows at various points in the analysis, but Canada has none of them in common with other donors – suggesting a diversity of motives within the comparison group. In contrast, the only factor Canada appears to have in common with other donors in *reducing* aid flows is recipient country GDP per capita, evident both in the full sample and in the 2000s.

Counterintuitively, one can make the argument that Canada shares in the non-effects of several determinants of their aid flows with other donors. Trade levels and disasters seem to have little consistent effect on any of these donors' aid flows. Apart from the UK, democracy has no measureable effect in all time periods aside from the 1970s. In terms of conflict, the evidence is mixed, with some donors providing greater aid to conflict countries at various points, but with Canada reducing aid in this instance in the 1990s. This suggests one can infer common motives through the absence of an effect of these factors – simply put, these factors did not shape Canadian or other donor aid flows to such an extent that the correlations are statistically significant.

Comparing Canada to the other donors reveals two interesting conclusions about the factors that contribute to Canadian provision of aid to a country. First, the only consistent factor over time appears to be a country's level of economic development. The poorer a country, the more aid it will receive. This holds for both Canada and the majority of the donors in my sample. In this sense, Canada is following the pack and providing aid along the lines of helping those most in economic need. Likewise, Canada resembles other donors in terms of what appears not to matter: trade, democracy, disaster, and conflict – none of these factors are robustly associated with multiple donors' aid allocation over time.

These results suggest that Canada is similar to the rest of the donor community in terms of the criteria affecting its decisions to maintain an aid relationship with a developing country. There is no massive discrepancy between the Canadian and other donor models, except that in the full sample Norway appears to take a more principled humanitarian stance, favouring those countries recovering from disaster and conflict. Emulating much of what is seen in the rest of the donor community, Canada's motives echo those of other comparable donors.

What Does Mimicry Say about Motives?

My findings suggest that, though the donors Canada has most closely resembled have varied over time, its patterns of aid allocation show that mimicry plays a strong role in shaping its aid programs. Indeed, since 1995, the extent to which Canada's aid network closely resembles other donors is on the increase. These similarities speak to motive behind Canada's provision of aid, in the sense that different donors carry reputations – deserved or not – for providing aid on a continuum of motives from realist national interest to humane internationalism. Analyzing Canada's changing aid allocation patterns reveals that, although there was a time in the 1980s and 1990s when Canada's aid allocation was most similar to the more humanitarian-oriented group of like-minded donors, that era has passed. Since 2000, the UK and the US have been the donors with which its aid allocation is most aligned – donors more closely associated with more realist interests.

This finding suggests a possible shift in the first principles of Canadian aid away from helping the neediest in an altruistic fashion to a more self-interested or commercially driven form of aid. Yet, in my cross-national analysis of the criteria most closely associated with the provision of Canadian aid, the self-interested factors seem less central. Indeed, none of trade, democracy, or conflict reduction featured as key factors explaining Canada's aid flows in the full sample of Canada's aid from 1965 to 2010.

This raises a possible contradiction or limitation within my study. The assumption that I can discern motive or principles from Canada's aid allocation based on which countries its aid network is most similar to takes for granted that Canada would be aiding recipient countries for the same motives as other donors in each case. This may not be valid. Perhaps Canada provides aid to a given country not because of a past colonial tie or a high level of trade between countries, but instead purely out of recipient need. These sorts of contradictions are more difficult to discern at the macro level and require a more detailed country-by-country micro-level analysis to flesh out specific motives. Still, my study, though exploratory, sheds new light on Canadian aid allocation over time and how that allocation helps explain the first principles of Canadian aid.

Though that is not a satisfying conclusion in terms of identifying any *one* motive underpinning Canadian aid, this chapter provides definitive empirical evidence of the shifting and varied nature of the motives of Canadian aid over time and how they can be discerned through examining which donors Canada resembles. By showing that Canada has mimicked other donors at different points by allocating aid based on different criteria, I have revealed new patterns of how Canada has positioned itself as a donor *vis-à-vis* other donor countries. The value of a long period of study with a larger number of data points, as employed in this chapter, is that, unlike the short-term cross-sectional approach more common to the Canadian aid literature, it shows how the patterns of allocation and the factors that shape aid flows are in flux. This chapter also reveals that, in spite of Canada's mimicry of other donors and shifting from a more humanitarian set of donors to those motivated by self-interest, the evidence of realist motives shaping aid flows at the recipient country level is less clear. It is this contradictory and dynamic aspect of Canadian aid programs and allocation that will require future researchers to continue to undertake crucial empirical analysis – even of the exploratory kind – using a wide array of data over a long period of time. Only by examining Canada's aid programs over the long term can something that might appear static be recast as a phenomenon that is dynamic. The fact that the donors Canada mimics have changed frequently over the past fifty years is perhaps not surprising, but the ability to discern the shifts in motives that changing aid allocation patterns suggest is a valuable contribution to expanding our understanding of Canadian aid.

Notes

1. I do not discuss the effects of the lagged dependent variable, as it is included in the models primarily to account for serial autocorrelation from year to year.
2. Full model results for each of these donors can be found in Appendix Tables A1–A4.

References

Action Aid. 2010. *Real Aid: Ending Aid Dependency*. London: Action Aid.

Alesina, Alberto, and David Dollar. 2000. "Who Gives Foreign Aid to Whom and Why?" *Journal of Economic Growth*, vol. 5, no. 1: 33–63.

Brown, Stephen. 2007. "'Creating the World's Best Development Agency'? Confusion and Contradictions in CIDA's New Development Policy." *Canadian Journal of Development Studies*, vol. 28, no. 2: 203–18.

Clist, Paul. 2011. "25 Years of Aid Allocation Practice: Whither Selectivity?" *World Development*, vol. 39, no. 10: 1724–34.

DiMaggio, Paul, and Walter W. Powell. 1983. "The Iron Cage Revisited: Institutional Isomorphism and Collective Rationality in Organizational Fields." *American Sociological Review*, vol. 48, no. 2: 147–60.

Dreher, Axel, Peter Nunnenkamp, and Rainer Thiele. 2011. "Are 'New' Donors Different? Comparing the Allocation of Bilateral Aid Between nonDAC and DAC Donor Countries." *World Development*, vol. 39, no. 11: 1950–68.

Gulrajani, Nilima. 2010. "Re-imagining Canadian Development Co-operation: A Comparative Examination of Norway and the UK." Toronto: Walter and Duncan Gordon Foundation.

Lumsdaine, David Halloran. 1993. *Moral Vision in International Politics: The Foreign Aid Regime, 1949–1989*. Princeton, NJ: Princeton University Press.

Macdonald, Ryan, and John Hoddinott. 2004. "Determinants of Canadian Bilateral Aid Allocations: Humanitarian, Commercial or Political?" *Canadian Journal of Economics*, vol. 37, no. 2: 294–312.

Marshall, Monty G., Keith Jaggers, and Ted R. Gurr. 2009. "Polity IV Project: Political Regime Characteristics and Transitions, 1800–2007." Electronic Dataset. Center for Systemic Peace.

McGill, Hunter. 2012. "Canada among Donors: How Does Canadian Aid Compare?" In Stephen Brown, ed. *Struggling for Effectiveness: CIDA and Canadian Foreign Aid*. Montreal and Kingston: McGill–Queen's University Press: 24–52

Morrison, David R. 1994. "The Choice of Bilateral Aid Recipients." In Cranford Pratt, ed. *Canadian International Development Assistance Policies: An Appraisal*. Montreal: McGill–Queen's University Press: 123–55.

Morrison, David R. 1998. *Aid and Ebb Tide: A History of CIDA and Canadian Development Assistance*. Waterloo, ON: Wilfrid Laurier University Press.

Neumayer, Eric. 2003. *The Pattern of Aid Giving: The Impact of Good Governance on Development Assistance*. London: Routledge.

Noël, Alain, Jean-Philippe Thérien, and Sébastien Dallaire. 2004. "Divided over Internationalism: The Canadian Public and Development Assistance." *Canadian Public Policy/Analyse de Politiques*, vol. 30, no. 1: 29–46.

OECD. 2013. "QWIDS: Query Wizard for International Development Statistics." Paris: OECD. Internet, http://stats.oecd.org/qwids/. Accessed August 10, 2013.

Pevehouse, Jon, Timothy Nordstrom, and Kevin Warnke. 2004. "The Correlates of War 2 International Governmental Organizations Data Version 2.0." *Conflict Management and Peace Science*, vol. 21, no. 2: 101–19.

Pratt, Cranford. 1994a. "Canadian Development Assistance: A Profile." In Cranford Pratt, ed. *Canadian International Development Assistance Policies: An Appraisal*. Montreal: McGill–Queen's University Press: 3–24.

Pratt, Cranford. 1994b. "Humane Internationalism and Canadian Development Assistance Policies." In Cranford Pratt, ed. *Canadian International Development Assistance Policies: An Appraisal*. Montreal: McGill–Queen's University Press: 334–70.

Pronk, Jan P. 2001. "Aid as a Catalyst." *Development and Change*, vol. 32, no. 4: 611–29.

Schraeder, Peter J., Steven W. Hook, and Bruce Taylor. 1998. "Clarifying the Foreign Aid Puzzle: A Comparison of American, Japanese, French, and Swedish Aid Flows." *World Politics*, vol. 50, no. 2: 294–323.

Sumner, Andy. 2012. "Where Do the Poor Live?" *World Development*, vol. 40, no. 5: 865–77.

Swiss, Liam. 2011. "Security Sector Reform and Development Assistance: Explaining the Diffusion of Policy Priorities Among Donor Agencies." *Qualitative Sociology*, vol. 34, no. 2: 371–93.

Swiss, Liam. 2012a. "The Adoption of Women and Gender as Development Assistance Priorities: An Event History Analysis of World Polity Effects." *International Sociology*, vol. 27, no. 1: 96–119.

Swiss, Liam. 2012b. "Gender, Security, and Instrumentalism: Canada's Foreign Aid in Support of National Interest?" In Stephen Brown, ed. *Struggling for Effectiveness: CIDA and Canadian Foreign Aid*. Montreal and Kingston: McGill–Queen's University Press: 135–58.

Thérien, Jean-Philippe, and Alain Noël. 1994. "Welfare Institutions and Foreign Aid: Domestic Foundations of Canadian Foreign Policy." *Canadian Journal of Political Science*, vol. 27, no. 3: 529–58.

Tierney, Michael J., Daniel L. Nielson, Darren G. Hawkins, J. Timmons Roberts, Michael G. Findley, Ryan M. Powers, Bradley Parks, Sven E. Wilson, and Robert L. Hicks. 2011. "More Dollars than Sense: Refining Our Knowledge of Development Finance Using AidData." *World Development*, vol. 39, no. 11: 1891–1906.

Woods, Ngaire. 2005. "The Shifting Politics of Foreign Aid." *International Affairs*, vol. 81, no. 2: 393–409.

World Bank. 2012. *World Development Indicators*. Washington, DC: World Bank.

Appendix – Table A1. Random Effects Models of Determinants of Norwegian Bilateral ODA Flows, 1965–2010

	Full Sample	1970s	1980s	1990s	2000s
Lagged Dyadic ODA Flow	0.66***	0.38***	0.54***	0.35***	0.58***
Logged Distance between Dyad Capital Cities	3.14***	2.09	5.14*	3.89**	8.79***
Polity IV Recipient Score	-0.05	0.22***	-0.06	-0.07	-0.26
Country Affected by Disaster	0.73*	-0.64	0.53	0.13	0.32
Presence of Intrastate Conflict	2.55***	-0.85	2.47*	2.23***	2.62
Logged Total Trade	-0.23	0.09	0.23	-0.42*	-0.18
Recipient GDP per capita	-0.53*	-1.01	-1.53*	-0.47	-2.43*
Logged Total Recipient ODA Volumes	0.19	-0.03	0.58	0.05	0.48
Logged Total Recipient Population	1.21***	2.30***	0.29	1.62***	2.36**
Constant	-44.76***	-42.35*	-48.54	-54.05***	-102.08**
Observations	2,501	473	617	729	429
R² Overall	0.64	0.59	0.69	0.69	0.64

* $p < 0.05$, ** $p < 0.01$, *** $p < 0.001$

Appendix – Table A2. Random Effects Models of Determinants of Swedish Bilateral ODA Flows, 1965–2010

	Full Sample	1970s	1980s	1990s	2000s
Lagged Dyadic ODA Flow	0.43***	0.23***	0.42***	0.33***	0.34***
Logged Distance between Dyad Capital Cities	3.19*	0.78	7.43*	4.47***	5.05
Polity IV Recipient Score	0.02	0.83***	-0.07	-0.02	-0.33
Country Affected by Disaster	-0.46	-1.10	-0.36	0.56	-3.46*
Presence of Intrastate Conflict	1.50	0.29	4.95*	1.35	-0.28
Logged Total Trade	0.21	-0.14	1.78*	0.07	0.30
Recipient GDP per capita	-2.15***	-1.81	-3.75**	-1.16*	-3.25*
Logged Total Recipient ODA Volumes	0.31	0.62	0.74	0.06	1.35
Logged Total Recipient Population	1.68***	4.02***	0.42	1.07*	1.93
Constant	-41.78*	-59.92	-60.28	-47.08**	-70.15
Observations	2,621	478	612	749	451
R² Overall	0.48	0.45	0.58	0.57	0.37

* $p < 0.05$, ** $p < 0.01$, *** $p < 0.001$

Appendix – Table A3. Random Effects Models of Determinants of British Bilateral ODA Flows, 1965–2010

	Full Sample	1970s	1980s	1990s	2000s
Lagged Dyadic ODA Flow	0.23***	0.66***	0.27***	0.76***	0.19*
Logged Distance between Dyad Capital Cities	7.99	0.04	8.51***	1.72	-6.28
Polity IV Recipient Score	0.86**	0.89**	-0.24	0.44*	1.23
Country Affected by Disaster	3.68	-2.69	-2.42	1.00	-10.50
Presence of Intrastate Conflict	-5.85	-4.42	7.49***	-3.50	-31.34
Logged Total Trade	-2.82	0.12	3.82***	0.01	10.00
Recipient GDP per capita	-0.17	-2.98	-6.81***	-3.35	-37.61**
Logged Total Recipient ODA Volumes	-0.37	1.40	0.67	-4.00**	-29.75**
Logged Total Recipient Population	16.33***	3.70*	2.08	7.34***	35.72***
Constant	-284.61***	-55.04	-82.38*	-22.17	316.51
Observations	2,866	522	667	822	502
R² Overall	0.22	0.72	0.63	0.59	0.15

* $p < 0.05$, ** $p < 0.01$, *** $p < 0.001$

Appendix – Table A4. Random Effects Models of Determinants of American Bilateral ODA Flows, 1965–2010

	Full Sample	1970s	1980s	1990s	2000s
Lagged Dyadic ODA Flow	0.48***	0.14***	0.95***	0.07*	0.02
Logged Distance between Dyad Capital Cities	11.44	42.29	-4.64	9.05	51.66
Polity IV Recipient Score	0.07	3.51*	-1.69	-0.52	-4.85
Country Affected by Disaster	0.27	-0.92	-5.62	-8.52	57.60
Presence of Intrastate Conflict	-7.46	-7.81	9.07	20.59	26.60
Logged Total Trade	1.28	4.53	0.36	11.88	24.50
Recipient GDP per capita	-19.77	37.38*	1.45	-12.24	-11.93
Logged Total Recipient ODA Volumes	-7.11	26.81***	-3.21	-6.09	-5.79
Logged Total Recipient Population	17.18	14.15	-0.98	9.06	13.92
Constant	-43.00	-1308.21**	105.74	-44.80	-567.04
Observations	3,806	722	866	1,048	633
R² Overall	0.31	0.30	0.76	0.08	0.02

* $p < 0.05$, ** $p < 0.01$, *** $p < 0.001$

CHAPTER VII

Continental Shift? Rethinking Canadian Aid to the Americas

Laura Macdonald and Arne Ruckert

One of the defining features of the Harper government's development assistance program, and of its foreign policy more broadly, has been a strong rhetorical shift towards an emphasis on Canadian economic interest in the promotion of foreign ties and in the delivery of foreign assistance. The Americas as a region has tended to serve as a proxy for this shift in focus. The higher levels of economic development of the region as a whole and growing Canadian trade and investment interests in the region, particularly in the mining sector, mean that increased aid to the Americas is commonly portrayed as a response to cold, hard Canadian self-interest, as opposed to the soft-hearted benevolence of assistance to Africa. Indeed, the Conservative government's Americas Strategy, launched in 2007, represented a partisan exercise insofar as Harper wished to distance himself from the Liberal governments under Chrétien and Martin, which emphasized Africa in an effort to focus on the poorest countries and to improve aid effectiveness, in line with the criteria of the OECD's Development Assistance Committee (Cameron 2007). Canadian development assistance to Latin America thus represents a good test case for the proposition that we have seen increased emphasis since 2007 on the economic self-interest of Canadians and Canadian firms, and less on the longer-term promotion of development and the well-being of the world's poorest citizens.

This article examines the case of Canadian development assistance to the Americas, with a focus on the policies of the Harper government. This case study represents a useful contribution to the debate on the domestic determinants of aid and the role of partisan motivations in shifting aid levels and priorities. We believe a study of the aid policy of a single state towards a single world region provides important insight into the complex and often contradictory motivations that shape aid policy, as well as more scope than purely quantitative analysis for understanding the ideational and discursive dimensions of governments' shifting priorities. In the case of Canadian development assistance to the Americas, we argue, quantitative analysis, which does not show the African region losing out to the Americas under the Harper government, needs to be supplemented with a more nuanced portrayal of changes in aid recipients and forms of assistance. We also suggest that Harper's transformation of Canadian aid policy has been incremental in nature, with a number of small but significant shifts accruing over time. More than seven years after Harper's ascendancy to power, we identify a marked shift in Canadian aid policy, with private-sector development and investment (especially in mining) and corporate social responsibility (CSR) in Latin America as strong areas of interest. This is not surprising, given some of the findings in the aid literature that highlight the institutional and cultural path-dependency of aid programs, which prevent drastic changes in aid delivery when opposition parties come to power (Thérien and Noël 1994).

The chapter begins with a short overview of debates regarding the motivations of development assistance policy, followed by a summary of the evolution of Canadian assistance in the Americas. We then provide more detail about current Canadian policies, focusing on three case studies: CIDA-supported partnerships between development NGOs and mining companies in Peru; Canadian assistance to Haiti, the biggest aid recipient in the region; and finally the controversial case of Honduras. We have selected these cases because they represent three of the most important aid recipients in the region and illustrate some of the competing logics behind Canadian aid. We conclude with a discussion of the implications of this analysis for rethinking Canadian development assistance policy.

Interests and Ideas in Development Assistance Policy

There is a long-running debate over governments' motives for delivering development assistance and the relative weight given to various factors in determining the nature of development policy. Van der Veen (2011) argues that analysts of aid often go astray by assuming that there is only one dominant motivation for aid, with the debate often polarized between advocates of self-interest and advocates of humanitarian principles. In addition, he argues, it is useful to use the concept of framing, with seven frames dominating policy makers' efforts to explain and defend aid policy: security, power, economic self-interest, enlightened self-interest, reputation/self-affirmation, obligation/duty, and humanitarianism (van der Veen 2011, 9–10).[1] Multiple frames can coexist, state motivations can shift over time, and some countries are more prone to certain motivations than others. Over the long term, national historical backgrounds play an important role in development assistance policy, but the ideological character of the party in power also influences shorter-term changes in style or direction.

It is commonly assumed that parties on the left are more generous in their development assistance policies than right-wing parties (Thérien and Noël 2000, 152). Much of this literature argues that right-wing parties are less likely to provide aid, implicitly assuming that aid is motivated by humanitarian motivations or at least long-term enlightened self-interest, overlooking the role of other factors like security or economic interest. However, Thérien and Noël (1994) carry out a quantitative analysis of donor assistance levels over several years and find no significant link between partisan orientation and foreign aid effort. They argue instead that a country's longer-term development of welfare-state institutions plays a more important role in explaining welfare state and aid spending patterns. Goldstein and Moss (2005, cited in Tingley 2010, 41) suggest that, in the United States, Republicans may be more generous towards Africa than Democrats because they may more effectively make the link between foreign policy objectives such as security interests and foreign aid. Fleck and Kilby (2006) similarly argue that while Democrats tend to be more driven by development concerns, Republicans are more driven by commercial interests. An analysis of the changing profile of Canadian development assistance to the Americas provides better insight into the competing motivations for aid and how the framing of aid motivations changes over time.

The Harper Government and Development Assistance to the Americas

Despite early expectations of some commentators (see Black and Tiessen 2006, 197), the Harper government has not reduced overall development assistance levels. In fact development assistance increased by 4.1 percent in real terms in 2012 over 2011, before the government's freeze came into effect (NSI and SELA 2013, 17). Nevertheless, the Tories have carried out an important shift in their framing of the aid program, capped by the incorporation of CIDA into the Department of Foreign Affairs and International Trade (DFAIT) and the creation of the Department of Foreign Affairs, Trade and Development (DFATD) in 2013.

Historically, levels of aid to the Americas were extremely low, as a result of the limited ties between Canada and Latin America (although ties with the Caribbean were stronger). By the 1990s, bilateral aid levels to the Americas increased as a result of instability in the Central American region and democratization and liberalization throughout the Americas (Cameron 2007, 237). However, the Liberal governments of Jean Chrétien and Paul Martin downplayed Canada's role in the Americas in both foreign and development assistance policies. The International Policy Statement (IPS) issued by Martin's government in April 2005 explicitly committed Canada to focus on Africa in its development assistance, including a commitment to double 2003–04 levels of ODA to that region by 2008–09 (Cameron 2007, 231). Also as part of the IPS, the government committed itself to increased concentration of aid, identifying a list of twenty-five "development partner" countries, justified largely on the basis of the level of poverty of the recipient.[2] Afghanistan, Iraq, and Haiti, which had been prominent aid recipients, were omitted from this list and classified as "failed and fragile states"; however, four countries in the Americas that were among the top twenty-five recipients of ODA were included (Bolivia, Honduras, Nicaragua, and Guyana) (Cameron 2007, 233–4). Senior CIDA officials stated that the agency did not have much of a future in the Americas (Cameron 2007, 235). Nevertheless, overall aid levels remained relatively constant (Cameron 2007), reflecting a path dependency dynamic.

Since Harper was elected, Latin America and the Caribbean have been highlighted again as an area of priority for Canadian foreign policy, but reflecting very different motivations and framing strategies from those of the late 1980s and early 1990s. The prime minister's extensive visit to the region in 2006 demonstrated his rapidly growing interest in hemispheric affairs, followed by the launch of a new "Strategy for the Americas" focused on three "interdependent strategic objectives or pillars": increasing economic prosperity, reinforcing democratic governance, and advancing common security (DFATD 2011a).

The government justified the Americas Strategy primarily in terms of advancing Canadian interests and values, rather than contributing to poverty reduction or development in the region. It identified the "prosperity pillar" as the "keystone" of the strategy. The proportion of Canada's overall trade going to the Americas increased from 1.7 percent in 2004 to 2.6 percent in 2009 (DFATD 2011a). As a result of the emphasis on the prosperity pillar, the main tangible outcome of the strategy has been the signing of a series of free trade agreements with countries in the Americas, including Colombia, Panama, Peru, and Honduras.

The government initially designed the Americas Strategy as a "whole-of-government" approach to the region, incorporating efforts by a wide range of federal government departments, with DFAIT as the coordinating ministry and under the political leadership of the Minister of State for the Americas. However, an internal DFAIT evaluation carried out in 2011 states that there is not much evidence that the whole-of-government approach has been implemented effectively, with few signs of greater cooperation and synergy across government departments, with the exception of the response to the Haitian earthquake. It identifies the lack of new dedicated funding to support the initiative as an important obstacle for the participation of most government agencies (DFATD 2011a). In this context, changes in allocation of ODA assume particular prominence and CIDA did receive new resources to support aid to the region (DFATD 2011a). In 2009, Minister Bev Oda announced a new list of countries of concentration, which signalled a shift in focus from Africa to the Americas as part of the government's "aid effectiveness agenda." Eighty percent of Canadian bilateral ODA would focus on these twenty countries. The new list included only seven African countries (down from the earlier fourteen and excluding some of the continent's poorest countries), five Asian countries, and six from the Americas (adding Peru and Colombia, and including the whole Caribbean region instead of just Guyana). In particular, the inclusion of Peru and Colombia, both middle-income countries with which Canada has signed free trade agreements, suggested a move from an emphasis on the needs of the poorest towards building relationships with countries that will benefit Canada's commercial interests (Berthiaume 2009).[3]

Canadian development assistance to the Americas is not justified in terms of poverty reduction, social assistance, or reduction of inequality, but primarily in terms of support to private sector development. The description of the Inter-American Regional Program on the DFATD (2012) website states,

> CIDA focuses on strengthening the region's enabling environment for economic growth and helping governments and private sector organizations connect to global markets. This includes standardizing and harmonizing investment and taxation policies, and regulatory frameworks so that the private sector can operate within a common set of rules and regulations, as well as strengthening public financial management by training public officials. (DFATD 2013a)

Despite these changes in justification for aid decisions and in aid recipients, as well as the greater rhetorical emphasis on the Americas, overall levels of ODA channelled to Africa did not decrease (see Figure 1). Latin America and the Caribbean did receive a greater share of Canada's aid budget, with the main loser being Asia, due mainly to the scaling down of aid to Afghanistan. Total assistance to the Americas has grown from around C$260 million in 2000 to over $800 million by 2010. Total assistance to countries of concentration increased from C$215 million to $570 million in this period (Blouin, Lopez Giral, and Bhushan 2012, 7). Both Africa and the Americas saw aid levels rise by about 2 to 3 percent between 2009 and 2012, while the share of aid to Asia declined in the same period, from 25 percent in 2009–10 to 20 percent in 2011–12 (NSI and SELA 2013, 18). Nevertheless, the high level of aid can be largely explained by the increase in assistance to Haiti, which was also the largest recipient of Canadian aid in 2009–10. The decision to increase aid to Haiti does not, as we discuss below, conform to the economic self-interest frame. Apart from Haiti, the share of the ODA budget has remained relatively constant for most recipients in the region, while absolute numbers have tended to increase.

Overall, development assistance policies under Harper have not thus far resulted in a significant increase in assistance to the Americas or reduction of aid to Africa. However, we have seen important changes in how aid is justified to the public, in the designation of recipient countries in the Americas, and in forms of assistance. An examination of the cases of three priority recipients – Peru, Honduras, and Haiti – reveals some of the complexity of motivations shaping aid decisions.

Figure 1: Canadian ODA to Different Regions in C$ Millions and Percentages

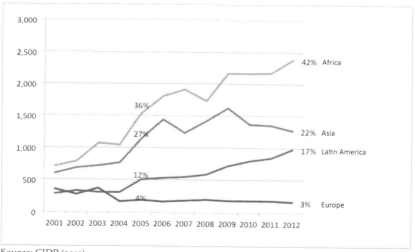

Source: CIDP (2013)

The Case of Peru: Promoting Extractive Industries and CSR

Peru arguably represents the best example of Canada's incremental shift in aid engagement in the Americas towards privileging private sector investments. Canada has significant mining interests in Peru, with Goldcorp, Barrick Gold, Candente Copper Corp, and various smaller companies operating in the country. In 2009, as part of CIDA's aid effectiveness agenda, Canada designated Peru as one of its twenty focus countries, despite its status as an upper middle-income country. As shown in Figure 2, this was followed by a rapid expansion of aid flows to Peru, from less than C$15 million in fiscal year 2009, to close to $30 million by 2012. The programming focus of Canada's newfound engagement with Peru lies in the areas of education and sustainable economic development, with the latter becoming the central focus in 2012. In fact, a quick scan of DFATD's project browser reveals that almost all projects (six out of eight) approved in 2012 and 2013 focus on private sector development and corporate social responsibility (CSR) in the mining sector (DFATD 2013b).

The government describes the overall goal of this engagement as "fostering the sustainable development of the extractive/natural resources sector to benefit all segments of the population and increasing government capacity to reduce social conflicts" (CIDA 2011a). This focus is part of the larger reorientation of aid policy under the Harper government towards CSR as a central area of concern, with initiatives that, DFATD claims, will contribute to sustainable economic growth, creating jobs and long-term poverty reduction (DFATD 2011b). In 2009, the government adopted a CSR strategy for the Canadian international extractive sector, with the objective of improving the competitive advantage of Canadian international extractive sector companies by enhancing their ability to manage social and environmental risks in developing countries (DFATD 2009). The CSR strategy is based on four pillars: to support initiatives aimed at enhancing the capacities of developing countries to manage the development of minerals and oil and gas, and to benefit from these resources so as to reduce poverty; to promote the widely recognized international CSR performance guidelines; to set up the Office of the Extractive Sector CSR Counsellor; and to support the development of a CSR Centre of Excellence (DFATD 2009; see also Goyette, this volume).

As part of a broader CSR pilot project to promote partnerships between civil society organizations and Canadian mining companies, DFATD is currently investing in a partnership in Peru between World Vision and Barrick Gold. The program focuses on increasing the income and standard of living of one thousand families affected by mining operations in the mining community of Quiruvilca. According to World Vision, the program "will help residents of Quiruvilca, Peru, especially women, youth, and people with disabilities, become more involved and influential in their own community planning. In addition to providing loans for people to start small businesses, there will be capacity-building for local leaders to ensure Quiruvilca follows a path of sustainable development in the long-term" (World Vision, cited in DFATD 2011b). In addition to such individual initiatives in Peru, there is also a host of regional initiatives under implementation, for example, the Andean Regional Initiative for Promoting Effective Corporate Social Responsibility. This initiative in Colombia, Peru, and Bolivia aims to strengthen the capacity of local governments and communities to implement sustainable development projects for the well-being of people living near extractive operations, and the sponsors claim it will improve dialogue between communities and the private sector. However, the real question is whether CSR projects are about ensuring better development outcomes for vulnerable populations, as claimed by its proponents.

Critics have raised a number of serious concerns regarding the quick proliferation of CSR initiatives. First and foremost, they question the need and desirability to subsidize CSR activities by some of the most profitable Canadian corporations, and suggest that such activities help the mining industry to put a positive spin on their negative environmental and human rights records (Carin 2012; see also Brown, this volume). It is also notable that the Canadian mining industry has intensely lobbied CIDA to fund CSR projects at mine sites and is now praising DFATD for doing so (Mining Watch Canada 2012). This is presumably related to the reputational problems of Canadian mining companies abroad. As Mining Watch Canada noted, "there is reason to believe that CIDA's funding of CSR projects at mine sites is a poorly articulated attempt by the Government of

Figure 2: Canadian ODA to Peru (by Donor Source in C$)

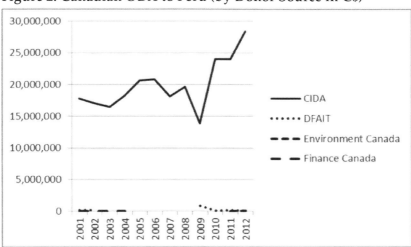

Source: CIDP (2013)

Canada to help mining companies appear to offset the development deficits they are creating at local and national levels" (Mining Watch Canada 2012, 8). Others see CSR initiatives as a reflection of an ongoing trend that has deepened under the Harper government, towards aggressively advancing the interests of Canadian multinationals in the global South and as a recipe for more violence and social conflict (Gordon 2012).

The Case of Haiti: Complexity of Aid Motivations

In contrast with the case of Peru, which appears to conform clearly to the frame of self-interest, the case of Haiti directly speaks to the complexity of Canadian aid motivations and raises questions about the oft-recited claim that Harper's aid policies in the Americas are solely driven by commercial self-interest (Gordon, 2012). Moreover, it shows that under Harper there is some programming continuity in the Americas with previous Liberal governments. Since Canada has few commercial interests in Haiti, the strong Canadian aid presence in that country must be explained by a combination of other factors (cultural and institutional), including the historical legacy of Haitian immigration to Canada, especially in Quebec, and the role that Haiti has played in Canada's focus on fragile states in the aftermath of the September 11 terrorist attacks. Since 2004, Haiti has been Canada's most important recipient of development assistance in the Americas, with annual allotments of more than C$100 million. In fact, under Harper, aid flows to Haiti (as documented in Figure 3 below) have more than doubled, reaching $250 million by 2010 (CIDP 2012).

Historically, Canadian assistance to Haiti has sought to promote sustainable development and human security, but since 2003 the focus has been predominantly on institutional strengthening and peacebuilding (Shamsie 2012). However, in the aftermath of the devastating earthquake of 2010, the focus has shifted towards rehabilitation and reconstruction, with programming in the areas of food security, health and education systems strengthening, and participation of vulnerable population in economic development through the provision of microcredit and financial services (CIDA 2011b). The fact that Haiti has remained the largest recipient of Canadian aid in the western hemisphere, despite its irrelevance to the Canadian economy, must be understood in relation to the support that the fragile state agenda has received from the Harper government.

While the focus on state fragility dates back to the International Policy Statement (discussed above) and as such represents a partisan effort by the previous Liberal government, CIDA under Harper has continued its engagement with fragile states, for example, through Canada's financial commitment to Afghanistan. As discussed above, in 2009, Haiti officially became a country of focus for Canadian aid efforts, yet funding started to drop in 2010, with cutbacks intensifying in fiscal year 2012 (see Figure 3). In January 2013, then Minister of International Cooperation Julian Fantino announced that funding for new development projects in Haiti would be frozen pending a review, expressing a frustration with the lack of progress in the country: "Canada expects transparency, accountability from the government of Haiti in exchange for future commitments" (Blatchford 2013). The reason for this decision is unclear, but in addition to concerns with lack of development progress and corruption, the Conservatives may have decided that they have little chance of gaining electoral benefits from increased assistance to Haiti in ridings with a large Haitian presence, particularly in Quebec. However, it could also be seen as a sign of a closer alignment of aid flows with commercial interests in the region.

Figure 3: Canadian ODA to Haiti (by Donor Source in C$)

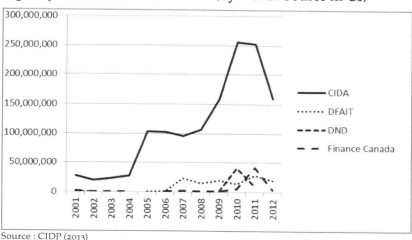

Source : CIDP (2013)

The Case of Honduras: Political Alliance Building

The case of Honduras further exemplifies the complexities and competing motivations for Canadian aid in the Americas. While Canada has a longstanding engagement in the country, reflecting its historically high levels of poverty, Honduras caught the attention of the Harper government in the aftermath of the 2009 *coup d'état,* during which Liberal president Manuel Zelaya was removed from power. Over a short period of time, aid to Honduras almost tripled, reaching C$40 million by 2012 (see Figure 4 below), making it the second-largest aid recipient in the region.

The programming focus in Honduras has traditionally been in the areas of food security and children and youth, with a special emphasis on reduction of maternal and child mortality and health information strengthening (CIDA 2011c). In the aftermath of the political instability associated with the constitutional crisis of 2009, some aid money has also been invested in the strengthening of the Honduran electoral system. The rapid increase to the Honduran aid envelope between 2008 and 2012 raises the question of what is driving the Canadian interest in Honduras.

On one hand, the focus on Honduras fits in well with the argument that, under Harper, Canada is slowly realigning its aid program with Canada's commercial interests. Canadian corporations are major economic players in Honduras, especially in mining, banking, and apparel manufacturing. According to the Economic Commission for Latin America and the Caribbean, since the mid-1990s Canada has consistently been one of the largest foreign investors in Honduras, accounting for almost 20 percent of all foreign direct investment in 2011 (ECLAC 2011). Mining companies like Goldcorp, Yamana, and Breakwater Resources have benefited from a mining law passed in 1998 that strongly favours foreign corporations. Like in Peru, the mining law and Canadian investments, particularly Goldcorp's San Martin open pit mine, have been the target of large protests by indigenous peoples and small farmers whose lands and livelihoods are threatened by the expansion of Canadian mining (Gordon 2009). However, *unlike* in Peru, the programming focus has not (yet?) shifted towards CSR initiatives. Canada also concluded negotiations in 2011 on a free trade agreement with Honduras, which aims to strengthen commercial ties between the two countries.

On the other hand, Canadian support for Honduras must also be seen as a partisan effort to prop up a country that, after the ouster of the left-leaning Zelaya, is ideologically in line with Harper's right-wing political agenda. It is notable that Canada and the United States were the only countries in the western hemisphere to recognize the legitimacy of Porfirio Lobo as the new president of Honduras after his conservative National Party won the highly contested elections in the wake of the *coup d'état*. For some, this signified a stamp of approval on the coup and the elections, made worse by the fact that the majority of the Honduran population boycotted the election, which was held under conditions that cannot be certified as meeting international standards of democratic fairness and freedom (Cameron and Tockman 2012). The wave of electoral successes of left-of-centre parties all over Latin America throughout the 2000s has meant that Harper has been increasingly isolated politically in the region and was looking for new partners in the hemisphere, which he found in post-coup Honduras. Nevertheless, the high rates of violence in the country and widespread human rights violations, as well as the questionable manner in which the Lobo government came to power, reveal the lack of emphasis on the democracy pillar in the government's Americas Strategy. The Honduran experience thus shows Harper government's political and economic interests conflicting with its espoused commitment to promoting democracy.

Figure 4: Canadian ODA to Honduras (by Donor Source in C$)

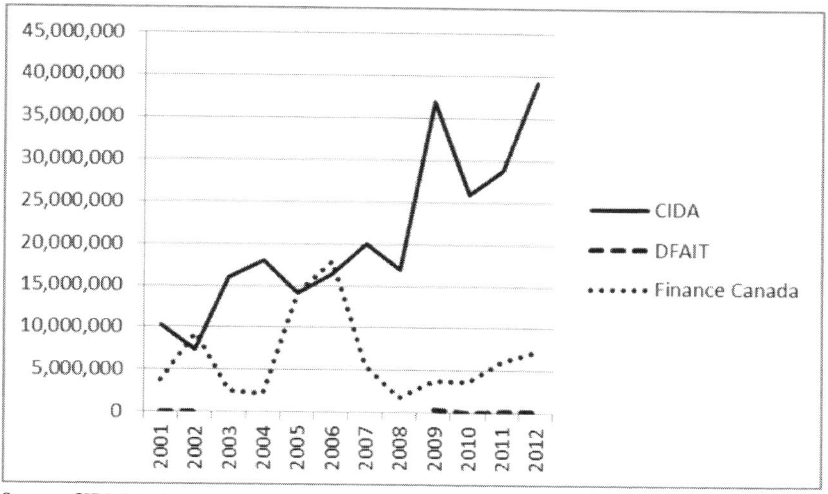

Source: CIDP (2013)

Conclusion

This analysis of Canadian development assistance to the Americas under the Conservative government of Stephen Harper suggests several lessons for the study of development assistance. While these conclusions may not be entirely generalizable, given the small number of case studies presented here, they do provide interesting indications of possible directions for future study. First, our analysis indicates the importance of unpacking simplistic assumptions like the idea that Conservative governments automatically wish to cut aid or that aid to Africa under the Liberals can be associated with selfless motivations, while a shift to an emphasis on the Americas under the Conservatives reflects a clear about-turn in Canadian government priorities towards commercial self-interest. As Stephen Brown points out, the "new policy blueprint" in the Martin government's 2005 International Policy Statement contained mixed messages and clear contradictions, with a strong emphasis on Canadian interests and support for neoliberal economic policies, while mentions of ethically based arguments were scarce (Brown 2007, 215). As well, the strong support for Haiti by the Conservatives, at least until 2013, challenges the assumption that ODA directed towards the Americas is entirely driven by selfish motives, since Canada has few economic interests in Haiti.

As such, our analysis provides considerable support for Thérien and Noël's (2000) argument in favour of the importance of path dependency and the relative immunity of development assistance policies from sharp U-turns in policy in the short term. This is particularly clear in terms of quantitative evidence, with the Harper government's increase in overall aid levels (until fiscal year 2011) and the relatively stable and increasing levels of aid for both Africa and the Americas. Nevertheless, a closer qualitative analysis of trends in choice of aid recipients and the character of aid to individual countries reveals an increasing use of ODA to the Americas in support of a conservative ideological agenda, particularly since Harper won a majority government in the 2011 elections. Although the government has increased aid to Haiti for reasons that are not framed in partisan terms, the cases of aid to both Peru and Honduras do, as we have discussed, display strong partisan motivations. Canada has signed free trade agreements in both countries and Canadian mining companies stand to benefit from greater cooperation with both of them, while Canadian support for Honduras reflects the Harper government's pursuit of ideological alliance building as a strategic objective pursued through rapid increases in aid. The intensification of self-interested behaviour under the Harper government in its development assistance policies towards the Americas thus reflects a gradual but strong movement away from the altruistic motives for aid and risks discrediting Canada as a relatively caring donor. Finally, our analysis supports van der Veen's constructivist approach and his emphasis on the importance of donors' framing strategies. While our study reveals that multiple and competing frames do exist within Canada's development assistance program, the evidence points to an important shift under the Harper government towards a strategy based on commercial self-interest.

Acknowledgments

We are grateful to Megan Pickup for her research assistance for this article. Thanks to Stephen Brown, Pablo Heidrich, and Jacobo Vargas Foronda for their helpful comments. We also thank the Social Sciences and Humanities Research Council of Canada for its financial support.

Notes

1. Van der Veen argues that the main function of frames is "to organize different pieces of information in a coherent fashion." Frames "help actors understand the world around them, can specify goals, and determine interests" (van der Veen 2011, 29).
2. The list included fourteen countries from Africa, six from Asia, four from the Americas, and Ukraine.
3. In June 2014, the government further amended the list, expanding it to twenty-five countries, to which 90 percent of bilateral aid would be directed. The only change in the Americas was the dropping of Bolivia as a country of focus.

References

Berthiaume, Lee. 2009. "CIDA Confirms Shift to Americas, Fewer Countries." *Embassy*, February 25.

Black, David R., and Rebecca Tiessen. 2007. "The Canadian International Development Agency: New Policies, Old Problems." *Canadian Journal of Development Studies*, vol. 28, no. 2: 191–212.

Blatchford, Andy. 2013. "Haiti PM Responds: Give Our Government More Say over Canadian Aid." *Globe and Mail*, January 8.

Blouin, Chantal, Dorotea Lopez Giral, and Aniket Bhushan. 2012. "Reducing Poverty and Inequality in Latin America: What Role for Canada?" *International Journal*, vol. 67, no. 3: 623–37.

Brown, Stephen. 2007. "'Creating the World's Best Development Agency'? Confusion and Contradictions in CIDA's New Policy Blueprint." *Canadian Journal of Development Studies*, vol. 28, no. 2: 213–28.

Cameron, John. 2007. "CIDA in the Americas: New Directions and Warning Signs for Canadian Development Policy." *Canadian Journal of Development Studies*, vol. 28, no. 2: 229–49.

Cameron, Maxwell A., and Jason Tockman. 2012. "Canada and the Democratic Charter: Lessons from the Coup in Honduras." In Peter McKenna, ed. *Canada Looks South: In Search of an Americas Policy*. Toronto: University of Toronto Press: 87–117.

Carin, Barry. 2012. "CIDA, NGOs and Mining Companies: The Good, the Bad and the Ugly." *iPolitics*. May 8. Internet, http://www.ipolitics.ca/2012/05/08/barry-carin-cida-ngos-and-mining-companies-the-good-the-bad-and-the-ugly/. Accessed November 2, 2013.

CIDA (Canadian International Development Agency). 2011a. "Peru: CIDA Report." Internet, http://www.acdi-cida.gc.ca/INET/IMAGES.NSF/vLUImages/Countries-of-Focus/$file/10-054-Perou-E.pdf. Accessed August 16, 2013.

CIDA (Canadian International Development Agency). 2011b. "Haiti: CIDA Report." Internet, http://www.acdi-cida.gc.ca/inet/images.nsf/vLUImages/Countries-of-Focus/$file/10-053-Haiti-E.pdf. Accessed August 16, 2013.

CIDA (Canadian International Development Agency). 2011c. "Honduras: CIDA Report." Internet, http://www.acdi-cida.gc.ca/Inet/IMaGeS.nSF/vLUImages/Countries-of-Focus/$file/10-043-Honduras-E.pdf. Accessed August 16, 2013.

CIDP (Canadian International Development Platform). 2013. "Canada's Foreign Aid 2012." Internet, http://cidpnsi.ca/blog/portfolio/canadas-foreign-aid/. Accessed August 15, 2013.

Daudelin, Jean. 2007. "Canada and the Americas: A Time for Modesty." *Behind the Headlines*, vol. 64, no. 4: 1–28.

DFATD (Department of Foreign Affairs, Trade and Development). 2009. "Building the Canadian Advantage: A Corporate Social Responsibility (CSR) Strategy for the Canadian International Extractive Sector." Internet, http://www.international.gc.ca/trade-agreements-accords-commerciaux/topics-domaines/other-autre/csr-strat-rse.aspx. Accessed October 17, 2013.

DFATD (Department of Foreign Affairs, Trade and Development). 2011a. "Evaluation of the Americas Strategy." Internet, http://www.international.gc.ca/about-a_propos/oig-big/2011/evaluation/tas_lsa11.aspx?lang=eng. Accessed August 15, 2013.

DFATD (Department of Foreign Affairs, Trade and Development). 2011b. "Minister Oda Announces Initiatives to Increase the Benefits of Natural Resource Management for Peoples in Africa and South America." Internet, http://www.acdi-cida.gc.ca/acdi-cida/acdi-cida.nsf/eng/CAR-929105317-KGD. Accessed August 15, 2013.

DFATD (Department of Foreign Affairs, Trade and Development). 2013a. "Inter-American Regional Program." Internet, http://www.acdi-cida.gc.ca/acdi-cida/acdi-cida.nsf/eng/JUD-82413253-NF8. Accessed August 14, 2013.

DFATD (Department of Foreign Affairs, Trade and Development). 2013b. "Peru — International Development Projects." International Development Project Browser. Internet, www.acdi-cida.gc.ca/cidaweb/cpo.nsf/fWebCSAZEn?ReadForm&idx=01&CC=PE. August 14, 2013.

ECLAC (Economic Commission for Latin America and the Caribbean). 2011. "Foreign Direct Investment in Latin America and the Caribbean." Internet, http://www.eclac.cl/publicaciones/xml/2/46572/2012-182-LIEI-WEB.pdf. Accessed October 17, 2013.

Fleck, Robert K. and Christopher Kilby. 2006. "How Do Political Changes Influence US Bilateral Aid Allocations? Evidence from Panel Data." *Review of Development Economics*, vol. 10, no. 2: 210–23.

Goldstein, Markus P. and Todd Moss. 2005. "Compassionate conservatives or conservative compassionates? US Political Parties and Bilateral Foreign Assistance to Africa." *Journal of Development Studies*, vol. 41, no. 7: 1288–1302.

Gordon, Todd. 2009. "Acceptable versus Unacceptable Oppression: A Lesson in Canadian Imperial Hypocrisy." *The Bullet*, no. 231, June 30. Internet, http://www.socialistproject.ca/bullet/bullet231.html. Accessed August 12, 2013.

Gordon, Todd. 2012. "Canadian Development Aid Takes on Corporate Colouring." *Toronto Star*, November 29. Internet, http://www.thestar.com/opinion/editorialopinion/2012/11/29/canadian_development_aid_takes_on_corporate_colouring.html. Accessed August 14, 2013.

Mining Watch Canada. 2012. "CIDA's Partnership with Mining Companies Fails to Acknowledge and Address the Role of Mining in the Creation of Development Deficits." Internet, http://www.miningwatch.ca/sites/www.miningwatch.ca/files/Mining_and_Development_FAAE_2012.pdf. Accessed August 15, 2013.

NSI and SELA. 2013. *Economic Relations between Canada and Latin America and the Caribbean.* Caracas: Permanent Secretariat of SELA. Internet, http://www.sela.org/view/index.asp?ms=258&pageMs=75205&new_id=116677. Accessed November 21, 2014.

Shamsie, Yasmine. 2012. "Canadian Assistance to Haiti: Some Sobering Snags in a Fragile-State Approach." In Peter McKenna, ed. *Canada Looks South: In Search of an Americas Policy.* Toronto: University of Toronto Press: 180–212.

Thérien, Jean-Philippe, and Alain Noël. 1994. "Welfare Institutions and Foreign Aid: Domestic Foundations of Canadian Foreign Policy." *Canadian Journal of Political Science,* vol. 27, no. 3: 523–53.

Thérien, Jean-Philippe, and Alain Noël. 2000. "Political Parties and Foreign Aid." *American Political Science Review,* vol. 94, no. 1: 151–62.

Tingley, Dustin. 2010. "Donors and Domestic Politics: Political Influences on Foreign Aid Effort." *Quarterly Review of Economics and Finance,* vol. 50, no. 1: 40–9.

van der Veen, A. Maurits. 2011. *Ideas, Interests and Foreign Aid.* Cambridge: Cambridge University Press.

CHAPTER VIII

Preventing, Substituting or Complementing the Use of Force? Development Assistance in Canadian Strategic Culture

Justin Massie and Stéphane Roussel

D̲ecades ago, analysts complained that security and foreign aid policies were generally conceived as distinct spheres of activity (Spicer 1966, 14–22). Since then, states have adapted their foreign policy to make development aid and security operations coherent tools aimed at similar politico-strategic goals. The "militarization" and "securitization" of aid and peacebuilding are now common, albeit often criticized, features of policies addressing conflict resolution and failed and failing states (Hook and Lebo 2010; Newman 2010; Woods 2005).

This change is due not only to the broader meaning of "security," but of security policies as well, which now encompass both "soft" and "hard" power strategies. In fact, the Western-led military operations in Afghanistan and Iraq have led to a surge of interest in counterinsurgency, which is increasingly being confused with "robust peacebuilding" (Gilmore 2011), thereby conceptually and operationally blending together two formerly very distinct state policies: war and aid. This trend, however, has not received sufficient attention in terms of foreign policy analysis. When did military operations and development assistance policies become integrated foreign policy tools? For what politico-strategic purposes? Despite a significant literature on human security, failed and failing states, peacebuilding, humanitarian wars, and even foreign aid as an instrument of foreign policy, the relationship between official development assistance (ODA) and the use of military force as converging tools of statecraft remains under-analyzed.

The purpose of this chapter is to propose an integrated framework for understanding the relationship between ODA policies and military interventions from a foreign policy perspective. Since we are interested in both the conceptual link and its application on the ground, we conduct our inquiry through the concept of "strategic culture." Using a constructivist approach to strategic culture, which focuses on how national cultures and identities constitute national interests and the appropriate means to pursue them, we suggest three main foreign policy strategies on the security-development continuum: foreign aid as (1) a means to *prevent* future military action and/or violence escalation; (2) a preferred *alternative* to the use of force in the attainment of states' national objectives; and (3) a *complement* to military action for similar political objectives. A systematic and historical analysis of Canada's foreign aid policy reveals, somewhat surprisingly, that a complementary approach to ODA and military interventions was pursued well before the advent of the "3D" approach (defence, diplomacy, development) in the 2000s. We illustrate the shift from a conflict prevention strategy to a complementary one by contrasting Canada's main defence and aid policies to its actual allocation of ODA and military interventions since the late 1940s.[1] We argue that strategic culture allows us to makes sense of this shift, notably by highlighting the country's predisposition to support a Western-led liberal order.

Foreign Aid and Strategic Preferences

With regard to security policies, states have pursued three types of development assistance strategies, depending on their strategic preferences. First, for much of the Cold War period, they treated foreign aid as a preventive tool. The conventional wisdom was that aid served to achieve security goals, such as the preservation of the West's spheres of influence against the Soviet Union or the prevention of conflict initiation and escalation (Boschini and Olofsgard 2007). Western states thus used ODA as an operational (immediate), rather than structural (long-term) preventive tool; moreover, they used it to combat communism rather than poverty. Notwithstanding valid critiques of those priorities, contemporary understandings of peacebuilding insist that development assistance is an essential tool to prevent conflicts and promote lasting and sustainable peace (Jeong 2005; OECD 1997, 2001). It should thus not be surprising if ODA continues to be used for conflict prevention.

A second strategy consists of using foreign aid as an independent tool, geared towards goals unrelated to security. ODA, from this perspective, represents a substitute for military force, used according to its own logic and aimed at other political, economic, and social objectives (Belloni 2007). When adopted, this strategy means that states do not implement the security-development nexus, explicitly or tacitly, in their foreign policies. Hence, rather than "securitizing" aid, states pursue alternative objectives, such as poverty reduction, gender equality, or economic development for their own sake. Only indirectly or unintentionally do these objectives contribute to peace and security.

Lastly, a third strategy entails the exact opposite of substitution: ODA is deliberately used simultaneously and in coordination with the use of military force in a conflict or post-conflict zone, towards common political objectives. This complementary strategy is precisely what the Development Assistance Committee of the Organisation for Economic Co-operation and Development recommended in its 1997 policy statement (OECD 1997, 3). Though this strategy faces critiques similar to the ones operational preventive strategies faced during the Cold War, it remains "key to attaining sustainable peace" according to a United Nations Security Council declaration (UNSC 2011). Peacebuilding, in other words, is conceived of as an integrated and coherent agenda involving mutually reinforcing development- and security-related policies. From this perspective, for example, antiterrorist policies and development assistance are inextricably linked.

The choice between these three strategies is significantly shaped by a state's identity-based strategic culture. Canadian development assistance has, according to many analysts, oscillated between the pursuit of material self-interest, altruistic goals, and identity promotion (Nossal 1988; Pratt 1999). It is often considered an integral part of Canada's "liberal internationalist" strategic culture. The latter implies that Canada shares a sense of responsibility to allocate a significant portion of its public resources to ODA, to support a liberal, Western-led international order, and to reflect Canada's ethno-cultural identity (Pratt 1994; Thérien 1989). It follows that Canada's foreign aid policy is expected to shadow the international aid regime's evolving norms, ranging from anti-communist preventive measures to purely socio-economic development (of donors and/or beneficiaries) and now to an integrated "3D" policy *vis-à-vis* failed and failing states (Jacquet 2002). A systematic examination of the security-development nexus in Canadian foreign policy broadly supports this expectation, with a noteworthy *caveat*: the Canadian government has preferred a complementarity strategy over the two alternatives, decades before its official formalization, albeit to varying degrees.

1945–1960: A Modest Preventive Tool

The first comprehensive statement about Canadian foreign policy is the "Gray Lecture," delivered in January 1947 by Louis St-Laurent, who was Secretary of State for External Affairs at that time. In this speech, St-Laurent exposed the basic principles of Canadian foreign policy and provided a first rationale for foreign aid: to create a favourable, stable environment for international trade, and hence for Canadians themselves. He argued, "the continued prosperity and well-being of our own people can best be served by the prosperity and well-being of the whole world" (St-Laurent 1947, 10). In this spirit, Western Europe and China were the first countries to receive Canadian economic assistance. The primary objective was to prevent these countries from falling into the USSR's growing sphere of influence, while at the same time supporting Canada's commercial interests (Bothwell 1998, 58).

Over the years, it became clear that Canada privileged a preventive strategy rather than a purely substitutive one aimed at its own economic development. During the 1950s, Canadian aid was essentially directed towards South-East Asian countries. The first concerted effort was the Colombo Plan, established in 1950. Canadian aid focused on three Indian subcontinent countries: Ceylon (Sri Lanka), India, and Pakistan (Dobell 1988, 353). This emphasis reflected more a commitment to the "new Commonwealth" than any economic rationale. In the context of the communist victory in China, the emergence of guerrillas in French Indochina and, later, the Korean War, the purpose of this aid program was to promote stability in societies plagued with poverty and viewed as vulnerable to Communist influence. In other words, Canada conceived of foreign aid as a conflict prevention tool, as well as a reflection of the country's British origins and anti-communist stance.

Yet Canada's aid program remained modest, to say the least. In 1950, development assistance amounted to only 0.13 percent of Canada's gross national income (GNI). Ten years later, it had risen to only 0.16 percent. These figures cast doubts on the level of strategic thought behind Canada's apparent conflict prevention strategy (Spicer 1966, 3). At best, it saw foreign aid as an instrument to prevent some key states from falling in the communist camp, as the Marshall Plan did for Western Europe. However, Canada could "free ride" on Anglo-American foreign aid policies, while benefiting from the newly acquired status of pro-Western aid donor.

It is worth noting that, though primarily aimed at conflict prevention, Canada's ODA went to some extent hand-in-hand with its newly found international security role: peacekeeping. While Ottawa agreed to take part in three UN military observation operations in the Middle East, the Kashmir area, and Lebanon, Canadian ODA policy did not target Lebanon or other Middle Eastern states during that period.[2] Moreover, despite actively taking part in the Korean War (1950–53), Canada only began to provide ODA to South Korea in 1964. Canada's aid policy was thus primarily aimed at conflict prevention, but the complementarity between its aid and military commitments in India and Pakistan remains noteworthy, as it indicates a parallel between its security and development policies, despite the lack of any official statement to that effect.

1961–1967: Expansion, Status Enhancement, and Conflict Prevention

In the late 1950s and early 1960s, Canadian aid programs grew significantly. Targeted first to Commonwealth members, Canadian development assistance was extended to French-speaking countries in Africa and was mostly motivated by conflict prevention and status enhancement rationales. "It was a logical step to take in view of Canada's bilingual and bicultural character," noted Canada's External Aid Office in 1967 (Cermakian 1968, 231). The most important motive, after 1965, was to counter the French-speaking province of Quebec's growing activity in the region and thus reaffirm Canada's status as a sovereign and bicultural state (Gendron 2006). Foreign aid was conceived by Prime Minister Pearson as an important tool for nation-building in the sense that it was aimed at showing French-speaking

Canadians that their country's (and not Quebec's) foreign policy was serving and representing their specific interests.

The expansion of Canada's development assistance programs to francophone Africa took place alongside greater peacekeeping commitments. In addition to ongoing participation in UN operations in the Kashmir area and the Middle East, Ottawa committed troops to six new peacekeeping missions, including for the first time in French-speaking Africa, with up to 500 soldiers operating in the Congo. Canadian forces would help to restore order in Congo and, as Sean Maloney observes, to prevent a NATO split, Soviet infiltration, and American involvement in the region. ODA followed a similar logic. Canadian officials agreed that "any aid money from North America would be funnelled through the UN to maintain the appearance of impartiality," but that Canada would "highlight Soviet machinations when they provided aid to the Congo" (Maloney 2002, 115–16).

Nevertheless, it is not clear that foreign aid acquired a new status *vis-à-vis* the use of force in the 1960s. The Canadian government was ready to contribute to peacekeeping missions to avoid direct involvement from great powers and thus prevent the escalation of regional tensions into worldwide conflicts (Canada 1964, 80). However, despite Canadian military involvement in Yemen, West New Guinea, and the Dominican Republic, none of these regions received Canadian ODA. While Canadian troops were deployed in the Middle East and Kashmir areas, India and Pakistan remained Canada's top two ODA recipients. Therefore, while we must note the correlation between Canadian military involvement in the Kashmir area and ODA to India and Pakistan, the nature of the former (a UN military observation), the continued aid to these two countries (both received continuous and substantial ODA from 1950 to 2010), the nature of the Colombo plan, as well as the absence of any Canadian strategic thought specifically linking peacekeeping to ODA, tend to indicate the prevalence of a conflict-prevention strategy in the 1960s.

1968–1976: The Articulation of Canada's First Security-Development Policy

While the early 1960s witnessed a significant increase in the relative budget dedicated to development assistance – which peaked in 1975 – it is not before the end of the decade that the Canadian government articulated a clear vision of its function as a security instrument. It created the Canadian International Development Agency (CIDA) in 1968 and published the first white paper two years later. Among the latter's central theme was that hard power alone could not defeat communism; soft power was also required (Pratt 1994, 340 n28). The idea was hardly new, but it nevertheless represented a major strategic change, formally and officially articulating a security-development policy focused on conflict prevention.

Soon after his election in 1968, Prime Minister Pierre Trudeau exposed his foreign policy objectives. The main one was to encourage the economic and social development of developing countries (Canada 1970, 11), an international projection of Canada's social justice system (Noël and Thérien 1995). Nevertheless, ODA's relationship with security remained crucial. The government feared that a reduction in the development effort would have "tragic consequences for peace and global order" (Canada 1970, 8). The 1971 *White Paper on Defence* added that Canadian Forces "can also give support to foreign policy objectives through increased assistance in economic aid programs" through their capabilities in "such fields as engineering and construction, logistic policies, trades and technical training, advisory services, project analysis and air transport" (Canada 1971, 14). Thus the Department of National Defence (DND) conceived of its assets, for the first time, as potentially supplementing development assistance programs, albeit without any reference to Canada's commitments in India, Pakistan, and the Middle East.

Despite budget increases and some notable discrepancies between CIDA and DND's approach to ODA, Canadian foreign aid remained relatively stable, as it continued to focus on conflict prevention. Ottawa did not allocate development aid to Middle Eastern countries until 1976, when it added Egypt to Canada's list of recipients, followed in 1981 by Lebanon and Jordan. The Indian subcontinent remained Canada's primary ODA area of concentration, while some French-speaking African states continued to rank among Canada's top ten ODA beneficiaries (OECD 2010b). And most notably, Canada added Indonesia to the list in 1972 in order to help prevent communist influence in the region and to maintain stability following the United States' withdrawal from the country (Nossal 1980, 226–27). In other words, in spite of the complementary approach invoked in the 1971 *White Paper on Defence,* and the fact that its aid and military policies were increasingly working in parallel on the Indian subcontinent and in the Middle East, Canada's ODA policy continued to focus on conflict prevention, while emphasizing the country's position as a reliable Western ally, and its bicultural status.

1977–1992: Towards a Complementary Strategy

Brian Mulroney's Conservative government upset the country's emerging security-development policy. Among the government's top ODA objectives during that period was the opening of new markets for Canadian businesses. While official discourse made some reference to the altruistic values of Canadian society, the government increasingly conceived of foreign aid as a tool to promote global and Canadian prosperity, as well as a secondary tool to prevent conflict initiation and escalation. A substitution strategy thus often took precedence over its security-related alternatives. CIDA's 1987 policy statement emphasized trade as a substitute to security-related aid purposes, but also directly addressed conflict prevention by stating that poverty reduction is a prerequisite to peace and, hence, development must be understood as a necessary condition for greater international security (CIDA 1987, 90). Most notably, however, the policy statement indicating the growing importance of human rights in Canadian foreign policy was increasingly perceived as a means to achieve strategic goals while avoiding direct military confrontation. By the mid-1980s, human rights had become a central piece of the Mulroney government's foreign policy, in particular the fight against apartheid in South Africa (Black 2001). Promoting human rights was then a substitute for ODA as a conflict prevention tool aimed at fostering peace and stability.

If, in terms of official policy statements, substitution took precedence over conflict prevention, the latter remained relevant at the operational level. African and Caribbean Commonwealth states, as well as francophone African countries, remained Canada's top ODA recipients, in addition to Indonesia. Exemplifying the continued anti-communist security policy, between 1980 and 1988, Canada substantially increased its aid to El Salvador – the third largest recipient of American ODA in 1985 – as well as its aid to Grenada following the US invasion in 1983 (OECD 2010b). Canada's ODA policy thus remained a soft-power tool, helping sustain the liberal politico-military order defended by the West against the Soviet Union (Thérien 1989, 19).

As conflict-prevention strategies persisted despite growing trade concerns, a complementary approach grew in importance, although remaining under-conceptualized. Numerous examples illustrating this trend include the following: CIDA targeted Lebanon following Canada's military involvement in the country in 1978 and the 1982–84 Western multinational force; Canadian ODA to Afghanistan resumed following the USSR's withdrawal from the country in 1988, as Canadian military personnel took part in the 1988–90 United Nations Good Offices Mission in Afghanistan and Pakistan (UNGOMAP); and Canada's participation in the United Nations Transition Assistance Group (UNTAG) in 1989 coincided with a thirteenfold increase of ODA allocated to Namibia that year, from $150,000 to $2 million (2009 constant USD, OECD, 2010b).

More important, Canada took part in significant military operations in the Middle East, the former Yugoslavia, and Somalia during that period. It contributed to the United Nations Iran-Iraq Military Observer Group (UNIIMOG), the 1990–91 Persian Gulf War, and the 1991–2003 United Nations Iraq-Kuwait Observer Mission (UNIKOM). Iraq received Canadian ODA from 1991 until the 1998 economic sanctions. The aid was resumed and greatly increased in 2003, following the US–UK invasion. Canada's military participation in the 1992–95 United Nations Protection Force (UNPROFOR) in the former Yugoslavia also coincided with ODA allocation in that area, beginning in 1993. Finally, as Canada contributed militarily to the 1992–95 United Nations Operation in Somalia (UNOSOM), the latter received a ninefold ODA increase in 1992 (OECD 2010b). In other words, despite a conceptual shift from preventive to substitutive rationales in Canadian official statements, Canada's actual aid and military policies indicate a growing preference towards a complementary strategy. This trend coincided with Canada's increasing military troop deployment in ever more UN and NATO peace operations.

1993–2000: Formalizing the Peacebuilding Complementary Approach

The 1990s witnessed two significant changes. First, after a brief period of euphoria following the end of the Cold War, the war in Yugoslavia and the multiplication of sources of tension in Europe and elsewhere raised new concerns. "Crisis prevention and management" became the new international priority. Canada was thus asked to contribute to numerous newly created UN and NATO peace operations. It responded positively, mainly due to its quest for reliable ally status (Massie 2009). The second change was purely domestic: The fight against public debt and the deficit became a major issue in Canada. The impact on development programs was immediate and drastic. Between 1992 and 2001, the percentage of GNI allocated to ODA was cut by more than half, falling from 0.46 percent to 0.22 percent (OECD 2010a).

These changes warranted a reassessment of the nature of the relationship between security and foreign aid. In the 1991–92 foreign policy review, the Mulroney government reaffirmed the function of foreign aid as being to "alleviate poverty as one of the root causes of political instability" (Canada 1993, 92). At the end of Mulroney's mandate, the conflict prevention strategy had thus re-emerged conceptually. Yet the growing complementary approach explains many new top ten ODA recipients, including the former Yugoslavia, Egypt, and Mozambique (OECD, 2010b). Regarding the latter, Canadian troops took part in the 1992–94 United Nations Operation in Mozambique, which monitored the ceasefire in the country.

In its 1995 *White Paper on Foreign Affairs*, the newly elected Chrétien government reaffirmed the now classic conflict prevention strategy (Canada 1995, 2). However, the most important new step was to pave the way for a very important concept, which was officially integrated in the Canadian official discourse in the following months: human security (Gervais and Roussel 1998). The concept of human security was mainly promoted by Minister of Foreign Affairs Lloyd Axworthy. He and his advisers were apparently reluctant to address the issue of the use of force as a means to implement human security. As a result, the Canadian military never really integrated the concept, since its place was never made clear within its strategic thought (Dewitt 2004). It was not until the Kosovo war, when the use of force was instrumental in putting an end to massive ethnic cleansing, that the relationship was formally addressed. Distinct from human development, the government now conceived of human security as potentially involving "the use of coercive measures, including sanctions and military force, as in Bosnia and Kosovo" (DFAIT 1999, 4 and 7–8). In other words, "hard" security policies and "soft" development aid were now distinct but complementary parts of a post-conflict peacebuilding agenda (Hynek and Bosold 2009).

Canada's newly crafted complementary strategy did materialize on the ground. Throughout the period, the Canadian Forces actively took part in several UN and NATO-led peace operations, concentrating the bulk of their troops in Rwanda, the former Yugoslavia, Haiti, East Timor, and Ethiopia/Eritrea, in addition to the 1999 Kosovo war. However, no obvious ODA policy shift was discernible in the mid-1990s. Former Yugoslavian states, Ethiopia, and Rwanda continued to receive steady development aid, ODA to Haiti increased slightly, and Timor-Leste was added to Canada's list of aid recipients in 2000. Yet, in 1995, none of them figured among Canada's top ten recipients (OECD 2010b). This contrasts sharply with the major recipient countries in 2000: Ex-Yugoslavian states ranked first and Haiti fifth (CIDA 2002, 49). The substantial increase in development assistance to the latter thus tends to illustrate the growing importance on the ground of a complementary strategy. Contrary to previous historical periods, Canadian authorities seemed, by the end of the 1990s, to have implemented a more coherent and consistent post-conflict peacebuilding strategy, in which aid was a central component of Canada's conflict-resolution policy.

2001–2013: Institutionalizing the Peacebuilding Complementary Approach

Many have argued that the attacks of September 11, 2001 marked a shift towards the securitization of peacebuilding (Jacquet 2002; Marclay 2008). However, the preceding analysis suggests that a development-security complementary approach had been at work in Canadian foreign policy years before 9/11, be it conceptually, operationally, or both. Nevertheless, 9/11 did have an impact on Canada's security-development strategy. Having put an end to its public finance deficit, the Canadian government almost restored its ODA budget to pre-austerity levels. Foreign aid amounted to 0.38 percent of Canada's GNI in 1995, 0.25 percent in 2000, 0.34 percent in 2005, 0.33 percent in 2010 (OECD 2010a), and 0.27 percent in 2013 (OECD 2014).

The attacks of 9/11 also marked a sea change in the conceptualization of the interdependence of security and development, around two broad assumptions: Poverty, and the frustration it creates, is among the major sources of terrorism; and failed and failing (i.e., impoverished) states provide a sanctuary and a recruitment ground for terrorism (Marclay 2008). This conceptualization reinforced the coherence of the security-development nexus and the complementary strategy that it entails. Indeed, Canada's first major post–9/11 foreign policy review, the 2005 International Policy Statement (IPS), identified three purposes for foreign aid: to prevent, at the socio-political level, conflicts from emerging, notably through the "responsibility to protect" rationale; to complement military initiatives, according to the "three block war" or "3D" approaches; and to allow Canada to make a distinctive and notable contribution to international peace and security (Canada 2005). In other words, it advanced both conflict-prevention and complementary strategies to further Canada's status as an active, distinctive, and cosmopolitan world actor.

It is thus not surprising that Afghanistan was Canada's prime ODA recipient country as early as 2002. It was soon replaced, ranking second to Iraq in 2003, following the US–UK invasion (CIDA 2005, 33). While Canada did not officially take part in this war, it contributed significantly to the war effort: Its military contribution exceeded those of all but three members of the "coalition of the willing" (Engler 2009, 45). Other major Canadian military interventions also coincided with increased ODA allocation, most notably in the Democratic Republic of the Congo (CIDA 2002, 34; 2004, 33; 2006, 33), Haiti (CIDA 2006, 33; 2011, 3), and Sudan (CIDA 2008, 39).

The prime example of the institutionalization of Canada's complementary strategy remains Afghanistan. Following the deployment of Canadian troops in the country in the fall of 2001, ODA to Afghanistan doubled every year from 2001 to 2003, and again between 2005 and 2007, following Canada's commitments in Kandahar. ODA increased from $6.66 million in 2000 to $345.39 million in 2007 (in 2009 constant USD). Though Afghanistan was not among Canada's thirty top recipient countries in 2001, it ranked third in 2002, second from 2004 to 2006 and in 2010, first in 2003 and from 2007 to 2009 (OECD 2010b), and second in 2011–12 (OECD 2014).

Conceptually demonstrating this institutionalization of Canada's security-development complementary strategy, Canada's 2008 counterinsurgency manual justifies the military's role in providing not only humanitarian assistance, but also the "delivery of aid." Indeed, it makes clear the distinction between humanitarian and development assistance, and instructs Canadian military personnel that "in order to avoid initial delays in development, the campaign plan from the outset must include details for sustainable development" (Canada 2008, 5-24, 5-28). The likely military tasks within these domains include the provision of water, fuel, and power, and the restoration of health and public buildings and services, as well as interim governance of commercial support and economic institutions, education institutions and infrastructure, and public civil service institutions (e.g., health, customs, media), in addition to humanitarian assistance and aid distribution (Canada 2008, 5-24). The 2012–13 government report to Parliament on ODA similarly emphasizes "ensuring security and stability" as one of Canada's five foreign aid objectives, though this priority amounted to less than 1 percent of CIDA's thematic priority spending, in contrast with 25 percent of DFAIT's thematic ODA allocations (Canada 2013, 5 and 12).

Nonetheless, CIDA's first program and management priority remained to support "Canada's strategic role in Haiti and Afghanistan" – the two most important recipients of bilateral ODA – and its first core program activity was to help "fragile states and crisis-affected communities" (totalling $788.2 million, close to 23 percent of CIDA's budget). This suggests that a complementary strategy has been institutionalized in CIDA's operating and governing structures. If this logic is correct, we should see reduced ODA allocations to both Haiti and Afghanistan following the end of Canada's military operations in both countries, and increased aid to new host countries of Canadian soldiers. While Libya received only humanitarian assistance from Canada throughout and after NATO's military intervention in that country, the inclusion of Ukraine as a country of focus for Canada's international development efforts suggests that the trend towards a complementary strategy is likely to last.

Conclusion

Canadian security-development policy broadly followed the evolving international norms and expectations of conflict prevention during the Cold War and post–9/11 eras. According to this conceptualization of Canadian foreign policy, international security and ODA are part of the same continuum. They represent different tools, complementing each other to reach the same goal: global stability through the promotion, enforcement, and maintenance of a Western-led liberal order. In part because of its unique strategic cultural predisposition, Canada concentrated most of its conflict prevention strategy in the spheres of influence of the US, the UK, and France, and actively took part in many UN and NATO-led peace operations. It furthermore developed and applied a complementary approach to post-conflict peacebuilding years before the attacks of 9/11, albeit in conjunction with a conflict prevention strategy.

Thus, the interdependence between security and development was stronger before 9/11 than conventional wisdom would have it. For only a brief period, roughly in the 1980s, did Canadian authorities officially conceive of and practice development assistance as a substitutive tool towards goals unrelated to security concerns. The systematic, historical examination of the concomitant variations between ODA and military policies demonstrates how Canada's strategic preferences predisposed it to prefer conflict prevention ODA strategies towards Cold War peacekeeping and a complementary strategy *vis-à-vis* contemporary peace operations, increasingly multidimensional, robust, and not neutral. This trend, at a minimum, implies that the Canadian government is likely to allocate future ODA to states where it deploys military troops, unless it finds alternative ways to secure its status as a reliable and active Western ally.

Notes

1. Space limitations prevent us from utilizing a process-tracing methodology to examine aid allocations and military interventions throughout the period under examination (1945 to 2013). We can thus merely suggest patterns of relationships between the two, as demonstrated by systematic geographic correlations, official documentation, and secondary sources, and identify periods of change. We cannot and do not suggest that the strategies pursued (preventive, substitutive, or complementary) have been intended as such by policy makers. Future research could study specific strategies adopted or discarded by examining in greater depth and detail the decision-making processes surrounding specific aid allocations and military interventions.

2. All data pertaining to Canadian military operations in this chapter are drawn from Canada's "Operation Database" website (Canada 2009), as well as www.canadiansoldiers.com.

References

Belloni, Roberto. 2007. "The Trouble with Humanitarianism." *Review of International Studies*, vol. 33, no. 3: 451–74.

Black, David R. 2001. "How Exceptional? Reassessing the Mulroney Government's Anti-Apartheid 'Crusade'." In Nelson Michaud and

Kim Richard Nossal, eds. *Diplomatic Departures: The Conservative Era in Canadian Foreign Policy, 1984–93*. Vancouver: UBC Press: 128–41.

Boschini, Anne, and Anders Olofsgard. 2007. "Foreign Aid: An Instrument for Fighting Poverty or Communism?" *Journal of Development Studies*, vol. 43, no. 4: 622–48.

Bothwell, Robert. 1998. *The Big Chill: Canada and the Cold War*. Toronto: Irwin Publishing.

Canada. 1964. *White Paper on Defence*. Ottawa: Department of National Defence.

Canada. 1970. "Foreign Policy for Canadians." In Jack L. Granatstein, ed. *Canadian Foreign Policy. Historical Readings*. Revised Edition. Toronto: Copp Clark Pitman, 1993: 54–72.

Canada. 1971. *Defence in the 1970s*. Ottawa: Information Canada.

Canada. 1993. "Foreign Policy Themes and Priorities 1991–92 Update." In Jack L. Granatstein, ed. *Canadian Foreign Policy. Historical Readings*. Revised Edition. Toronto: Copp Clark Pitman: 87–104.

Canada. 1995. *Canada in the World*. Ottawa: Supply and Service Canada.

Canada. 2005. "Development." *Canada's International Policy Statement*. Ottawa: Supply and Service Canada.

Canada. 2008. *Counter-Insurgency Operations*. Ottawa: Department of National Defence.

Canada. 2009. "Operations Database." Ottawa: National Defence and the Canadian Forces, Internet, http://www.cmp-cpm.forces.gc.ca/dhh-dhp/od-bdo/index-eng.asp. Accessed May 5, 2011.

Canada. 2013. *Report to Parliament on the Government of Canada's Official Development Assistance – 2012–2013*. Ottawa: Department of Foreign Affairs, Trade and Development.

Cermakian, Jean. 1968. "Canada's Role in the Foreign Aid Programmes to the Developing Nations: A Geographical Appraisal." *Cahiers de géographie du Québec*, vol. 12, no. 26: 225–34.

CIDA. 1987. *To Benefit a Better World*. Ottawa: Supply and Service Canada.

CIDA. 2002. *Statistical Report on Official Development Assistance, Fiscal Year 2000–2001*. Gatineau, QC: CIDA.

CIDA. 2004. *Statistical Report on Official Development Assistance, Fiscal Year 2002–2003*. Gatineau, QC: CIDA.

CIDA. 2006. *Statistical Report on Official Development Assistance, Fiscal Year 2004–2005*. Gatineau, QC: CIDA.

CIDA. 2008. *Statistical Report on Official Development Assistance, Fiscal Year 2005–2006*. Gatineau, QC: CIDA.

Dewitt, David B. 2004. "National Defence vs. Foreign Affairs: Culture Clash in Canada's International Security Policy?" *International Journal*, vol. 59, no. 3: 579–96.

DFAIT. 1999. *Human Security: Safety for People in a Changing World*. Ottawa: Supply and Service Canada.

Dobell, W.M. 1988. "Canadian Relations with South Asia." In Paul Painchaud, ed. *De Mackenzie King à Pierre Trudeau, Quarante ans de diplomatie canadienne (1945–1985)*. Quebec City: Presses de l'Université Laval: 347–373.

Engler, Yves. 2009. *The Black Book of Canadian Foreign Policy*. Vancouver: Fernwood and RED Publishing.

Gendron, Robin S. 2006. *Towards a Francophone Community: Canada's Relations with France and French Africa, 1945–1968*. Montreal and Kingston: McGill–Queen's University Press.

Gervais, Myriam, and Stéphane Roussel. 1998. "De la sécurité de l'État à celle de l'individu : L'évolution du concept de sécurité au Canada (1990–1996)." *Études internationales*, vol. 29, no. 1 : 25–52.

Gilmore, Jonathan. 2011. "A Kinder Gentler Counterterrorism: Counter-insurgency, Human Security and the War on Terror." *Security Dialogue*, vol. 42, no. 1: 21–37.

Hook, Steven W., and Franklin Barr Lebo. 2010. "Development/Poverty Issues and Foreign Policy Analysis." In Robert Allen Denemark, ed. *The International Studies Encyclopedia*. Chichester, UK, and Malden, MA: Wiley-Blackwell.

Hynek, Nikola, and David Bosold. 1999. "A History and Genealogy of the Freedom from Fear Doctrine." *International Journal*, vol. 64, no. 3: 142–60.

Jacquet, Pierre. 2002. "L'aide au développement dans la gouvernance globale." *Ramsès 2003*. Paris: Dunod/Institut français des relations internationales.

Jeong, Ho-Won. 2005. *Peacebuilding in Postconflict Societies: Strategy and Process*. Boulder: Lynne Rienner.

Maloney, Sean M. 2002. *Canada and UN peacekeeping: Cold War by Other Means, 1945–1970*. St. Catharines, ON: Vanwell Publishing.

Marclay, Eric. 2008. "Le virage vers les questions de sécurité de l'aide publique au développement." In François Audet, Marie-Eve Desrosiers, and Stéphane Roussel, eds. *L'aide canadienne au développement*. Montreal: Presses de l'Université de Montréal: 241–61.

Massie, Justin. 2009. "Making Sense of Canada's 'Irrational' International Security Policy. A Tale of Three Strategic Cultures." *International Journal*, vol. 64, no. 3 : 625–45.

Newman, Edward. 2010. "Peacebuilding as Security in 'Failing' and Conflict-Prone States." *Journal of Intervention and Statebuilding*, vol. 4, no. 3: 305–22.

Noël, Alain, and Jean-Philippe Thérien. 1995. "From Domestic to International Justice: the Welfare State and Foreign Aid." *International Organization*, vol. 49, no. 3: 523–53.

Nossal, Kim Richard. 1980. "Les droits de la personne et la politique étrangère canadienne : Le cas de l'Indonésie." *Études internationales*, vol. 11, no. 2: 223–38.

Nossal, Kim Richard. 1988. "Mixed Motives Revisited: Canada's Interest in Development Assistance." *Canadian Journal of Political Science*, vol. 21, no. 1: 35–56.

OECD. 1997. *Conflict, Peace and Development Co-operation on the Threshold of the 21st Century: Policy Statement*. Paris: OECD.

OECD. 2001. *The DAC Guidelines: Helping Prevent Violent Conflict*. Paris.

OECD. 2010a. "Aggregate Aid Statistics: ODA by Donor." *OECD International Development Statistics* (database), doi: 10.1787/data-00063-en. Accessed May 5, 2011.

OECD. 2010b. "ODA Official Development Assistance: Disbursements." *OECD International Development Statistics* (database), doi: 10.1787/data-00069-en. Accessed on May 5, 2011.

OECD. 2014. "Net Official Development Assistance from DAC and Other Donors in 2013 – Preliminary Data for 2013." *Publications and Statistics*, 8 April.

Palmer, Glenn, Scott B. Wohlander, and T. Clifton Morgan. 2002. "Give or Take: Foreign Aid and Foreign Policy Substitutability." *Journal of Peace Research*, vol. 39, no. 1: 5–26.

Pratt, Cranford. 1994. "Humane Internationalism and Canadian Development Assistance Policies." In Cranford Pratt, ed. *Canadian International Development Assistance Policies: An Appraisal*. Montreal and Kingston: McGill–Queen's University Press: 334–70.

Pratt, Cranford. 1999. "Competing Rationales for Canadian Development Assistance." *International Journal*, vol. 54, no. 2: 306–23.

St-Laurent, Louis. 1947. "The Foundation of Canadian Policy in World Affairs (Gray Foundation Lectureship)." *Statements and Speeches*, vol. 47, no. 2.

Spicer, Keith. 1966. *A Samaritan State? External Aid in Canada's Foreign Policy*. Toronto: University of Toronto Press.

Thérien, Jean-Philippe. 1989. "Le Canada et le régime international de l'aide." *Études internationales*, vol. 20, no. 2: 311–40.

United Nations Security Council. 2011. "Statement by the President of the Security Council." S/PRST/2011/4, February 11.

Woods, Ngaire. 2005. "The Shifting Politics of Foreign Aid." *International Affairs*, vol. 81, no. 2: 393–409.

CHAPTER IX

Why Aid? Canadian Perception of the Usefulness of Canadian Aid in an Era of Economic Uncertainty

Dominic H. Silvio

Introduction

Early in the autumn of 2008, the world experienced the most important financial and economic downturn since the 1930s. This economic downturn became a harsh reality for individuals and governments across the globe as profits shrank, workers lost their jobs, and tax revenues fell. In response, many governments in donor countries spent billions of dollars on fiscal stimulus packages to mitigate the economic carnage within their own economies. As these governments refocused their efforts on domestic problems, many analysts and aid recipients feared that increased demand for domestic spending would undercut previous commitments to development aid and leave aid-dependent countries to fend for themselves. In fact, in 2011 the decade-long trend of annual increases in aid to developing countries was broken, with a drop of nearly 3 percent (OECD 2012).

There is growing evidence in many countries that the state of the economy can have a powerful impact on public attitudes towards anything international, but particularly development assistance. Bad economic news can have negative effects on public attitudes towards aid; and positive news, positive effects (Smillie 2003; Zealand and Howes 2012). Since the beginning of the Canadian aid program in the early 1950s, it has received considerable public support (Lavergne 1989; Smillie 1998ab, 2003). However, the perception of the usefulness of aid has not been endorsed by Canadians without reservation. Given the fact that, after 2010, the Canadian government cut the budgets of specific programs in Canada, which might have an impact on services to Canadians, it makes sense to analyze Canadians' perception or attitudes towards the usefulness of aid, since it is their tax dollars that are being given away.

The intention of this chapter is to track the wider context of Canadian perception of the usefulness of aid, from the time of the global financial crisis in 2008 until 2012, to see whether there has been a decline in public support for development assistance, or a shift from positivism to negativism. Positivism here refers to the holding of optimistic attitudes towards foreign aid and support for the aid program. This positive support can be manifested in various ways. Customarily, as in many other policy fields, citizens' support for government efforts such as foreign aid is gauged by public opinion polling. However, in theory, support for aid could be expressed through the regular mechanisms of political accountability practiced in democratic societies, including elections (Czaplińska 2007). This, of course, is subject to the condition that development aid is a part of party programs, that voters take it into account when marking the ballot, and that it is possible to distinguish this factor as more decisive than others. In reality, however, in electoral campaigns, aid is overshadowed by other, mostly domestic, policy concerns (Czaplińska 2007; Noël et al. 2004). Furthermore, people support aid through their attitudes and individual decisions and choices made in their private daily life. Donations to non-governmental organizations (NGOs) can serve as a proxy for public attitudes towards development aid (Czaplińska 2007). In addition, one can make non-financial contributions to the works of NGOs through volunteering. One can also contribute ideas and criticism, for example, by engaging in the public debate or by writing letters to government policy officials. Furthermore, individual informed decisions concerning development issues also include ethical consumer behaviour, such as the purchase of fair trade goods. Negativism, on the other hand, refers to pessimistic attitudes towards aid issues and thus a lack of support for the aid program. It can result in active opposition to development assistance or in apathy on development-related issues.

The chapter explores whether public attitudes towards development aid in Canada are less favourable, or more specifically negative, as a result of the financial crisis. The analysis is based on available public opinion survey data retrieved from Canadian Opinion Research Archives (CORA), as well as from other agencies such as Ipsos Reid, the Canadian International Development Agency (CIDA), Innovative Research, Angus Reid, and Vision Critical. Furthermore, it is important to note that the analysis focuses on development aid or official development assistance (ODA) in general, and not the purpose or what it is spent on.

The chapter is divided into four sections. The first section provides background information on public support for aid as discussed in the literature. The second section looks into public support of the aid program in Canada from 1993 to 2002, while the third section analyzes public attitudes towards the volume of aid spending from the eve of the financial crisis in 2007 until 2012. The fourth and final section tracks the amount of Canadian ODA since 2007.

Background on Public Support for Development Assistance

Donor government aid policies are often determined by a combination of competing forces within the international system, as well as the domestic environment. As with other foreign policies, domestic public opinion is an important factor influencing the "aid effort" of donor governments (Mc Donnell et al. 2003). According to the Organisation for Economic Co-operation and Development (OECD 2008b), public awareness of, and support for, development cooperation is the best guarantee for ensuring continued political and legislative support for development assistance. This support has to be demonstrated both during good and bad economic times. In order to gauge this support, most OECD countries began carrying out public opinion surveys over a number of years on the level of public support provided to their official foreign aid programs. By and large, the surveys have been very positive for aid activists: They have shown that aid programs receive the support of the majority of their populations. Governments and aid activists claim it proves that there is no evidence of "aid fatigue," as is often claimed in the media (McDonnell et al. 2003; Smillie 1998b). Non-governmental organizations (NGOs) often cite this high level of public support in their lobbying for increased government expenditures on aid or to obtain government financial support for their own activities.

Research shows that the public knows virtually nothing about foreign aid and that what they think they know is actually incorrect.

Some commentators claim that public opinion about foreign aid does not matter. There is a variety of different views in political science concerning the extent to which public opinion influences policy creation. Powlick (1991) has suggested that public opinion is usually latent and that politicians act in ways that will avoid stirring it up and thus drawing attention to themselves. In his view, they will consider the opinions of the public in their decision making, but will also try to change these opinions if they go against the policy that the politician deems best. Wall (1973) has argued that voters are usually ignorant about aid programs, but even if they are knowledgeable about them, will rarely allocate their vote according to a political party or a candidate's views on aid. Otter (2003) has argued that the public tends to be uninformed about foreign aid programs and thus does not serve as a good source of policy for politicians.

Even so, public opinion has been deemed to be important in supporting and legitimizing government expenditures on bilateral and multilateral aid programs and for efforts to reform aid (Hudson and van Heerde 2012). International survey data from DAC countries suggest that public support for development assistance is, on average, above 70 percent and has been stable since the 1990s. The development community, via international organizations and state agencies, has committed itself to monitoring public attitudes because public opinion has been deemed critical for the continued success of development cooperation and for realizing the ODA target of 0.7 percent of gross national income for all OECD Development Assistance Committee (DAC) countries. A 1999 United Nations Development Programme report illustrates the point:

> The system of international development cooperation – whether we think of the current existing one or a new, expanded one – cannot exist without broad-based political support. Building such support, of course, requires a basic understanding of the nature of people's – the public's – attitudes toward international development cooperation. (quoted in Stern 1998, v)

Consequently, since the mid-1990s, monitoring public support has become common practice for most donor countries and major international organizations such as the OECD Development Centre (Fransman and Solignac Lacomte 2004; McDonnell et al. 2003), the

European Union (EU) Eurobarometer surveys, the UK's Department for International Development (DFID) and the World Bank (Paxton and Knack 2008).

Canadian Support for Development Assistance

Tracking of Canadian opinion towards development aid has been an ongoing initiative since the beginning of the Canadian aid program. However, between 2005 and 2012, the emphasis in the survey questions has shifted from asking respondents whether they supported the aid program to how well the government is doing in terms of the amount of ODA it gives. These different questions require separate analysis. This section will only focus on questions about the level of support Canadians offered to the development aid program from 1993 to 2002. The questions on the amount of support for ODA from 2007 to 2012 will be addressed in the next section.

Looking at older but sporadic opinion polls, the few survey analyses that were conducted on Canadian public attitudes towards development assistance tend to reinforce the idea that aid is a consensus issue in Canada. Canadians are usually presented as supporting foreign aid, and their attitudes are depicted as being fairly stable over time (see Table 1). At the end of the 1980s, for instance, Réal Lavergne (1989, 38) noted that "one usually finds between 75 percent and 80 percent of the population to be in favour of current or increased aid levels." The number of respondents in favour of increased levels, he added, "has remained approximately constant over the last twenty years" (Lavergne 1989, 40). A decade later, Ian Smillie (1998a, 58) concluded in the same vein that, in spite of some fluctuations in Canadians' support for aid, "the long-term trend has shown little significant change upward or downward, and it remains at the relatively high levels that have prevailed for the better part of two decades."

Table 1. Public Support for Development Assistance, 1993–2002[1]
(In percentages)

Categories	1993	1994	1995	1997	1998	2002
Strongly support	35	26	21	46	28	29
Mild support	44	38	36	26	47	54
Mild opposition	10	17	20	14	14	8
Strongly oppose	7	16	21	15	9	6

Source: Environics Research Group (2004)

According to Otter (2003, 122), in a 1995 survey, 82 percent of Canadians supported constant or increased aid levels, and support has remained stable in subsequent years. Although this number expresses overwhelming support, levels of support tend to be lower when respondents are explicitly asked if they would be willing to pay higher taxes to support aid increases (Noël et al. 2004). Macdonald (1995, 123) has argued that Canadians view themselves as "uniquely suited to solve many of the world's problems, particularly the problems of the non-European world." This legacy dates back at least to the government of Prime Minister Lester B. Pearson, who made peacekeeping and development assistance the hallmarks of Canadian foreign policy.

Overall, the Canadian public does appear highly supportive of foreign aid. An Ipsos Reid survey presented to the Department of Foreign Affairs and International Trade in September 2001 confirms the earlier findings of Lavergne and Smillie. According to the survey, 76.4 percent of Canadians consider it important for their country to pursue the promotion of assistance to poorer countries, while only 11.2 percent think that this foreign policy objective is not important (12.4 percent are neutral). Fifty-three percent of the respondents also agree that Canada should give more aid to developing countries, while only 26 percent disagree (21 percent are neutral). CIDA's polling in March 2002, conducted by Environics, showed that more than eight in ten Canadians (83 percent) continue to support long-term development assistance and a slightly higher number of Canadians (85 percent) express support for humanitarian assistance (Environics 2002).

Over time, Canadian attitudes towards development assistance have not varied, especially when compared to Canadian aid policy. This, however, does not mean that the public does not respond to the policy context. Public attitudes do fluctuate from one year to another. Various surveys have shown higher levels of support in the early 1990s and lower levels in the mid-1990s. In the 1993–95 period, in particular, when the fight against the budget deficit was the a top government priority, the proportion of Canadians who thought that the government spent the right amount or not enough to assist developing countries dropped to around 50 percent (from 76 percent in 1989). In a context of unprecedented financial restrictions, Canadians were more preoccupied with domestic than with foreign policy issues (Noël et al. 2004). In short, in the words of Noël et al. (2004, 9),

"Canadians appear supportive of foreign aid in principle, at a level that is constant over time, but their generosity remains guarded."

There are also additional surveys that support the trends described in the above table. For instance, according to Environics Research Group (2004), almost eight in ten Canadians (78 percent) indicate that they support Canada's aid program for poor countries, while two in ten (20 percent) are opposed. Support declined dramatically in September 2003 (59 percent), but subsequently returned to previous levels. A 2007 Canadian Defence and Foreign Affairs Institute survey conducted by Innovative Research Group indicated that 70 percent of respondents surveyed felt Canada had an obligation to help poor countries (CDFAI/Innovative, 2007). According to Gulrajani (2012), while this support may appear substantial, aid often polls at the top of the list when it comes to areas targeted for cutbacks. This finding is similar to a survey on British public attitudes to development that highlight aid as a highly supported area of government expenditures that is given low priority when presented against domestic priorities (DFID 2010). Furthermore, in a poll conducted by the North–South Institute in 2006, respondents were asked, "should Canada increase its official development assistance (ODA) to 0.7 percent of GNI by 2015?" Surprisingly, 53 percent said yes and only 5 percent said no. A large segment, about 42 percent, actually wanted the government to commit to achieving the increase before 2015 (North–South Institute 2006).

Canadian Opinion on the Volume of Aid Spending, 2007–2012

As mentioned earlier, the phrasing of survey questions on development aid by the major polling firms has shifted since 2004. Instead of focusing on the level of public support for development aid programs *per se*, they now place the emphasis on the *amount* of ODA the government gives. That is, should government give more, less or the same amount of aid. As a result, the responses differ and are very difficult to compare with the older survey data. In addition, the range of available data is limited. Hence, in order to resolve this, I have used additional data that have been collected sporadically from other opinion poll surveys in order to buttress or support some of the arguments that are raised and thus strengthen my analysis. Table 2 below presents the overall findings on public opinion of Canadians towards aid spending. The available data runs from 2007 to 2010 because the data for both 2011 and 2012 have not been released and it is not clear if the government has even commissioned a survey. However, I have decided to use survey data from other sources such as Innovative Research Group, Make Poverty History, and Inter-Council Network to fill the gap.

Table 2: Public Opinion on Volume of Aid Spending, 2007–2010
(In percentages)

Categories	2007	2008	2009	2010
More	21.0	21.7	29.3	24.4
Less	29.1	23.3	19.9	17.2
Same	46.8	52.3	45.6	54.4
Base	1,180	2,023	740	2,020

Source: Environics Focus Canada (2007–2010).

Based purely on visual analysis of the numbers, it is clear that the opinions of Canadians as to how much the government should spend on foreign aid shows a non-linear trend. For instance, the lowest percentage of Canadians who thought that the government should do more or increase its level of aid commitment was in 2007, when only 21 percent expressed that opinion. However, as the data show, the opinion of those who wanted the government to do more in terms of aid commitment began to increase, with the highest percentage (29.3 percent) in 2009, right when Canada was experiencing the effects of the economic downturn. Even though the reason behind this dramatic rise is not clear, this might be the result of an increase in transnational campaigns, such as Make Poverty History (MPH), ONE, and Product Red. This was short-lived, as the percentage of those in favour of increases in aid dropped considerably in 2010, to 24.4 percent (Environics Focus Canada 2007–2010).

Another area of interest is the number of those surveyed who opined that the government should spend the same amount or just maintain the same level of commitment. There is also a non-linear trend with those who suggest that the government should spend the same amount. For instance, in 2007, 46.8 percent of those surveyed favoured the status quo, with a significant increase to 52.3 percent in 2008. However, in 2009, the proportion dropped to 45.6 percent, almost identical to the 2007 values, rising again in 2010 to 54.4 percent. Similar to earlier analysis, it is clear that as the financial crisis started, the percentage of Canadians who wanted the government to maintain the status quo in ODA rose significantly, possibly due to fear that the economic downturn was going to negatively affect Canadians. However, in 2009, after realizing that Canada would not be hit as hard as other Western countries (e.g., the US and EU members), or perhaps due to the effects of anti-poverty campaigns, the percentage of those supporting the status quo dropped considerably, whereas the percentage of those who favoured increases in the aid budget rose to 29.3 percent. However, this was only temporary, because the numbers reversed course after the 2009 federal budget, when cuts to services were announced.

In 2007, 29.1 percent of surveyed Canadians wanted the government to spend less. This was an anomaly, because since then, despite the financial crisis, the numbers have been declining, from 23.3 percent in 2008 to 17.2 percent in 2010. Thus, despite the crisis and resulting economic downturn, the majority of Canadians favoured either the status quo or an increase in aid.

Based on this data, it is clear that the public is more likely than not to be comfortable with the level of aid currently being provided, and since 2009, has become more so. For instance, in 2010, over half (54.4 percent) considered the level of spending to be about right – meaning Canada should give the same amount of ODA (up 8 points from 2009). The proportion who believe the amount of foreign aid is not enough – meaning Canada should give more – has declined (24.4 percent, down 5 percent from 2009), while one in six (17.2 percent, down 3 percent from 2009) maintain that Canada is spending too much and should give less (Environics Focus Canada 2007–2010).

Furthermore, in 2009, a non-random Internet poll conducted by Innovative Research Group for the Munk Centre for International Studies found that about 49 percent of respondents supported the idea of more than doubling aid to reach the late Prime Minister Lester B. Pearson's goal of 0.7 percent of the size of the Canadian economy – an increase to about $10 billion per year (Clark 2009).[2] Furthermore, a poll conducted by Angus Reid in collaboration with MPH in 2010 found that 61 percent of Canadians agree that the government should increase the amount of money it spends on international aid programs (Make Poverty History and Angus Reid 2010). This high level of support is consistent with previous findings (Lavergne 1989; Smillie 1998a, 2003) that Canadian support of foreign aid has been fairly stable over time.

Even when the budgetary context is less difficult, domestic programs tend to take higher priority. Canadians are supportive of foreign aid, but they simply do not rank it very high among their various concerns. As can be seen in Figure 1, in 2012, only 15 percent of Canadians thought world poverty should be a priority for the federal government. These international development objectives ranked well below a series of domestic priorities, including many that were not even within the jurisdiction of the federal government. The main public concerns had to do with health care (a priority for 55 percent of respondents), the economy (45 percent), government accountability (34 percent), the environment and education (both at 29 percent), and employment (28 percent) (Inter-Council Network 2012).

Figure 1: The Public Policy Priorities of Canadians

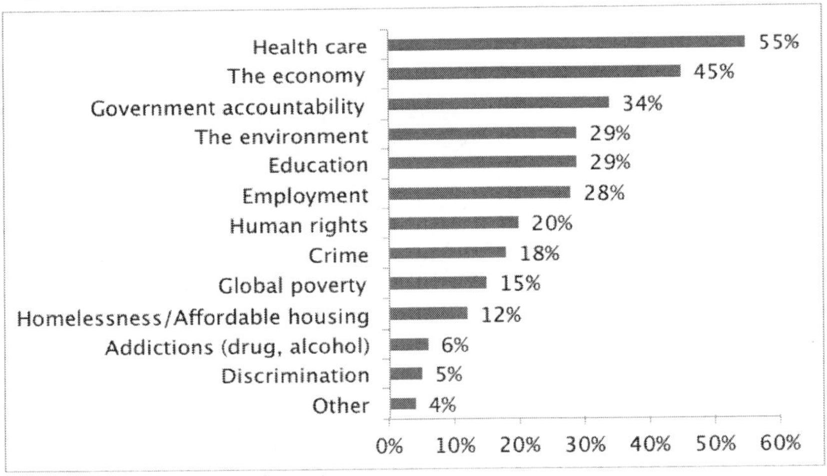

Source: Inter-Council Network (2012).

As Smillie (1998b, 23) noted, public support for development aid in Canada tends to be "a mile wide and an inch deep." When aid budgets are reduced, there is little public protest, suggesting that support is soft. The contrast between the high support expressed by Canadians and the relatively low importance they give to the issue seems in line with this assessment. The fact that Canadians give more importance to domestic issues than to international development issues such as the reduction of world poverty is not surprising (Noël et al. 2004).

In short, it is important to note that many differences in poll results have to do with the way a question is asked. For a long time, pollsters' questions were straightforward and simple to answer. For instance, the March 1969 Canadian Gallup Poll asked respondents if they thought that Canada should help other countries achieve a higher standard of living or not. However, modern firms like Environics ask respondents if they thought that aid to developing countries was not necessary. Another poll, by a different firm, asked the same question this way: "Do you support or oppose Canada providing assistance to poor countries?" Recent questions on foreign aid from polling firms are less straightforward, which in turn may mislead respondents. In some instance, they tried to gauge respondents' knowledge in terms of the amount the government gives in ODA as well as their willingness to contribute to the program. These questions are more likely to generate different response rates when compared.

The Volume of Canadian ODA Spending, 2007–2011

It is evident from the analysis above that Canadian support for both the aid program and the need to increase the government's aid contribution is fairly high. However, in order to assess the significance or impact of this support during the economic downturn, the total amount of ODA is a very important variable to analyze.[3] I therefore examined data on total Canadian ODA accessed from OECD statistical collections. Because the financial crisis started in the autumn of 2008, I included data from 2007 to see if there had been considerable changes in total ODA. Table 3 below shows the amount of ODA and the percentage of gross national income (GNI) from the eve of the financial crisis until 2012.

Table 3. Canadian ODA Contribution and GNI Percentage

Year	Total ODA	GNI
	Thousands of USD	Percentage
2007	4,079.69	0.29
2008	4,794.71	0.33
2009	4,000.07	0.30
2010	5,208.57	0.34
2011	5,457.16	0.32
2012 (preliminary)	5,667.60	0.32

Source: OECD/DAC Statistics (2012b).

As the numbers show, ODA as percent of GNI fluctuated between 0.29 percent and 0.34 percent between 2007 and 2012. In both 2008 and 2010, aid increased modestly. The only anomaly occurred in 2009, when Canada gave only US$4 billion in development aid; however, it was higher in terms of GNI (0.30 percent) when compared to the 2007 volume and GNI. Thus, regardless of the economic downturn, Canada at least maintained its consistency in the amount of ODA it provided every year. In fact, while Canadian aid increased slightly after its last drop in 2009, the ratio of ODA to GNI at 0.32 percent in 2012 still put it in fourteenth place among the twenty-four members of the OECD/DAC's (OECD 2012c).[4] This position is not one that a country espousing internationalism, soft power, and multilateral commitments could view with any sort of pride. In contrast, a number of small northern European countries have already well surpassed both the OECD average and the target of 0.7 percent. Furthermore, the Canadian government has decided to freeze the amount of ODA in 2010 and as part of its effort to eliminate the federal deficit by 2015, it plans to cut 7.5 percent of the aid budget, or $377.6 million, from the $5.16 billion international assistance envelope by that year.

Conclusion

What does this mean for the future of Canadian aid policy? As noted earlier, Canadian aid policy is neither influenced by, nor mirrors, public opinion. However, this does not necessarily mean that the government does not listen to public opinion. In fact, the government does pay careful attention to public opinion to determine how much latitude it has to ignore that opinion on various issues, such as aid spending. Development assistance is an area of low salience to the public, based on the priority given to it by Canadians, and the government seems to grasp that (see Figure 1 above). Hence, I do not expect public opinion to influence Canadian aid policy in the near future, unless public support for development aid shifts from being "a mile wide and an inch deep" to "a mile deep."

There is now a rich vein of polling information, going back at least three decades, concerning what Canadians think about foreign aid. While many of the findings appear somewhat contradictory or ambiguous, there is good evidence that a majority of Canadians support development aid programs. This general support for aid and its specificities fluctuates somewhat, depending on two variables – feelings of confidence in the economy, and the trends and issues in the news. However, in the main, support is steady and relatively high. Overall, despite the severity of the recent economic crisis, public support for development cooperation and the desire to increase Canadian ODA remains high: Around 61 percent of Canadians still believe development is important, while about 50 percent still believe in honouring or going beyond existing aid commitments to the developing world. As Noël et al. (2004) noted, the fact that public support for more generous levels of foreign aid is lower than the support for the very principle of development assistance is to be expected, since the commitment invoked in the budget increase question is more explicit and important. The gap between these two questions, however, indicates that the Canadian consensus over foreign aid is weaker and more fragile than what is often suggested.

In fact, there appears to be no correlation at all between public support for development aid and actual government ODA expenditure, which showed some modest increases between 2009 and 2012, although not sufficient to reach the OECD/DAC target. In agreement with other authors (e.g., Smillie 1998ab, 2003), two possible conclusions might be drawn. First, public opinion means very little to governmental policy formulation where ODA is concerned, perhaps not surprisingly in light of Canadian public opinion, which consistently gives the government a high performance rating on the aid file, while assigning it the lowest priority among both domestic and foreign policy issues. Second, public opinion, while widely supportive of issues such as development assistance, is not, in reality, very strong. Little protest has followed budget cuts. This might not have made any difference, however. In recent years, ODA has had to compete with large cuts in educational spending and health care in Canada, where protests have been loud and organized, and equally ineffective. However, the decision of the government to eliminate roughly 7.5 percent, or $377.6 million, from the international assistance envelope by 2015 will water down all these marginal achievements. In short, I find no decline in the level of support for both Canadian aid programs and the volume of ODA. Further, there is a generally positive feeling towards development aid.

Notes

1. The question posed was: Through its aid program, Canada provides goods, services, and the transfer of knowledge and skills to poor countries. This helps poor countries make long-term economic and social progress that will enable them to eventually meet their own needs. On a scale of one to six, where one means "very strongly oppose" and six means "very strongly support," what is your level of support for Canada's aid program for poor countries?

2. The poll used an Internet panel with 1,383 respondents, a sample size that is typically considered accurate within 2.6 percentage points, 19 times out of 20. However, an Internet panel is not a random sample and therefore does not have a statistically valid margin of error. The poll was conducted in preparation for Munk Debates series.

3. The OECD defines ODA as those flows to developing countries and multilateral institutions provided by official agencies, including state and local governments, or by their executive agencies. Each of the transactions must meet the following tests: (a) its main objective is the promotion of the economic development and welfare of developing countries; and (b) it is concessional in character and conveys a grant element of at least 25 percent (OECD 2008b).

4. Canada's net ODA rose by 4.1 percent in 2012, mainly due to an increase in debt relief and a commitments to major regional initiatives, and ranked sixth in terms of total ODA given (OECD 2012).

References

CDFAI/Innovative. 2007. *Canadian Views on Foreign Aid*. Internet, http://www.cdfai.org/PDF/Poll%20on%20Foreign%20Aid.pdf. Accessed November 8, 2013.

Clark, Campbell. 2009. "Canadians Disapprove of Linking Foreign Aid to Trade." *Globe and Mail*, June 1. Internet, http://www.theglobeandmail.com/news/national/canadians-disapprove-of-linking-foreign-aid-to-trade/article1162521/. Accessed November 8, 2013.

Czaplińska, Agata. 2007. "Building Public Support for Development Cooperation." Instituto Complutense de Estudios Internacionales (ICEI). Internet. http://eprints.ucm.es/11859/1/PP02-07.pdf. Accessed July 16, 2014.

Department for International Development. 2010. *Public Attitudes towards Development*. London: TNS UK. Internet, https://www.gov.uk/government/uploads/system/uploads/attachment_data/file/67684/public-attitudes-april10.pdf. Accessed November 8, 2013.

Environics Focus Canada. 2002. "Public Opinion on Foreign Aid." Toronto: Environics Institute.

Environics Focus Canada. 2007–2010. "Public Opinion on Foreign Aid." Internet, http://search2.odesi.ca/search/search.html?q=Environics+Focus+Canada&field=SE&coll=odesiall&coll=DLI&coll=DLI_aggregate&coll=CGP&coll=CAD&coll=external&coll=cora&coll=icpsr&date-gt=2007&date-lt. Accessed November 8, 2013.

Environics Research Group. 2004. *Canadian Attitudes toward Development Assistance*. Gatineau, QC: CIDA. Internet, http://www.oecd.org/dev/devcom/39436670.pdf. Accessed November 8, 2013.

Fransman, Jude, and Henri-Bernard Solignac Lecomte. 2004. *Mobilising Public Opinion against Global Poverty*. Paris: OECD. Internet, http://www.oecd.org/pcd/31744527.pdf. Accessed November 8, 2013.

Gallup Canada. 1969. "Canadian Gallup Poll, May 1969." Internet, http://odesi2.scholarsportal.info/webview/index.jsp?object=http://142.150.190.128:80%2Fobj%2FfStudy%2Fcipo-334-E-1969-03&mode=documentation&v=2&top=yes. Accessed November 8, 2013.

Gulrajani, Nilima. 2012. "Improving Canada's Performance as a Bilateral Donor: Assessing the Past and Building for the Future." In Stephen Brown, ed. *Struggling for Effectiveness: CIDA and Canadian Foreign Aid*. Montreal and Kingston: McGill–Queen's University Press: 53–78.

Hudson, David, and Jennifer van Heerde. 2012. "A Mile Wide and an Inch Deep: Surveys of Public Attitudes Towards Development Aid." *International Journal of Development Education and Global Learning*, vol. 4, no. 1: 5–23.

Inter-Council Network. 2012. *Canadian Engagement on Global Poverty Issues*. Internet, http://www.acgc.ca/09/images/file/Final_ICN_Global_Poverty_Poll_Report_Sept6_12.pdf. Accessed November 8, 2013.

Lavergne, Réal. 1989. "Determinants of Canadian aid policy." In Olav Stokke, ed. *Western Middle Powers and Global Poverty: The Determinants of the Aid Policies of Canada, Denmark, the Netherlands, Norway and Sweden*. Uppsala: Scandinavian Institute of African Studies and Norwegian Institute of International Affairs: 33–84.

Macdonald, Laura. 1995. "Unequal Partnerships: The Politics of Canada's Relations with the Third World." *Studies in Political Economy*, no. 47: 111–41.

Make Poverty History, and Angus Reid. 2010. "Poll Shows Canadians Support Increasing Foreign Aid and Want Canada to Show Leadership on Child and Maternal Health." Internet, http://www.makepovertyhistory.ca/story/poll-shows-canadians-support-increasing-foreign-aid-and-want-canada-to-show-leadership-on-chil . Accessed November 8, 2013.

McDonnell, Ida, Henri-Bernard Solignac Lecomte, and Liam Wegimont. 2003. *Public Opinion and the Fight against Poverty*. Paris: OECD.

Noël, Alain, Jean-Philippe Thérien, and Sébastien Dallaire. 2004. "Divided over Internationalism: The Canadian Public and Development Assistance." *Canadian Public Policy*, vol. 30, no. 1: 29–46.

North–South Institute. 2006. "Should Canada Increase Its Official Development Assistance (ODA) to 0.7% of GNI by 2015?" Internet, http://www.nsi-ins.ca/english/poll-result.asp. Accessed July 22, 2009.

OECD. 2008a. "Effective Aid Management: Twelve Lessons from DAC Peer Reviews." *OECD Journal on Development*, vol. 9, no. 1: 42–62.

OECD. 2008b. "Is It ODA?" Internet, http://www.oecd.org/dac/stats/34086975.pdf. Accessed November 8, 2013.

OECD. 2012a. "Aid to Poor Countries Slips further as Governments Tighten Budgets." Internet, http://www.oecd.org/dac/stats/aidtopoorcountries slipsfurtherasgovernmentstightenbudgets.htm. Accessed November 8, 2013.

OECD. 2012b. "Development: Key Tables from OECD." Paris: OECD. Internet, http://www.oecd-ilibrary.org/development/development-aid-net-official-development-assistance-oda-2012_aid-oda-table-2012-1-en. Accessed November 8, 2013.

OECD. 2012c. "Total Flows by Donor (Canada)." Internet, http://stats.oecd.org/Index.aspx?QueryId=42230&lang=en#. Accessed November 8, 2013.

Otter, Mark. 2003. "Domestic Public Support for Foreign Aid: Does It Matter?" *Third World Quarterly*, vol. 24, no. 1: 115–25.

Paxton, Pamela, and Stephen Knack. 2008. "Individual and Country-level Factors Affecting Support for Foreign Aid." Policy Research Working Paper, 4714. Washington, DC: World Bank. Internet, http://www-wds.worldbank.org/servlet/WDSContentServer/WDSP/IB/2008/09/08/000158349_20080908113828/Rendered/PDF/WPS4714.pdf. Accessed November 8, 2013.

Powlick, Philip J. 1991. "The Attitudinal Bases for Responsiveness to Public Opinion among American Foreign Policy Officials." *Journal of Conflict Resolution*, vol. 35, no. 4: 611–41.

Smillie, Ian. 1998a. "Canada." In Ian Smillie, Henny Helmich, Tony German and Judith Randel, eds. *Public Attitudes and International Development Co-operation*. Paris: OECD: 55–59.

Smillie, Ian. 1998b. "Optical and Other Illusions: Trends and Issues in Public Thinking about Development Co-operation." In Ian Smillie, Henny Helmich, Tony German, and Judith Randel, eds. *Public Attitudes and International Development Co-operation*. Paris: OECD: 21–39.

Smillie, Ian. 2003. "Canada." In Ida McDonnell, Henri-Bernard Solignac Lecomte, and Liam Wegimont, eds. *Public Opinion and the Fight against Poverty*. Paris: OECD: 73–80.

Stern, Marc. 1998. *Development Aid: What the Public Thinks*. New York: United Nations Development Programme.

Wall, David. 1973. *The Charity of Nations: The Political Economy of Foreign Aid.* New York: Basic Books.

Zealand, Kathryn, and Stephen Howes. 2012. "End of the Aid Boom? The Impact of Austerity on Aid Budgets." Canberra: Australian National University Development Policy Centre. Internet, http://devpolicy.anu. edu.au/pdf/2012/policy_briefs/PB5-The-impacts-of-austerity-on-aid-budgets.pdf. Accessed November 8, 2013.

CHAPTER X

The Management of Canadian Development Assistance: Ideology, Electoral Politics or Public Interest?

François Audet and Olga Navarro-Flores

Introduction

Several decisions made by the Canadian government have initi-ated an important debate on what some call a shift in foreign aid. Coinciding with the Conservative government's arrival in power, this shift has been especially noticeable since 2005. In particular, the gov-ernment has closed Rights & Democracy and transformed it into the Office of Religious Freedom, cut women's sexual and reproductive health programs, provided new support for the extractive industry, increased funding to faith-based non-governmental organizations, and folded the Canadian International Development Agency (CIDA) into the Department of Foreign Affairs and International Trade (DFAIT), renamed the Department of Foreign Affairs, Trade and Development (DFATD). Despite the importance of these changes, relatively little research has been conducted on the Conservative government's impact on international aid policies.

Inspired by recent trends in public administration, this chapter analyzes the decisions at the core of this shift in the Canadian gov-ernment's aid policy management. More specifically, we use some of these decisions to illustrate how the concept of development man-agement can help interpret the Conservative government's choices regarding official development assistance (ODA). We specifically consider whether they were made on the basis of ideology, electoral politics, or the public interest. Our goal is to reflect on Canadian aid from a public administration perspective and, more broadly, to participate in the debate on Canadian foreign policy.

The chapter is divided into three sections. The first contextualizes the issue of foreign aid in major debates surrounding the public administration of ODA and proposes a three-pronged analytical framework. The second section outlines some observable components of the shift in Canadian aid. The third section analyzes these changes.

Foreign Aid: A Public Administration Issue

Foreign aid is the voluntary transfer of resources from one country to another through a range of activities, programs, financial channels, and goods and services, as well as debt cancellation (Kim 2009, 556). Through the donor countries' public administrations, government departments or agencies manage international programs. In addition, the study of foreign aid is a public administration concern, as it can bring about positive change, change public policy, and encourage good governance (Knack 2004; Neumayer 2002).

For over three decades, New Public Management (NPM) has been the prevailing theoretical and practical public administration paradigm (Osborne and Gaebler 1992). This approach contends that the private sector's management model is more effective than the one generally used by the public sector. Following in the tradition of Anglo-Saxon countries, the model mainly implies a separation between political involvement (steering) and the operational/administrative function (rowing). In this perspective, such separation facilitates empowerment and consequently enhances the effectiveness of small operational units in charge of public policy (Bezes 2009). In addition to the adoption of NPM, the advent of the debate on aid effectiveness was another strong influence of the private sector's emphasis on efficiency within public management.

In the context of public administration, Thomas (1996, 96) characterized ODA management as *Development Management*, a union between management and international development that implies the inclusion of aid-related values, such as equity, political participation, and gender equality. Development managers in public administration thus distinguish themselves through specific attributes and skills connected to challenges and realities that are different from those found in other areas of the public sector. They must therefore reconcile notions of NPM efficiency with "Third World" ideals (Dar and Cooke 2008, 15). However, de Vries (2008, 151) characterizes NPM as an authoritarian and institutionalized ideological practice which depoliticizes all development activities by transforming a "utopian" project, in line with the recipient countries' situation, into a "hierarchical" project that reflects donor standards. In short, NPM increases the separation between the steering (politics) and rowing (operations/administration). This situation raises questions such as: Which partner countries should be prioritized? Which crises should receive assistance? Which organizations should implement these projects? Should the political level be involved in defining programs and choosing partner agencies? Should development managers be given ultimate responsibility for these choices? Finally, in case of failure or criticism, as is often the case in foreign aid, who should be held accountable?

Who decides? Is it administrators, politicians, or both? Should decisions be made jointly, in consultation with DFAIT and CIDA experts? If politicians make the decisions, political interests should be taken into account, following the ruling party's ideology (de Vries 2008; Massie 2011). If development managers make the decisions, they should be based on development considerations, which entails separating politics from the administrative functions. If, however, decisions are made jointly by politicians, development managers, and other public administrators, bureaucratic efficiency must be considered. It is thus possible to analyze the development management decision-making process from three perspectives: political ideology, the separation between political and administrative functions, and bureaucratic efficiency. In the next section, we apply this analytical framework to better understand the Canadian government's approach to the management of official development assistance.

Observable Phenomena in Management of Official Development Assistance

As mentioned above, a shift has taken place in Canadian aid since the Conservatives came to power. We compiled many of their decisions and, to facilitate reading and break down the available information on their analysis, we divided them into two basic types. We based the categories on the Canadian government's justification at the time of the decision's announcement: (1) economic rationale (e.g., privatization, exports, role of the private sector); (2) efficiency rationale (e.g., responsible management of the public purse, government downsizing, improved performance). We added a third category for decisions not justified by economic or efficiency rationales.

Table 1 shows the Canadian government's main decisions from 2010 to 2013, taken from CIDA's website (CIDA 2013) and grouped by rationale. Other decisions may have been taken that are not listed on the CIDA website. The decisions shown below represent solely those that were publicly announced.

Without going over all the decisions presented in Table 1, some important facts are worth highlighting to support our analysis. One of the key factors that emerges from this list of decisions has to do with the public administration's management effectiveness. Influenced by the NPM perspectives, the budget cuts and merger of CIDA and DFAIT to downsize government, along with the fact that 13 percent of the ODA budget went unspent, seek to improve program management efficiency and reduce operating costs. At the

Table 1: Main Canadian Government Decisions on ODA Management

Justification of Decisions	Key Decisions Announced
Economic rationale	2010 • Minister Oda unveils CIDA's Sustainable Economic Growth Strategy (October) 2012 • Minister Fantino announces UBC-SFU to partner with government on new extractive institute (November) PM announces support for economic growth and development in the Americas (April) 2013 • The government announces it will broaden and deepen its partnership with the private sector to promote development, following the release of the parliamentary report "Driving Inclusive Economic Growth: The Role of the Private Sector in International Development" (March) • The Harper government consults experts on private sector–led international development (March) • Harper government and World Economic Forum committed to improving prosperity in developing countries through responsible resource development (March) • PM announces support for responsible natural resource development in Africa (January)

Table 1: (continued)

Justification of Decisions	Key Decisions Announced
Efficiency rationale	**2010** Minister Oda announces next step to CIDA's Aid Effectiveness; CCIC funding is cut (July), among other consequences **2011** • CIDA joins the International Aid Transparency Initiative (November 2011) **2012** • The Minister announces that CIDA is moving forward with its commitment to transparency and accountability by publishing its implementation schedule for an internationally agreed aid transparency standard (December) • The government announces its support for the Open Aid Partnership in order to promote transparency and good governance of official development assistance (March) • The government announces KAIROS and Alternatives funding cuts on grounds that they do not meet CIDA program requirements **2013** • Merger of CIDA and DFATD in the March 2013 budget • Minister Fantino explains that CIDA funds projects, not organizations, when questioned about increase in funding of faith-based organizations and a homophobic group • The 2013–14 Federal Budget forecasts significant cuts in funding for foreign aid, $378 million (nearly 10%) decrease in CIDA's annual budget
Other rationales or none	**2011** • Closure of Rights & Democracy • Elimination of funding for NGOs KAIROS and Alternatives, which ran humanitarian programs in Palestine **2012** • Establishment of the Office of Religious Freedom • Minister Baird Announces Closing of International Centre for Human Rights and Democratic Development (April 3) • Reformulation of support programs for sexually abused women • Unilateral policy in support of Israel **2013** • The government reveals that $419 million of Canadian aid budget lapsed in 2012, equivalent to about 13% of the budget • Canada Committed to Protecting and Promoting Religious Freedom (April)

Source: Compiled from the CIDA and DFAIT websites and interpreted by the authors

time of writing this chapter, the government had yet to announce the merger's financial impact.

The table also reveals Canada's new policy towards Israel, which tends to influence and justify a good number of related decisions. Foreign Minister John Baird has stated that "Canada is a better and stronger ally of Israel's than the United States" (Blanchfield 2012). This new Conservative policy seems to be ideological. Massie (2011) points out how the Harper government's position towards Israel contrasts with Canada's previous balanced policy.

Finally, the table highlights cuts in the funding of several Canadian non-governmental organizations (NGOs), including the Canadian Council for International Co-operation (CCIC). These decisions are based on the Canadian government's pro-Israel ideology or other ideological perspectives, for instance, its rejection of bottom-up approaches such as those of the CCIC, a longtime CIDA strategic partner organization for defining and applying aid policy.

The above helps us characterize the Conservative government's behaviour and establish that efficiency issues and the Conservative Party's ideology heavily influence aid management decisions. We analyze this in the next section.

The Difficult Application of Development Management

As mentioned above, NPM and development management are the dominant public administration paradigms. This translates into the application of specific development values related to foreign aid, in addition to the NPM-influenced agenda of bureaucratic efficiency and the ideal of a separation between political and administrative functions. Using core concepts from both theoretical fields, Table 2 provides a framework to interpret Canadian government decisions that have drastically altered the Canadian aid landscape.

A review of Table 2 reveals at least three main development management challenges in Canada: (1) The NPM utopian separation of political and administrative functions, which enables (2) the influence of political ideology and (3) policies seeking "bureaucratic efficiency" at all cost.

An Impossible Separation of Functions

In this context, it would appear that the ideal of the separation between the political and the administrative is impossible to achieve.

Table 2: Framework for Analyzing Canadian Government Decisions

Categories	Criteria	Responsibilities	Main Issues and Debates from Key Decisions
Aid effectiveness (Development Management)	New Public Management (Hood 1991): - Project quality - Government downsizing - Privatization - Budget cuts - Underspending	Public administration (CIDA/DFAIT) and politicians	Selection and funding of projects on the basis of project proposals without taking into account the organizations Sidelining of public sector expertise Political predisposition towards the private sector Fragile balance between values and interests that are not unanimously accepted
	On the basis of public interest (Bozeman 2007) and development management ethics (Thomas 1996)	Public administration (CIDA/DFAIT) and politicians	
Political interests (NPM)	Interest groups and electoral considerations (Cochran 1973)	Politicians	"Swing of the pendulum"; some groups were disadvantaged during the Liberal era Unfair representation Religious ideology Possible intervention in the process by politicians for "self-preservation"
	Political ideology (Collins and Kakabadse 2006)	Politicians	
Separation of functions (NPM)	Administrators have the required technical information to make decisions (Hood 2011)	Public administration (CIDA/DFAIT) and politicians	Avoid the politicization of aid Maintain expertise in the Canadian public administration Possible intervention in the process by politicians for "self-preservation" reasons

Source: Authors' compilation.

However, is there a genuine interest in separating these functions? To answer the questions, it is instructive to examine Harper government decisions and one case in particular of political intervention in aid program management, in which Bev Oda, then Minister of International Cooperation, overturned a CIDA administrative funding decision regarding KAIROS, an NGO working in Palestine, by inserting the word "not" (see Fitzpatrick 2011). The political rhetoric that denies political intervention is contradicted by politicians' actions. This specific case shows how difficult it is for the Harper government to remain outside of the administrative structure. Citing the importance of working with administrators, Sharp (1981) advocates joint decision making. He explains that public administration is even more important when the parties in power alternate. The administrators (the rowing) guarantee the development and maintenance of expertise, which can be used by politicians (the steering), who come and go. How, then, to explain the government's concealment of its interventions? Hood (2011, 7) explains that politicians, because of their need to be re-elected, worry about being criticized. Not wanting to be blamed for political intervention, the Conservatives might prefer to hide their influence on decision making.

Table 2 also illustrates how officials and politicians have a complementary role in decision making regarding the formulation and implementation of aid effectiveness policies. In fact, the international debate on aid effectiveness, in which Canada participates, involves a plethora of measures that require the government's political commitment (such as harmonization with other donors, ownership policies), as well as program administration through mechanisms for funding, monitoring, and evaluation, as well as program administration tools.

However, the invocation of "Canadian values" and aid effectiveness to justify certain decisions – the increase in funding to faith-based organizations, the closure of organizations that are not aligned with the Conservatives' ideology or pro-Israel policy – must be interpreted through a different framework. Some of the Conservative government's decisions seem ideological. This suggests that religious ideology plays a dominant role in the Harper government.

A Political Ideology Steeped in Political Interests
Collins and Kakabadse (2006, 112) describe the dangers of a rigid and dogmatic political ideology based on religious views, insofar as those who subscribe to a Manichean logic of good and evil seem incapable

of nuance or respect for other religions and ideologies, which they perceive to be in conflict with their own values. Such behaviour leads either to the exclusion of those who do not share the same beliefs or attempts to convert them.

Collins and Kakabadse's (2006) argument sheds new light on certain Canadian government decisions. First, the selection of new proselytizing organizations to implement aid programs cannot be justified on the basis of effectiveness. Though Canadian aid was initially based in religious motivations, most Canadian NGOs abandoned their religious roots in the late 1970s. However, after the Conservatives were elected, the number of faith-based organizations delivering aid increased significantly. Between 2005 and 2010, funding to proselytizing organizations increased by more than 70 percent, and non-evangelical faith-based organizations received a 40 percent increase, while secular organizations received only a 4 percent increase (Audet et al. 2013). While there is no consensus on the evidence regarding the growth in funding for faith-based organizations (Vander Zaag 2013), religious groups clearly influence Canadian international cooperation (Berger 2006) and NGOs more generally (Clarke 2006), and the role and the effect of evangelical groups on the Canadian Conservative government is well documented (Malloy, 2013; Potter 2011).

The Harper government justifies the funding decisions on the basis of the quality of the project proposals, not on the organizations themselves. Project-based criteria would suggest an aid effectiveness rationale. However, that justification does not hold, since new organizations have by definition less experience, which decreases the effectiveness of aid delivery. The funding of evangelical organizations thus fits well with Collins and Kakabadse's (2006) description of Manichaean ideology.

Second, the defunding of Canadian NGOs KAIROS and Alternatives was probably due to their support of Palestinian communities, which was not consistent with the Harper government's ideological view of the Israeli-Palestinian conflict.[1] The closure of Rights & Democracy and its subsequent transformation into the Office of Religious Freedom is also not surprising in this context, as it too opted for a balanced human rights policy regarding the Israeli-Palestinian conflict. DFATD's new Office of Religious Freedom, led by a supporter of the Catholic Church, will be easier to keep in line with the government's ideology.

Third, some NGOs' refusal to toe the Conservative line has had other repercussions, as well. Some Canadian organizations have lost government funding for their projects relating to sexual and reproductive health, notably those providing access to safe and legal abortion for women who have been sexually assaulted or are HIV-positive. This decision can be attributed to the Conservatives' ideological position on abortion. Organizations such as Doctors of the World Canada, which has much expertise in maternal health and fighting HIV, can no longer rely on funding from the Canadian government for those issues.

The situation is similar with humanitarian organizations. Indeed, a large number of faith-based organizations have joined the Policy and Advocacy Group for Emergency Relief (PAGER), an ad hoc committee for coordination and policy composed of Canadian humanitarian organizations, DFAIT, and CIDA. Since 2005, the number of faith-based PAGER members has risen from three to fourteen. With this dilution of Canadian humanitarian professionals, PAGER appears to have lost its *raison d'être*. The space for dialogue between experts to discuss policy and operational issues has turned into a list of CIDA-funded organizations that the government favours. Relatedly, DFAIT removed from its website the list of organizations it endorsed, which included about fifteen Catholic and evangelical organizations, most of which had only recently been added to the list.

These changes and their link to the Conservative government's ideology can be interpreted in two ways. The first has to do with the electoral impact of criticism (self-preservation). Thus, given the obvious objections to these decisions, how should one interpret such behaviour? On the one hand, politicians worry about the impact of their decisions if it compromises their chances of re-election. However, criticism probably has a lesser impact on their image than the faith-based groups that approve of these changes. Indeed, the Conservatives are probably seeking to please their electoral base. The second view helps us understand how political intervention imbues the Canadian public administration of ODA with Conservative values. How does this compare with previous governments? As explained by Jeffrey (2011), the Conservatives have merely "removed" the Liberal bias and introduced a Conservative one in its place. As such, the Conservative government is no different from previous ones or from other international donors. The Harper government is part of mainstream economic development discourse in which ODA is an instrument of economic self-interest. In the Conservative Party's ideology, this implies favouring organizations that echo their religious values.

The Quest for Bureaucratic Efficiency

The third issue affecting development management in Canada concerns aid effectiveness. Requirements for the effective management of aid and the government's desire to reduce expenditures in a context of economic crisis can explain the reorganization of aid management (CIDA/DFAIT), as well as the budgets cuts themselves. However, these decisions can also be defended from a public interest perspective. From this point of view, taxpayers should expect judicious use of public funds, especially in times of economic crisis. Similarly, decisions and policies encouraging the private sector, especially the mining sector, are part of the Conservative government's economic development strategy. Aligning aid policy with the private sector and the extractive industry can also be justified on effective grounds.

From an NPM perspective, the private sector produces more cost-effective results, thereby improving the effectiveness of aid programs. It is politically expedient for the government to embrace rhetorically the strict management of public funds and the downsizing of the state bureaucracy. However, downsizing creates new public service problems because the layoff of experts impairs institutional memory and reduces the government's ability to make informed decisions (Tait 1997). Public interest is therefore not necessarily served by the market, but rather by institutionalization, meaning general social acceptability, recognition, and support, and not just from government officials. However, even if the aid effectiveness rhetoric appeals to a segment of the population, it must in the long term reflect a political project broadly embedded in society.

Conclusion

This chapter analyzes the shift in Canadian official development assistance. It finds that some decisions can actually be justified by the promotion of the role of private sector or by NPM's emphasis on government downsizing and program efficiency. However, other decisions result from electoral concerns and a Conservative ideology that pervades development management decisions. This chapter also highlights the complexity of the separation between politics and public administration.

Our analysis suggests that, beyond the rhetorical level, it is indeed difficult, perhaps even impossible, to avoid political intervention in the public service's operational workings. Admittedly, the ideological nature of government decisions has caused tensions within and between sectors among traditional aid actors. However, the arrival of new private actors will create an interesting new dynamic. Will these new players demand more consultation, dialogue, and collaboration between the political and administrative functions? How will they influence aid policy? Will the government be able to set up innovative public policies that cater to society as a whole rather than just its electoral base and interest groups? What will be the concrete impact on the effectiveness of Canadian aid? To that end, other studies must explore the links between the Conservative Party and its electoral base to better understand the relationship between politicians and the electorate.

Acknowledgments

This chapter is an adaptation of an article by François Audet and Olga Navarro-Flores, "Virage dans la gestion de l'aide canadienne publique au développement: tensions et dynamiques d'une nouvelle idéologie," *Canadian Foreign Policy Journal*, vol. 20, no. 1 (2014), pp. 61–72, copyright © Norman Paterson School of International Affairs (NPSIA). It is reprinted by permission of Taylor & Francis Ltd. (www. tandfonline.com) on behalf of NPSIA. The authors and editors are grateful to Taylor & Francis for allowing it to appear here and to David Carment for helping them obtain the permission. The authors also wish to thank Professor Étienne Charbonneau from the UQÀM School of Public Administration for his judicious advice on an earlier draft of this chapter.

Notes

1. In the case of KAIROS, it might also be related to the organization's support of Guatemalan communities protesting the actions of a Canadian mining company.

References

Audet, François, Francis Paquette, and Stéfanie Bergeron. 2013. "Religious Nongovernmental Organisations and Canadian International Aid, 2001–2010: A Preliminary Study." *Canadian Journal of Development Studies*, vol. 34, no. 2: 291–320.

Berger, Ida. 2006. "The Influence of Religion on Philanthropy in Canada." *Voluntas: International Journal of Voluntary and Nonprofit Organizations*, vol. 17, no. 2: 110–27.

Bezes, Philippe. 2009. *Réinventer l'État. Les reformes de l'administration française.* Paris: Gallimard.

Blanchfield, Mike. 2012. "Le Canada meilleur que les États-Unis pour Israël." *La Presse*, February 3. Internet, http://www.lapresse.ca/actualites/quebec-canada/politique-canadienne/201202/03/01-4492516-le-canada-meilleur-que-les-etats-unis-pour-israel.php. Accessed July 23, 2013.

Bozeman, Barry. 2007. *Public Values and Public Interest: Counterbalancing Economic Individualism.* Washington, DC: Georgetown University Press.

CIDA. 2013. "Médias." Internet, http://www.acdi-cida.gc.ca/medias. Accessed November 16, 2013.

Clarke, Gerard. 2006. "Faith Matters: Faith-Based Organisations, Civil Society and International Development." *Journal of International Development*, vol. 18, no. 6: 835–48.

Cochran, Clarke E. 1973. "The Politics of Interests: Philosophy and the Limitations of Science of Politics." *American Journal of Political Science*, vol. 17, no. 4: 745–66.

Collins, Paul, and Nada K. Kakabadse. 2006. "Perils of Religion: Need for Spirituality in the Public Sphere." *Public Administration and Development*, vol. 26, no. 2: 109–21.

Dar, Sadhvi, and Bill Cooke, eds. 2008. *The New Development Management: Critiquing the Dual Modernization.* London: Zed Books.

de Vries, Pieter. 2008. "The Managerialization of Development, the Banalization of its Promise and the Disavowal of Critique as Modernist Illusion." In Sadhvi Dar and Bill Cooke, eds. *The New Development Management: Critiquing the Dual Modernization.* London: Zed Books: 150–77.

Fitzpatrick, Meagan. 2011. "Who is KAIROS, the Organization Bev Oda Did (Not) Give Funding?" *National Post*, April 15. Internet, http://news.nationalpost.com/2011/02/15/who-is-kairos-the-organization-bev-oda-did-not-give-funding/. Accessed July 23, 2013.

Hood, Christopher. 1991. "A Public Management for All Seasons?" *Public Administration*, vol. 69, no. 1: 3–13.

Hood, Christopher. 2011. *The Blame Game: Spin, Bureaucracy, and Self-Preservation in Government.* Princeton, NJ: Princeton University Press.

Jeffrey, Brooke. 2011. "Strained Relations: The Conflict Between the Harper Conservatives and the Federal Bureaucracy." Paper presented at the Canadian Political Science Association Annual Conference. Waterloo, ON, May 17. Internet, http://www.cpsa-acsp.ca/papers-2011/Jeffrey.pdf. Accessed August 14, 2013.

Kim, Pan Suk. 2009. "Introduction: The Aid–Good Governance Conundrum: Searching for More Realistic Discourse." *International Review of Administrative Sciences*, vol. 75, no. 4: 555–63.

Knack, Stephen. 2004. "Does Foreign Aid Promote Democracy?" *International Studies Quarterly*, vol. 48, no. 1: 251–66.

Malloy, Jonathan. 2013. "The Relationship between the Conservative Party of Canada and Evangelicals and Social Conservatives." In James Farney and David Rayside, eds. *Conservatism in Canada*. Toronto: University of Toronto Press: 184–206.

Massie, Justin. 2011. "Un énoncé conservateur de politique étrangère." *Center for International Policy Studies Blog*, November 28. Internet, http://cips.uottawa.ca/un-enonce-conservateur-de-politique-etrangere. Accessed August 14, 2013.

Neumayer, Eric. 2002. "Is Good Governance Rewarded? A Cross-National Analysis of Debt Forgiveness." *World Development*, vol. 30, no. 6: 913–30.

Osborne, David, and Ted Gaebler. 1992. *Reinventing Government: How the Entrepreneurial Spirit is Transforming the Public Sector*. New York: Plume.

Potter, Evan H. 2011. "Religion and Canadian Diplomacy: Promoting Pluralism on the Global Stage." In Patrick James, ed. *Religion, Identity, and Global Governance: Ideas, Evidence, and Practice*. Toronto: University of Toronto Press: 271–91.

Sharp, Mitchell. 1981. "The Role of Mandarins: The Case for Non-Partisan Senior Public Service." *Policy Option*, vol. 2, no. 2: 42–44.

Tait, John. 1997. "A Strong Foundation: Report of the Task Force on Public Service Values and Ethics (the Summary)." *Canadian Public Administration*, vol. 40, no. 1: 1–22.

Thomas, Alan. 1996. "What is Development Management?" *Journal of International Development*, vol. 8, no. 1: 95–110.

Vander Zaag, Ray. 2013. "Canadian Faith-Based Development NGOs and CIDA Funding." *Canadian Journal of Development Studies*, vol. 34, no. 2: 321–47.

SECTION III

CANADA'S ROLE IN INTERNATIONAL DEVELOPMENT ON KEY THEMES

CHAPTER XI

Gender Equality and the "Two CIDAs": Successes and Setbacks, 1976–2013

Rebecca Tiessen

Introduction

For more than four decades, the Canadian International Development Agency (CIDA) played an important role in promoting women's rights and gender equality in development projects around the world, albeit with several setbacks that I document in this chapter. Over the forty-seven years of its existence, CIDA progressed from a "women in development" (WID) approach to a gender equality approach to development programming. However, between 2009 and 2013, two key developments set back the progress CIDA had made in this area: (1) the partial, but significant, erasure of the term "gender equality" from official policies and government speeches when the Harper Conservatives shifted their language to "equality between women and men";[1] and (2) the introduction of the Muskoka Initiative on maternal health, signalling a further retreat from gender equality programming by targeting mothers as "victims" and beneficiaries of development services rather than active agents in the design and implementation of development programs.[2] These initiatives heralded the return of a WID approach, at best, and the increasing prevalence of a charity model under which the government assigns money to solve development problems without the active participation and engagement of local communities in the design and implementation of their own development projects. Under the Harper Conservatives, the government has thus fundamentally retreated from Canadian best practices in the promotion of gender equality.

Notwithstanding these steps backward, mid-level CIDA officials found ways to continue to promote gender equality in their development programs, even if the official discourse of equality between women and men did not allow them to articulate it as such. Of central importance to this analysis is the way this language shift and new policy approach played out in what I refer as the "two CIDAs." An important distinction must be made between the first CIDA, the public face of CIDA and the projection of specific policies or approaches to gender equality by senior CIDA staff and government officials, and the second CIDA, comprised of mid-level professionals working within CIDA, many of whom made gender equality a priority in their work, despite shifting and/or disappearing commitments to gender equality in official policies and programs. As such, mid-level bureaucrats (the "second CIDA") continue to carry the gender equality "torch" in ways that may allow it to survive in the newly formed Department of Foreign Affairs, Trade and Development (DFATD). A record of resilience, combined with staff commitments to promoting gender equality, has the potential to serve as a platform for a renewed commitment to gender equality in DFATD. However, the individual commitments of those working in government rest on their continued, often surreptitious, efforts to support the advancement of gender equality. If these dedicated individuals leave CIDA/DFATD, as several individuals interviewed for this study have indicated is happening, and if they are not replaced with practitioners equally committed to gender equality, it will be increasingly difficult to keep gender equality on the official, and unofficial, agenda of DFATD's development programs.

In order to gain insights into the perspectives and experiences of mid-level bureaucrats, seven interviews were conducted between 2012 and 2013 with individuals who were working or had worked for CIDA or the Department of Foreign Affairs and International Trade (DFAIT) on development programming prior to the merger. Of particular interest to this study was how the shift in language from the internationally accepted term "gender equality" to the Harper government's language of "equality between women and men" translated into practice in development programming generally, and projects designated as part the Conservatives' flagship Muskoka Initiative specifically.

Putting and Keeping Gender on the Agenda

CIDA made a formal commitment to support equality between women and men through a "women in development" (WID) approach in 1976. Leading up to this approach was a growing understanding among CIDA practitioners of how gender relations affected development project success. Quite simply, mid-level CIDA staff members who completed evaluations of development projects in the early 1970s quickly realized that development projects that had not addressed gender relations were likely to fail (interview response). In the 1970s, awareness of gender inequality and the gender division of labour became a central feature of CIDA's development programs, a commitment that was sustained in subsequent decades by dedicated mid-level CIDA staff.

On the international stage, women's contributions to development were also becoming a topic of great interest. By the 1970s, several important feminist critiques had emerged, documenting the failure of development projects to incorporate the needs of women (Boserup 1970, for example). By the mid-1970s, international policy attention shifted to the role of women in development, as evidenced in the 1975 First World Conference on Women in Mexico City and subsequently the UN declaration of the Decade for Women (Karl 1995). This new interest in women in development led to a critique of the presumed gender-neutrality of development policies and programs (Karl 1995). Development had been anything but neutral in terms of its impact on men and women, targeting women for specific reproductive and community-oriented tasks (such as craft-making or food preparation), while the "real" development work of productive activities (such as agricultural projects) were designed with men in mind (Escobar 1995). Over time, failures in development projects brought into question the efficacy of a gender-neutral development approach and CIDA was one important player on the world stage in identifying this important oversight. In recognizing the significance of gender relations to development project success, CIDA issued its own WID strategy in 1976, focusing on providing guidance in the promotion of women's participation in the design and implementation of development projects.

CIDA's WID approach of the 1970s not only acknowledged men's and women's different roles and development impacts, it provided a comprehensive framework for involving women in all stages of the project cycle.[3] Subsequently, in 1981, Canada ratified the UN Convention on the Elimination of All Forms of Discrimination Against Women (CEDAW); in 1983, CIDA established a WID Directorate in order to develop and support the agency's 1984 Policy on Women in Development; and in 1986 CIDA launched the five-year WID Plan of Action (DFATD 2013a). Over time, development practitioners and scholars shifted their focus from women's participation in development to a better understanding of gender inequality: how development paradigms supported unequal treatment of women and men (Mukhopadhyay, Steehouwer, and Wong 2006),[4] and an advanced understanding of gender roles as socially constructed (Karl 1995) and dependent on social, cultural, and political settings (Young 1997). These new feminist insights marked the transition from a WID approach to a Gender and Development (GAD) approach (Jacquette and Staudt 2006).

In 1994, CIDA re-established a WID and Gender Equity Division after a series of reorganizations within the agency (Srineevasan 1999). Following Canada's participation in the Fourth World Conference on Women in Beijing in 1995, CIDA revised and expanded its 1984 WID Policy to include the concept of gender equity, effectively laying the groundwork for the 1995 Policy on Women in Development and Gender Equity (DFATD 2013a). The pivotal commitment to gender equality for CIDA came in 1999 with CIDA's Policy on Gender Equality (GE), which offered guidance on using gender equality as a crosscutting theme and an integral part of all CIDA policies, programs, and projects. The 1999 GE Policy acknowledged that women and men have different perspectives, needs, interests, roles, and resources, and that development programming must address these differences (DFATD 2013b). The hard work that went into developing the GE Policy can be attributed to a commitment to gender equality among mid-level CIDA staff members.

Over time, critiques of CIDA's 1999 policy and programs began to emerge. In particular, CIDA's official evaluation of the implementation of its Gender Equality Policy (Bytown and CAC 2008) and the civil society response by the Informal CSO Working Group on Women's Rights (WGWR 2009) identified a number of areas for improvement within CIDA's gender equality efforts. CIDA was criticized for having a tendency to compartmentalize its gender equality processes; a propensity to spread the responsibility of gender mainstreaming too thinly across the organization; and a lack of clarity from CIDA to its stakeholders and development recipients regarding their gender equality documents and programs.

CIDA staff members and critics alike attributed the shortcomings on the gender front to the lack of funding for GE programming. Indeed, the official evaluation of CIDA's gender policy noted that the agency, while recognizably committed to long-term GE initiatives, had not committed resources to GE-designated programming initiatives that were commensurate with its stated GE policy objectives (Bytown and CAC 2008). It attributed the failure largely to senior management officials who had not made gender equality a priority and so allocated insufficient financial and human resources to GE in programs and projects (Bytown and CAC 2008). The WGWR took stock of this lack of gender funding within CIDA, noting that in 1998–2005 CIDA's total gender equality expenditures represented only 4.7 percent of CIDA-managed official development assistance, combined with an ongoing reduction in GE funding between 1999 and 2006 (WGWR 2009, 5). This trend within CIDA led to a number of lost funding opportunities for NGOs and CSOs intimately connected with CIDA's gender equality initiatives (Plewes and Kerr 2010).

Furthermore, though CIDA attempted to make gender equality a crosscutting issue throughout the organization, it suffered from a lack of consistent leadership at the highest management levels, an inconsistency of expertise and approaches across organizational branches, the multitasking of gender equality specialists and focal points, and the lack of a coherent strategy for rolling out gender equality initiatives, with no concerted plan of action clearly defining roles and responsibilities across all management levels and in the field (Bytown and CAC, 2008). CIDA, like many international agencies and development organizations, was criticized for integrating gender equality – or gender mainstreaming – "everywhere but nowhere" (Tiessen 2007). Maneepong and Stiles (2007) note in their evaluation of CIDA project monitoring that some of the major challenges of integrating gender included ingrained institutional attitudes that regarded GE as unimportant. They found that senior managers failed to appreciate the importance of gender dimensions and achieved relatively little in advancing women's equal participation in decision making and reducing gender inequities in access to – and control over – resources. Similarly, Kelleher and Stuart (2008) identify CIDA's organizational culture as a significant barrier to progress on gender equality.

Despite the committed efforts of many CIDA staff members, implementing short-term, technical projects rarely resulted in the agency addressing the political and attitudinal changes necessary for advancing gender equality. Nonetheless, the 1999 GE Policy was noteworthy for its advanced work in promoting gender analysis as a crosscutting tool for project design, since it helped planners identify constraints and structure projects so that objectives could be met and measured (CIDA 1999). Critiques of CIDA's GE policy, however, argued that attention to GE weakened during implementation (Bytown and CAC 2008). This "front-ending" of CIDA's interest in gender, combined with a failure to allocate sufficient resources for the promotion of gender equality, led some NGOs to lessen their focus on gender equality throughout the process as well, adding to the difficulty of effectively implementing CIDA's gender equality initiatives (Kelleher and Stuart 2008).

A second important set of critiques of CIDA's development programs centres on the government's obsession with results-based management (RBM), formulaic approaches, and technical fixes, rather than tackling the root causes of gender inequality (see Tiessen and Tuckey forthcoming). As such, the focus on aid effectiveness through RBM does not always equip practitioners to deal with complications arising from difficult cases, nor the scope to create programs with gender equality as the outcome. Some of the problems CIDA officials encountered in the employment of RBM included an "oversimplification and misunderstanding of how development outcomes occur and confusion over accountability for results; overemphasis on results that are easy to quantify at the expensive of less tangible, but no less important outcomes; ... and mechanical use of results indicators for reporting purposes in ways that fail to feed into strategic thinking and organizational practices" (Lavergne 2002, 3–4). CIDA had placed a greater focus on development results than on processes, inputs, and efforts (Bazinet, Sequeira, and Delahanty 2006), a trend that has been highlighted in CIDA's own review of its gender policy and frameworks as well (Bytown and CAC 2008). In spite of the challenges brought about by an RBM approach to development, mid-level CIDA officials fought to keep gender equality on the agenda by making RBM work in their favour. If the focus of senior government officials was on results, then CIDA mid-level management staff members were able to find ways to make gender equality a priority by ensuring that gender equality was an outcome of development programs (interview with CIDA official).

The challenges faced by mid-level CIDA officials took a new turn in 2009 as they slowly realized that the language of gender equality had largely evaporated and been replaced with "equality between women and men." The shift in language can be traced to Canadian ministers' speeches and official government material beginning in 2006 (see Carrier and Tiessen, 2012). Mid-level CIDA officials were told by senior managers at CIDA to replace the term "gender equality" with "equality between women and men" (Collins 2009; Tiessen and Carrier 2013), and reports were returned with "gender equality" erased and replaced with "equality between women and men." A more obvious and concerted attempt to make the shift in language more clear occurred in 2009 at a time when the Conservative government was attempting to distance itself from language it deemed too similar to that of the Liberal Party. It changed several terms used in foreign policy material, replacing "child soldiers" with "children in armed conflict," removing "humanitarian" from "international humanitarian law" and changing "gender-based violence" to "violence against women." The new language signalled more than a departure from Liberal Party terminology; it demonstrated a move away from international discourse widely used and accepted within the United Nations and constituted a departure from Canadian best practices in the promotion of gender equality (see Carrier and Tiessen 2012). The change in language also created a dilemma for mid-level professionals working at CIDA who understood the value of the policy and practice of gender equality. The shift was sufficient to cause some CIDA staff to leave the agency in protest.[5] Other staff members at CIDA expressed their confusion over the change in language and resisted the policy shift in their day-to-day work. While the official CIDA no longer addressed gender equality, some mid-level CIDA officials continued to promote GE in their work. I examine this resistance and dedication in the section that follows.

The Contributions of Mid-Level CIDA Officials to the Promotion of Gender Equality

Despite the challenges noted above, CIDA continued to play an important role in promoting gender equality in development programs, and many mid-level CIDA officials kept pressing for gender equality in development outcomes. When asked whether host communities were familiar with Canada's shift in language from "gender equality" to "equality between men and women," interview participants noted that the shift in language was not apparent to development beneficiaries. Mid-level CIDA staff considered the shift significant, nonetheless, because of how the discourse translates (or has the potential to translate) into practice. Interviews with current and former CIDA staff members highlighted the struggles they faced in promoting gender equality in their work, while reporting in a language of "equality between women and men." Only one of the interview participants said the change in language had little impact on how things were carried out. "It's just a word, it's just wording. It didn't change anything … [in their own work]." This interview participant notes that it did, however, affect how CIDA staff members wrote up their memos to the minister, but they remained committed to doing "the same type of programming," even if it had to be done surreptitiously. This CIDA official's comments and those of other CIDA mid-management staff confirmed that the "two CIDAs" were indeed at work.

However, the shift in language to "equality between women and men" was not the only challenge facing CIDA practitioners. Under the Harper Conservatives, projects that Bev Oda approved while minister "were things that were specifically for women" (interview participant) and were not about promoting gender equality. Other discussions with CIDA officials confirmed this observation. Anything that had to do with gender equality sat on the minister's desk for long periods of time without obtaining approval for funding (interview participant). Other studies have noted that removing the words "gender equality" from funding proposals was essential if NGOs wanted to improve their chances of having their projects approved (Caplan 2010; Carrier and Tiessen 2012; Plewes and Kerr 2010). The kinds of projects that CIDA funded under the Conservative government were those that demonstrated service delivery and outputs such as "health care services to so many women, getting so many girls to school … [because] that's something you can count and it was what could be promoted and approved" (interview participant). Several interview participants noted that the Harper Conservatives did not support projects that might not have numbers attached, such as gender mainstreaming or capacity building, because they believed these approaches to development would not resonate with Canadian taxpayers. In a related critique, a former CIDA staff member reflected on the short-term thinking that characterized the political decision making of senior officials. Under previous governments, there was a higher tolerance for transformational projects that would take fifteen years to complete. The Harper government did not want transformation in terms of gender equality; instead, as the interview participants noted, it was interested in measuring progress and outputs and meeting predetermined short-term goals (a charity model), rather than the development transformation aimed at increased participation and empowerment of marginalized people (Black and Tiessen 2007).

Other mid-level CIDA officials remarked that there were few people in senior management advocating gender equality and that expertise on gender equality was not a requirement for them. A lack of leadership on gender equality means that the language could easily change with little official resistance. However, a commitment to GE among those who deliver development programs kept the implementation of gender equality a priority in many development initiatives. Some programs, however, faced greater difficulty keeping gender equality on the agenda. The Maternal, Newborn and Child Health Initiative (MNCH, also known as the Muskoka Initiative) is one such example. At around the same time that Canada witnessed a shift in language from "gender equality" to "equality between women and men," the Muskoka Initiative became a touchstone of the Harper government, which introduced the MNCH program at the Muskoka G8 Summit in 2010. Initially, Canada's commitments to the initiative were vague. Over time, the commitment to nutrition for women and babies became one of the key projects in this program, with much less attention to sexual and reproductive health education, family planning, abortion, and treatment for victims of sexual and gender-based violence (for which Canada had expressed a commitment in its National Action Plan on Women, Peace and Security[6]).

The Muskoka Initiative became highly contentious, characterized by selective praise for its efforts to address the fifth Millennium Development Goal (MDG), namely to improve maternal health and to increase health services available to women and newborns, and by deep criticism for its failure to adequately address sexual and reproductive health, pregnancy prevention, and abortion (see Carrier and Tiessen 2012). Among the criticisms was the gender essentialism that exemplified the MNCH programs and, in effect, conceptualized mothers and pregnant women as helpless victims. Some even argued that the initiative had little to do with women, let alone gender equality, treating women like "walking wombs" (interview participant) rather than active agents in the development of policies, programs, and projects to promote improved maternal health options and to address the reasons why women are unable to access maternal health services. The Muskoka Initiative further solidified the shift from a development model to a charity approach, as it lacks any direct reference to gender equality and fails to address root causes of women's disadvantaged position in society relative to men, factors that might indicate whether or not women will access health services in the first place. Brodie and Bakker (2008) refer to a trend towards the "progressive disappearance of the gendered subject, both in discourse and practice," a process we have witnessed in Canada's foreign policy commitments since 2006 under the Harper Conservatives (Carrier and Tiessen 2012). In sum, the Muskoka Initiative failed to penetrate the gendered societal norms that prevent women from accessing health services even when they are available and has limited potential for improving the quality of life for women who still have little or no say over reproductive rights and child spacing. A focus on gender equality in development programming has the potential to correct for this shortcoming by involving education programs and including women in the design and implementation of development projects. While some CIDA mid-level officials have been able to continue to address gender inequality in their day-to-day work with development communities, several of the participants noted that the MNCH initiative made it exceedingly difficult to address gender issues, since the MNCH projects did not lend themselves to gender equality approaches.

Conclusion: Several Steps Backwards

The shift in language from "gender equality" to "equality between women and men" between 2009 and 2013 provides an interesting case of a diminishing commitment to internationally recognized development priorities such as gender equality. As the Harper Conservatives set themselves apart from previous governments by changing the policy rhetoric and announcing new initiatives such as the Muskoka Initiative, a fundamental shift from a development model to a charity approach can be observed—one that is concerned with "saving women" through modern, technological advances without understanding the underlying causes of gender inequality and how they contribute to women's reproductive health.

It is perhaps both ironic and fitting that CIDA's demise has coincided with a return to the language of equality between women and men – a language that reflects more of a 1970s WID approach. However, CIDA's efforts to promote gender equality, such as the pioneering work of CIDA's GE policy in 1999 and the struggles of mid-level CIDA officials to keep gender equality on the agenda since the early 1970s, are significant and worthy of celebration. Certainly, CIDA has faced numerous challenges in its efforts to promote gender equality over the decades, many of which are documented in this chapter.

It is not clear, however, how gender equality (or equality between women and men) will play out in the context of the newly amalgamated Department of Foreign Affairs, Trade and Development (DFATD). As this chapter has demonstrated, there has been a retreat from gender equality efforts, as evidenced in two key Conservative government initiatives between 2009 and 2013: (1) a deliberate and notable shift from the internationally recognized language of gender equality to equality between women and men; and (2) a move away from development programming to charity projects through the Muskoka Initiative on maternal health, for which gender issues are ignored and pregnant women are treated as the objects of policy attention rather than active agents in the design and implementation of projects. Both of these constitute a step back to WID thinking and language at best.

In spite of these regressive policy initiatives driven by senior bureaucrats (or the "first CIDA"), mid-level CIDA staff members (the "second CIDA") demonstrated a longstanding commitment to the promotion of gender equality and continued to promote gender equality in their work even when RBM tools, bureaucratic obstacles, or shifts in official policy approaches threatened their efforts. This record of resilience, combined with staff members' commitments to promoting gender equality, has the potential to serve as a platform for a renewed commitment to gender equality in DFATD. However, organizational restructuring at DFATD and the exodus of CIDA personnel who have made gender equality their life's work will make it increasingly difficult to keep gender on the official and unofficial agendas of DFATD's development programs. Furthermore, the changing landscape of Conservative programs that increasingly promote charity towards mothers and children (such as the MNCH), rather than human rights, equality, and development, is narrowing the programmatic scope within which committed staff members are able to promote gender equality. The events between 2009 and 2013 under the Harper Conservatives, therefore, highlight the erosion of CIDA's best practices in the promotion of gender equality.

Acknowledgments

I would like to thank the CIDA/DFATD staff members who agreed to be interviewed for this study under condition of anonymity. I also want to thank Krystel Carrier and Sarah Tuckey for their excellent research assistance and the Social Sciences and Humanities Research Council for providing funding to carry out this research. I am also deeply indebted to Diana Rivington for her helpful comments on an earlier version of this chapter and for many insightful conversations about the successes and setbacks in CIDA's efforts to promote gender equality in development.

Notes

1. While references to gender equality can still be found on the Department of Foreign Affairs, Trade and Development (DFATD) website and in some official documents, the language of "equality between women and men" became the official discourse of the Harper Conservatives in 2009. This shift in language was remarkable and significant from a foreign policy perspective, for practitioners who struggled to report on gender (in)equality without using the term "gender" and for translating policies into programs. However, the discursive turn was not exhaustive, and by 2013 the government reintroduced some references to gender equality into official documents. This chapter focuses on the implications of this change in approach under the Harper Conservatives, both discursively and in terms of specific policy and program commitments, such as the MNCH initiative.
2. It is important to note that the Muskoka Initiative and subsequent speeches and policy documents rarely, if ever, use the term "women" on its own, referring instead to "mothers" or "pregnant women."
3. Interviews with former CIDA staff members who were involved in the early years of CIDA's WID programs.
4. Clark-Kazak (this volume) provides additional background to – and a critical reflection on – the WID approach.

5. Claims of individuals leaving CIDA over the change in language from gender equality to equality between men and women arose on several occasions. Interview participants noted they knew colleagues who had left the agency over this discourse shift. In informal discussions, former CIDA staff members and consultants working on gender equality also said they knew colleagues who had left CIDA for this reason.
6. DFAIT spearheaded Canada's National Action Plan on Women, Peace and Security, but the latter failed to address the reason women and girls are at risk of insecurity and thus lacked coherent gender equality analysis.

References

Bazinet, Lucie, Tamara Sequeira, and Julie Delahanty. 2006. "Promoting Institutional Change: CIDA's Framework for Assessing Gender Equality Results." *Development*, vol. 49, no. 1: 104–7.

Black, David R., and Rebecca Tiessen. 2007. "The Canadian International Development Agency: New Policies, Old Problems." *Canadian Journal of Development Studies*, vol. 28, no. 2: 191–212.

Boserup, Esther. 1970. *Women's Role in Economic Development*. London: Earthscan.

Bytown Consulting and CAC International. 2008. *Evaluation of CIDA's Implementation of Its Policy on Gender Equality: Executive Report*. Gatineau, QC: CIDA.

Caplan, Gerald. 2010. "The Harper Government, Women's Rights and the Cost of Speaking Out." *Globe and Mail*, June 4. Internet, http://www.theglobeandmail.com/news/politics/the-harper-government-womens-rights-and-the-cost-of-speaking-out/article1592858/. Accessed June 29, 2010.

Carrier, Krystel, and Rebecca Tiessen. 2012. "Women and Children First: Maternal Health and the Silence of Gender in Canadian Foreign Policy." In Heather Smith and Claire Turenne Sjolander, eds. *Canada in the World: Perspectives on Canadian Foreign Policy*. Don Mills, ON: Oxford University Press: 183–200.

CIDA. 1999. *CIDA's Policy on Gender Equality*. Hull, QC: CIDA.

CIDA. 2010. *Equality Between Women and Men*. Internet, http://www.acdi-cida.gc.ca/acdi-cida/ACDI-CIDA.nsf/eng/JUD-31192610-JXF and http://www.acdi-cida.gc.ca/equality. Accessed June 22, 2010 and September 26, 2013.

DFATD. 2013a. *Gender Equality—Chronology, Selected Key Dates*. Internet, http://www.acdi-cida.gc.ca/acdi-cida/acdi-cida.nsf/eng/REN-218124915-PBF. Accessed September 26, 2013.

DFATD. 2013b. *CIDA's Policy on Gender Equality.* Internet, http://www.acdi-cida.gc.ca/acdi-cida/ACDI-CIDA.nsf/eng/EMA-218123616-NN9. Accessed September 26, 2013.

Escobar, Arturo. 1995. *Encountering Development: The Making and Unmaking of the Third World.* Princeton, NJ: Princeton University Press.

Hales, Jennifer. 2007. "Rhetoric and Reality: World Bank and CIDA Gender Policies." *Convergence,* vol. 40, nos. 1–2: 147–69.

Jaquette, Jane S., and Kathleen Staudt. 2006. "Women, Gender, and Development." In Jane S. Jaquette and Gale Summerfield, eds. *Women and Gender Equity in Development Theory and Practice: Institutions, Resources, and Mobilization.* Durham, NC: Duke University Press: 17–52.

Karl, Marilee. 1995. *Women and Empowerment: Participation and Decision Making.* London: Zed Books.

Kelleher, David, and Rieky Stuart. 2008. *Gender Equality, Promise to Practice: A Study of the Progress toward Gender Equality of CCIC Members.* Ottawa: Canadian Council for International Co-operation.

Lavergne, Réal. 2002. *Results-Based Management and Accountability for Enhanced Aid Effectiveness: A Reference Paper for CIDA Officers Engaged in Capacity Development and Program-Based Approaches Such as SWAps.* Hull, QC: CIDA.

Maneepong, Chuthatip, and J. Mark Stiles. 2007. "Navigating Uncharted Waters: Project Monitoring at CIDA." *Canadian Journal of Program Evaluation,* vol. 22, no. 1: 177–94.

Mukhopadhyay, Maitrayee, Gerard Steehouwer, and Franz Wong. 2006. *Politics of the Possible – Gender Mainstreaming and Organisational Change: Experiences from the Field.* Amsterdam: KIT.

Plewes, Betty, and Joanna Kerr. 2010. "Politicizing, undermining gender equality." *Embassy,* May 5. Internet, http://embassymag.ca/page/print-page/equality-05-05-2010. Accessed June 29, 2010.

Srineevasan, Gauri. 1999. "Review Essay: Aid and Ebb Tide: A History of CIDA and Canadian Development Assistance." *Canadian Journal of Development Studies,* vol. 20, no. 2: 403–12.

Tiessen, Rebecca. 2007. *Everywhere/Nowhere: Gender Mainstreaming in Development Agencies.* Bloomfield, CT: Kumarian Press.

Tiessen, Rebecca, and Sarah Tuckey. Forthcoming. "Losing Gender along the Way: CIDA, Gender Mainstreaming and the Securitization of Development." In Rosalind Warner, ed. *Ethics and Security in Canadian Foreign Policy.* Vancouver: UBC Press.

Tiessen, Rebecca, and Krystel Carrier. 2013. "The Erasure of 'Gender' in Canadian Foreign Policy and Why It Matters." Paper presented at the International Studies Association Conference, San Francisco, CA, April 3–6.

WGWR. 2009. *Strengthening Canada's International Leadership in the Promotion of Gender Equality: A Civil Society Response to the Evaluation of the Implementation of CIDA's 1999 Policy on Gender Equality.* Ottawa: Informal CSO Working Group on Women's Rights. Internet, http://www.ccic.ca/_files/en/what_we_do/002_gender_cida_analysis_cso_response.pdf. Accessed November 3, 2013.

Young, Kate. 1997. "Gender and Development." In Nalini Visvanathan, Lynn Duggan, Laurie Nisonoff, and Nan Wiegersma, eds. *The Women, Gender and Development Reader.* London: Zed Books: 51–54.

CHAPTER XII

From "Children-in-Development" to Social Age Mainstreaming in Canada's Development Policy and Programming? Practice, Prospects and Proposals

Christina Clark-Kazak

Introduction

Despite the importance of age and generation in development processes, very few development agencies attempt to mainstream age in the same way as they do gender. The United Nations High Commissioner for Refugees (UNHCR) is the only development actor that has an explicit age, gender, and diversity mainstreaming policy. Among bilateral donors, only Canada and Australia have thematic policies directly focused on children. Canada's emphasis on children and youth as a priority area in its international development policy and programming provides a potential point of departure for innovation and leadership on age issues. However, a discourse analysis of Canada's *Child and Youth Strategy* indicates that it is primarily based on a "children-in-development" approach. This approach is limiting because it overlooks children and young people's important development roles and tends to "target" them in isolation from broader social relationships, structures, and processes. This chapter proposes ways that Canada could leverage its well-established political commitment to children and aid (which spans a decade and both Liberal and Conservative governments) to more effectively mainstream age and generation issues into its development policy and programming. In this way, social age mainstreaming offers Canada an opportunity to carve out a new leadership role, especially in the context of the new Department of Foreign Affairs, Trade and Development.

The Importance of Age in Development Processes

Age is central to development processes for several reasons. First, demographic realities vary significantly with development context. While least developed countries have largely youthful populations, the most developed areas have a greater percentage of older people (UNPD 2013). For example, according to the most recent report by the United Nations Population Division (2013, 30), the median age in more developed countries is 40.5, compared with a median age of 19.7 in the least developed countries.

Second, for biological or social reasons, people of different ages may experience poverty differently (Sumner 2010). For example, children under the age of five have specific nutritional needs that may not be adequately met in contexts of poverty. At the other end of the spectrum, in some cultures male elders are given preferential treatment in collective meals, allowing them to eat more and better quality food than younger and female members of the same household.

Third, development initiatives have differential impacts on people at different stages of the life course. For example, León and Younger (2007) and Himaz (2008) have assessed the impact of grants to poor households on children's health in Ecuador and Sri Lanka, respectively. They conclude that increases in household income do not necessarily translate into better health outcomes for all members of a family. Indeed, Degraff and Levison (2009) argue that development projects that provide employment for women may result in increased child labour. This finding is reinforced by Wydick's (1999) study of the perverse impact of microenterprise initiatives on children's schooling in Guatemala, due to what he calls a "family-labor-substitution effect."

Fourth, intergenerational and family relationships can influence, and be influenced by, development policies and programs. For example, Ikels's (2006) research analyzes changing intergenerational relationships in China, where modernization and population ageing are occurring simultaneously. In some African contexts, the introduction of formal schooling has undermined the value children and young people attach to traditional forms of knowledge espoused by older generations. This has resulted in renegotiated power relations between young and old (Abbink 2005). Finally, in cross-cultural development contexts, groups and individuals attribute varied social meanings to different stages of the life cycle and hold diverging beliefs about the roles deemed beneficial and appropriate for different generations (James and Prout 1997a; Vera-Sanso 2006). These socially constructed approaches to age can have an impact on development projects and, in turn, can be changed by development processes.

Conceptual and Theoretical Framework

Drawing on the importance of variations in social constructions of age across time and place, I have developed the concept of social age to complement the predominant focus on chronological age. Many development agencies use the latter, based on international legal documents, such as the Convention on the Rights of the Child, which defines a child as a human being under the age of eighteen. Chronological age is administratively efficient, as it provides a clear eligibility criterion for inclusion in (and exclusion from) development programming. It is also a convenient, albeit imperfect, proxy for biological development: length of time of existence gives some indication of human development, despite individual variations.

However, a large body of scholarly literature critiques this dominant emphasis on chronological age in development policy and programming for a number of reasons. First, given non-existent or inadequate birth registration in many developing contexts, people may not know their exact chronological age. This fact may also reflect cultural norms in which chronological age is less important than biological or social markers of ageing, such as puberty and marriage. Many scholars have thus provided a second critique by emphasizing the social construction of age across time (Ariès 1979; Cunningham 1995) and place (Boyden 1997; James and Prout 1997b). Third, chronological age implies homogeneity, despite the diversity across individuals and groups (Rogoff 1990; Woodhead 1997). For example, the under-eighteen definition enshrined in the Convention on the Rights of the Child lumps together individuals at very different stages of development: from an infant to post-pubescent young person who may already be married with children of his or her own, and thus socially and culturally considered to be an adult. Similarly, many definitions of older people set fifty-five or sixty-five as the threshold, despite low life expectancies in many developing countries.

Is it possible to reconcile these seemingly opposing conceptions of age within aid programming on the one hand and scholarly literature on the other? I suggest that one way forward is to make an analytical distinction similar to sex and gender. While sex refers to the biological realities of being male, female, or intersex, gender refers to the socially constructed roles and attributes attached to males, females, and those who identify as neither. Similarly, chronological age is an imperfect proxy for biological development. It should be complemented by an additional analysis of social age: the socially constructed roles and attributes ascribed to different stages of the life course, as well as intra- and inter-generational relationships (see Clark-Kazak 2009b).

As I have argued elsewhere (Clark-Kazak 2009b), social age mainstreaming in development policy and practice would involve a comprehensive analysis of age and generational issues. The first step entails gathering basic demographic information, including chronological age, biological development indicators such as infant mortality and life expectancy, and marital, familial, and employment status (since these are important social age markers). This age-disaggregated data should be collected for the population as a whole, as well as for the specific development issue (e.g., education, health, labour, or sanitation). Second, social age analysis involves an investigation into the social meanings ascribed to biological human development and chronological age. What are the culturally specific definitions of childhood, youth, adulthood, and old age? Are there socially prescribed roles for different generations that may be codified in norms or laws? A third element of social age analysis entails an exploration into how biological and socially constructed differences may affect differential experiences and impacts of development initiatives for children, young people, adults, and elders. Fourth, social age analysis involves an evaluation of the generational division of labour. Productive and reproductive roles will also be informed by other subject positions, particularly gender and class. The division of labour is important in understanding power structures within a given community, as well as the differential opportunities and time available to participate in various development activities. Finally, social age analysis requires an understanding of dynamic intra- and inter-generational relationships. These relationships provide the context for development initiatives, which, in turn, may provoke changes in these relationships, as discussed above.

Social age analysis has the potential to make development initiatives more effective and less discriminatory by taking into account the physical and socially constructed differences that may affect poor people's experiences of poverty and development initiatives. Just as gender analysis should be undertaken even when – and, perhaps, *especially* when – a development project is not focused on sex or gender, similarly a social age analysis is a necessary part of development programming and planning. For instance, in many parts of the world, children are primarily responsible for fetching water. However, when deciding the location of water sources, development agencies rarely consider the physical development of children, nor the socially constructed power relations that may make children vulnerable to physical and sexual violence. Instead, water points are often placed far away from areas of high population density for sanitary reasons. This isolation could exacerbate the physical and socially constructed vulnerabilities that children encounter when fetching water. An age-based analysis would help to identify these issues so that they could be factored into decisions about the location of water sources.

Canada among Aid Agencies: A Comparative Analysis of Approaches to Age and Development

Indeed, despite the importance of social age in development processes, few aid agencies have an explicit or implicit policy on age. This contrasts with well-established gender mainstreaming efforts in all aid agencies.[1] My research indicates that only the United Nations High Commissioner for Refugees (UNHCR) has an explicit age component to its age, gender, and diversity mainstreaming (AGDM) policy. Established in 2004, UNHCR's AGDM aims "to ensure a broad participatory, rights- and community-based approach within UNHCR operations, based on an analysis of protection risks from the standpoint of age, gender and other social factors" (Thomas and Beck 2010, 1). It entails a fundamental conceptual and behavioural shift in the way UNHCR does its programming, and has only been partially successful (Clark-Kazak 2009a; Groves 2004; Thomas and Beck 2010).

Among bilateral development cooperation agencies, there is no well-developed approach to age. I have undertaken a comprehensive survey of all bilateral donors who are members of OECD/DAC. For each country, I identified direct policies or thematic priorities related to age, as well as indirect policies or priorities (such as primary education, which can be assumed to be targeted mostly at children). This analysis revealed that only Australia and Canada have specific policies on children, with Australia focusing on child protection in the delivery of aid, rather than in development programming, as in the Canadian approach.

Within the Millennium Development Goals (MDGs), there is also a lack of systematic attention to social age across the life cycle. Two goals have an implicit and explicit focus on children (respectively, MDG 3 "Universal Primary Education" and MDG 4: "Reduce Child Mortality"). Similarly, only two targets implicitly and explicitly mention children and young people (Target 3A, "Eliminate gender disparity in primary and secondary education"), and Target 1B, "Achieve full and productive employment and decent work for all, including women and young people"). Other generations are invisible in the MDGs.

A Decade of "Children in Development" in Canada's Aid Policy and Programming

Since 2000, Canada has had an explicit focus on children in its aid programming, making it a priority that has been upheld by both Liberal and Conservative governments over a sustained period of time. The Canadian International Development Agency (CIDA) document, *CIDA's Social Development Priorities: A Framework for Action*, listed child protection as one of four social development priorities (CIDA 2000). In 2002, these social development priorities were retained, along with gender as a crosscutting theme, in *Canada Making a Difference in the World: A Policy Statement on Strengthening Aid Effectiveness* (CIDA 2002). The next major policy statement, *Canada's International Policy Statement*, dropped child protection as a priority (Foreign Affairs Canada 2005). However, in 2009, a news release on a "new effective approach to Canadian aid" resurrected a focus on "children and youth" (CIDA 2009). The details of this are spelled out in the CIDA strategy entitled, "Securing the Future of Children and Youth" (CIDA 2010), which identified three areas of focus: (a) improve child and maternal health; (b) quality education and learning opportunities; and (c) rights and protection of children and youth. This section highlights the key findings of a discourse analysis of this strategy.

While Canada's focus on children and youth is somewhat innovative in the development cooperation sphere, it is still limiting. An analysis of the Children and Youth Strategy illustrates how Canada has adopted a "children in development" approach. I first undertook a content analysis to determine the frequency and location of the following words: child(ren), girl, boy, youth, young, adolescent, teenage, adult, family, generation, age, parent, mother, father, elder, old. Then, I employed grounded theory to identify the dominant themes that emerged from the document. Not surprisingly, "child(ren)" has the highest word count in Canada's *Children and Youth Strategy*, appearing eighty-six times in the seven-page document (not including references to the title of the document). The second most frequently used term is "youth," which appears thirty-nine times, almost exclusively in the formulation "children and youth," as in the title of the strategy. Indeed, there are only five references to "youth" that are not preceded by children. All of these references pertain to risks of young people turning to violence (CIDA 2010, 1, 7) and educational and learning opportunities for youth (CIDA 2010, 5–6) in order for them to become "productive members of their societies" (CIDA 2010, 7). "Young" appears nine times: five times to describe young women, twice to refer to young men and twice to refer to young people. "Adolescent" is used only once in reference to females. This gender difference is also apparent when analyzing the frequency of reference to girls (twenty-three times) versus boys (twice).

Other generations are much less represented in the document. "Adult" is mentioned only once – and this in reference to children "grow[ing] into active and productive young adults" (CIDA 2010, 1). There are no references to elders or older people. Parents are mentioned only three times: in relation to transmission of HIV (CIDA 2010, 1), in reference to children and young people's future potential as "better parents" (CIDA 2010, 5), and as potential barriers to girls' schooling (CIDA 2010, 5). The document contains no references to "father." In contrast, mothers are mentioned nine times, always pertaining to health issues, including mother-to-child transmission of HIV/AIDS, maternal health, and benefits to children of healthy mothers.

Several themes emerge from a close reading of the document. First, children and young people are most often represented as "human becomings" (Qvortrup 1994). In other words, the strategy emphasizes their future potential as adults, but also the risks they could pose to society if they do not receive education and adequate health care. At many points in the document, the rationale for Canada's focus on children is explicitly linked to future development, as in the following statement: "Investing in children and youth today is investing in the future stability, quality of life, and economic self-sufficiency of developing countries" (CIDA 2010, 2). It pays very little attention to children and young people's *current* development roles. In this way, it instrumentalizes children and young people, under-estimates their agency, and presents them primarily as a vehicle for future development. This is reinforced by the three priority areas. The strategy presents education and health as social development goods to be provided to children. In relation to the "safety and security" priority, children are conceptualized as victims in need of protection, instead of as active rights-holders.

Second, there is a gender bias in the document towards females. On one hand, this could be intended to recognize and counteract gender discrimination against girls in many developing countries. However, it also ironically reinforces negative stereotypes. For example, in presenting the priority given to maternal health, the document almost always explicitly links mothers' well-being to children's benefits, as in the following statement: "Maternal health is vital to the survival, health, and development of children. When a mother dies in childbirth, her child is four times more likely to die also" (CIDA 2010, 2). This extract implies that women's health is important primarily because of their biological reproductive roles, rather than as a development priority in and of itself. As Tiessen (this volume) argues, some people believe that Canada's approach to maternal health "had little to do with women, let alone gender equal-ity, treating women like 'walking wombs' ... rather than active agents in the development of policies, programs, and projects to promote improved maternal health options and to address the reasons why women are unable to access maternal health services."

Similarly, Canada's Children and Youth Strategy links invest-ments in girls to broader community development objectives, rather than presenting them as important for girls' sakes alone: "Investments in ... young women have a ripple effect, reaching their families, their communities, and their future children" (CIDA 2010, 2). Moreover, the document's focus on girls under-emphasizes the risks and challenges boys face. For example, it states, "72 mil-lion children – 54 percent of them girls – still do not have access to schools" (CIDA 2010, 2). While it is significant that more girls than boys face barriers to formal schooling, we should not overlook the over 33 million boys who, according to the document, are not accessing education.

Third, there is very little attention to intergenerational relationships in the strategy. This is indicated quantitatively in the very few references to parents, and the lack of references to fathers and grandparents. Similarly, children and young people are often presented in isolation, without recognizing the importance of familial and community relationships. While it is somewhat understandable that children and young people are the focus of the document, given the priority theme, it does not make developmental sense (in both meanings of the term) to exclude other generations from policy and programming.

Canada's Children and Youth Strategy thus adopts a "children in development" approach, which has shortcomings similar to those of the "women in development" era of the 1970s. At that time, following the publication of Ester Boserup's (1970) research on the gendered division of labour, "women in development" (WID) emerged in development theory and practice to describe a concern with "integrating" women into ongoing development initiatives (Kabeer 1994; Rathberger 1990). While the WID approach was an improvement on earlier development practices that ignored women altogether, it focused attention exclusively on women, rather than on gender norms and relationships between women and men. Moreover, WID approaches encouraged greater implication of women in productive work, ignoring the reproductive roles that women already undertook, thereby contributing to their "double burden."

Similarly, Canada's "children-in-development" approach is limiting for a number of reasons. First, it only takes into account children, rather than a broader focus on age across the life course. Indeed, elderly people are not represented in the strategy at all, despite their important development roles and differential needs. This is particularly problematic in the context of an ageing world population and projections that developing countries will experience population ageing more rapidly than their developed counterparts (UNPD 2013, 6). Second, while the document takes an important first step in recognizing the significance of children and young people, it tends to target them in isolation. While some child-specific programming may be necessary, it can result in a ghettoization – rather than a systematic mainstreaming – of children's issues. Moreover, there is little recognition that children are already part of development processes and that they are connected to other generations through relationships and social structures. Relatedly, a third shortcoming of the "children-in-development" approach is that it does not recognize and address unequal power relations within and between generations. This is partially associated with the lack of agency attributed to children and young people in the document.

Towards Social Age Mainstreaming?

Despite the shortcomings of Canada's current "children in development" approach, it could be a first step towards social age mainstreaming, just as WID eventually gave way to gender mainstreaming. Could Canada exhibit leadership on age issues as it did on gender and development in the 1970s and 1980s (despite Canada's recent backtracking on this issue – see Tiessen, this volume)? This section explores the opportunities and challenges of this approach, especially in the context of CIDA's amalgamation with the Department of Foreign Affairs and International Trade.

This latter process provides both an opportunity and a challenge. On the one hand, age mainstreaming requires "changing the way one does business," as the former High Commissioner for Refugees commented in relation to UNHCR's age, gender, and diversity mainstreaming (cited in Thomas and Beck 2010, 2). The fact that the structure of Canadian aid is changing may provide opportunities for reform. On the other hand, if Canada's development policy and programming becomes too aligned with trade and strategic diplomatic interests, the impetus for social age mainstreaming may be lost.

Within the broader development community, there are opportunities for Canadian leadership. First, Canada has one of only two aid agencies with a child-specific strategy. It has also provided some push towards UNHCR's AGDM strategy, given Canada's role on the UNHCR Executive Committee. Second, while limited, the MDGs do contain some age-specific targets (as highlighted above), which could provide some opportunities to leverage further action on age issues. An additional opportunity lies in the fact that Canada is legally mandated to undertake a gender assessment in all of its initiatives. Given the fact that social age analysis is inspired by gender mainstreaming, it could be possible to save some time and resources by undertaking gender and social age assessments together. That being said, it will require more resources and innovation, which may be difficult to muster, especially in a political climate of austerity. Moreover, it should be recognized that Canadian aid workers may already suffer from "mainstreaming fatigue," as they are faced with integrating many different elements – including gender, environment, conflict-sensitivity, and HIV/AIDS analysis – under time and resource constraints.[2]

Indeed, there are many critiques of mainstreaming in development policy. Although intended to effect deep organizational and structural change (Hartsock 1981), mainstreaming may actually depoliticize radical agendas by incorporating "language" into technocratic planning and programming without changing the reality on the ground (Hankivsky 2005). Mainstreaming has also been critiqued for its "fuzzy" approach (Booth and Bennett 2002), resulting in mixed or counterproductive application in practice, or being "everywhere but nowhere" (Tiessen 2007). In some cases, gender is simply equated with "women" without adequate attention to "the wider context of power relations caused by societally defined ... gender roles" (Groves 2005, 7; see also Clark-Kazak 2009a). Finally, the complexity of mainstreaming requires a long-term, multi-staged process (Donaghy 2004; Moser 2005).

Conclusions and Recommendations

It is clear that social age mainstreaming in Canada's development policy and programming will not be an easy or fast process. However, it could be one way for Canada to make an important contribution to international aid approaches and to exhibit leadership beyond its fairly modest aid budget. Social age mainstreaming also presents an opportunity for Canadian politicians and civil servants to rethink the way we deliver aid, especially in the context of the expanded Department of Foreign Affairs, Trade and Development (DFATD).

Given the challenges of mainstreaming articulated above, it is important to demonstrate clearly the importance of age in development processes and the dangers of current age-blindness. While there is a growing body of scholarly literature on age and development, more data is needed, particularly in relation to elderly people in development contexts (see Lloyd-Sherlock 2000). Lessons from the

UNHCR AGDM experience (Thomas and Beck 2010) and CIDA's gender mainstreaming (Tiessen, this volume) indicate that the implied organizational change requires champions at high political and policy levels, as well as working-level civil servants. To implement social age mainstreaming effectively, advocates for greater age-sensitivity in Canada's international development assistance need to identify key people within Canada's aid bureaucracy and provide them with the necessary data and tools. Given the important implementation role of non-governmental and private sector partners, allies from outside government could also encourage change within the new DFATD. These constituencies include organizations with an explicit mandate on age, such as members of the Child Rights Consortium, as well as organizations focused on elderly people, for instance, HelpAge Canada. Canadian officials could also consult with colleagues at UNHCR to see the degree to which their migration-specific policies could have broader applicability in development assistance.

Finally, in the context of budget cuts and numerous critiques of Canada's aid policy and programming, it is important for champions of social age mainstreaming to present it as a positive way for Canadian aid to reinvent and reinvigorate itself. Canada's Child and Youth Strategy, despite its "children-in-development" shortcomings described in this chapter, could be a first step towards a more comprehensive and innovative way to make Canadian aid more inclusive and ultimately more effective.

Acknowledgments

This research was made possible by a grant from the Social Sciences and Humanities Research Council. I am grateful to David Black, Stephen Brown, Rebecca Tiessen, and students in my "Global Politics of International Development" course for helpful comments on earlier drafts of this chapter and the ideas behind it. All errors and omissions are my own.

Notes

1. This does not necessarily mean that gender mainstreaming has been effective. See, for example, Tiessen (2007), as well as Hankivsky (2005), Hartsock (1981), and Moser (2005).
2. This is based on my experiences as a CIDA employee, as well as interviews conducted when developing an action plan for conflict sensitivity (Clark 2007; Clark-Kazak 2008).

References

Abbink, Jon. 2005. "Being Young in Africa: The Politics of Despair and Renewal." In Jon Abbink and Ineke van Kessel, eds. In *Vanguard or Vandals: Youth, Politics and Conflict in Africa*. Leiden: Brill: 1–35.

Ariès, Philippe. 1979. *Centuries of Childhood*. Translated by Robert Baldick. Harmondsworth: Penguin.

Booth, Christine, and Cinnamon Bennett. 2002. "Gender Mainstreaming in the European Union: Towards a New Conception and Practice of Equal Opportunities?" *European Journal of Women's Studies*, vol. 9, no. 4: 430–46.

Boserup, Ester. 1970. *Woman's Role in Economic Development*, London: Allen and Unwin.

Boyden, Jo. 1997. "Childhood and the Policy Makers: A Comparative Perspective on the Globalization of Childhood." In Allison James and Alan Prout, eds. *Constructing and Reconstructing Childhood*. London: Falmer Press: 187–226.

Canadian International Development Agency. 2000. *CIDA's Social Development Priorities: A Framework for Action*. Gatineau, QC: CIDA.

Canadian International Development Agency. 2002. *Canada Making a Difference in the World: A Policy Statement on Strengthening Aid Effectiveness*. Gatineau, QC: CIDA.

Canadian International Development Agency. 2009. "A New Effective Approach to Canadian Aid." Speaking Notes for the Honourable Beverley J. Oda, Minister of International Cooperation, at the Munk Centre for International Studies, May 20, 2009, Toronto. Internet, http://www.acdi-cida.gc.ca/acdi-cida/acdi-cida.nsf/eng/NAT-5208469-GYW. Accessed November 7, 2013.

Canadian International Development Agency. 2010. *Securing the Future of Children and Youth: CIDA's Children and Youth Strategy*. Gatineau, QC: CIDA.

Clark, Christina. 2007. "Conflict-Sensitive Action Plan." Gatineau, QC: CIDA.

Clark-Kazak, Christina. 2008. "Analyse des conflits dans le contexte de la programmation de l'ACDI au Sénégal." Gatineau, QC: CIDA.

Clark-Kazak, Christina. 2009a. "Representing Refugees in the Life Cycle: A Social Age Analysis of United Nations High Commissioner for Refugees Annual Reports and Appeals, 2000–2008." *Journal of Refugee Studies*, vol. 22, no. 3: 302–22.

Clark-Kazak, Christina. 2009b. "Towards a Working Definition and Application of Social Age in International Development Studies." *Journal of Development Studies*, vol. 45, no. 8: 1–18.

Cunningham, Hugh. 1995. *Children and Childhood in Western Society since 1500*. London: Longman.

Degraff, Deborah, and Deborah Levison. 2009. "Children's Work and Mother's Work – What Is the Connection?" *World Development*, vol. 37, no. 9: 1569–87.

deMause, Lloyd. 1974. "The Evolution of Childhood." In Lloyd deMause, ed. *The History of Childhood: The Evolution of Parent-Child Relationships as a Factor in History*. London: Souvenir Press: 1–52.

Donaghy, Tahnya Barnett. 2004. "Applications of Mainstreaming in Australia and Northern Ireland." *International Political Science Review*, vol. 25, no. 4: 393–410.

Foreign Affairs Canada. 2005. *Canada's International Policy Statement: A Role of Pride and Influence in the World*. Ottawa: Foreign Affairs Canada.

Groves, Leslie. 2005. "UNHCR's Age and Gender Mainstreaming Pilot Project 2004: Synthesis Report." Geneva: Office of the United Nations High Commissioner for Refugees.

Hankivsky, Olena. 2005. "Gender vs. Diversity Mainstreaming: A Preliminary Examination of the Role and Transformative Potential of Feminist Theory." *Canadian Journal of Political Science*, vol. 38, no. 4: 977–1001.

Hartsock, Nancy. 1981. "Political Change: Two Perspectives on Power." In N. Benevento, ed. *Building Feminist Theory: Essays from Quest*. New York and London: Longman: 3–19.

Himaz, Rozana. 2008. "Welfare Grants and Their Impact on Child Health: The Case of Sri Lanka." *World Development*, vol. 36, no. 10: 1843–57.

Ikels, Charlotte. 2006. "Economic Reform and Intergenerational Relationships in China." *Oxford Development Studies*, vol. 34, no. 4: 387–400.

James, Allison, and Alan Prout. 1997a. "A New Paradigm for the Sociology of Childhood? Provenance, Promise and Problems." In Allison James and Alan Prout, eds. *Constructing and Reconstructing Childhood*. London: Falmer Press: 7–32.

James, Allison, and Alan Prout. 1997b. "Re-presenting Childhood: Time and Transition in the Study of Childhood." In Allison James and Alan Prout, eds. *Constructing and Reconstructing Childhood*. London: Falmer Press: 227–46.

Kabeer, Naila. 1994. *Reversed Realities: Gender Hierarchies in Development Thought*. London: Verso.

León, Mauricio, and Stephen D. Younger. 2007. "Transfer Payments, Mothers' Income and Child Health in Ecuador." *Journal of Development Studies*, vo. 43, no. 6: 1126–43.

Lloyd-Sherlock, Peter. 2000. "Old Age and Poverty in Developing Countries: New Policy Challenges." *World Development*, vol. 28, no. 12: 2157–68.

Moser, Caroline. 2005. "Has Gender Mainstreaming Failed?" *International Feminist Journal of Politics*, vol. 7, no. 4: 576–90.

Qvortrup, Jens. 1994. "Childhood Matters: An Introduction." In Jens Qvortrup, Marjatta Bardy, Giovanni Sgritta, and Helmut Wintersberger, eds. *Childhood Matters: Social Theory, Practice and Politics*. Aldershot, UK: Avebury: 1–23.

Rathgeber, Eva M. 1990. "WID, WAD, GAD: Trends in Research and Practice." *Journal of Developing Areas*, vol. 24, no. 4: 489–502.

Rogoff, Barbara. 1990. *Apprenticeship in Thinking: Cognitive Development in Social Context*. Oxford: Oxford University Press.

Sumner, Andy. 2010. "Child Poverty, Well-Being and Agency: What Does a '3-D Well-Being' Approach Contribute?" *Journal of International Development*, vol. 22, no. 8: 1064–75.

Thomas, Virginia, and Tony Beck. 2010. "Changing the Way UNHCR Does Business? An Evaluation of the Age, Gender and Diversity Mainstreaming Strategy, 2004–2009." Geneva: UNHCR.

Tiessen, Rebecca. 2007. *Everywhere/Nowhere: Gender Mainstreaming in Development Agencies*. Bloomfield, CT: Kumarian.

United Nations Population Division. 2013. *World Population Prospects: The 2012 Revision*. New York: United Nations.

Vera-Sanso, Penny. 2006. "Experiences in Old Age: A South Indian Example of How Functional Age is Socially Structured." *Oxford Development Studies*, vol. 34, no. 4: 457–72.

Woodhead, Martin. 1997. "Psychology and the Cultural Construction of Children's Needs." In Allison James and Alan Prout, eds. *Constructing and Reconstructing Childhood*. London: Falmer Press: 63–84.

Wydick, Bruce. 1999. "The Effect of Microenterprise Lending on Child Schooling in Guatemala." *Economic Development and Cultural Change*, vol. 47, no. 4: 853–69.

CHAPTER XIII

Canada's Fragile States Policy: What Have We Accomplished and Where Do We Go from Here?

David Carment and Yiagadeesen Samy

Introduction

Though bold and innovative, the Canadian International Development Agency's (CIDA) early investments in fragile states analysis and network development held the organization to a level of high expectation, which has clearly failed to materialize in the form of a more effective policy. While sad for some, CIDA's demise and absorption into the Department of Foreign Affairs, Trade and Development (DFATD) is even more unfortunate because its mandate, goals, and objectives were never properly understood or realized by the Harper government. If CIDA's fragile states policy has not been a success, it is not for lack of trying by individuals within CIDA.

Our main argument is that CIDA faced serious conceptual, political, and organizational challenges in designing and implementing its fragile states policy. Though Canada allocated a significant and increasing amount of aid to fragile states in the last decade, the government squandered the opportunities for effective programming in fragile states due to those challenges.[1] The newly created DFATD has unfortunately failed to realize early investments it made in fragile states and, rather than reinvigorate Canada's engagement, the Harper government has essentially abandoned them. For example, the Stabilization and Reconstruction Task Force (START) failed to live up to its expectations and has been essentially sidelined. Even if it is perhaps too early to tell what will actually happen, the June 2014 announcement of Canada's new priority countries for its aid is perhaps indicative of a shift towards commercial interests, rather than an increased focus on the most fragile states.

Impatience for results and a lack of understanding of what the Canadian government was supposed to do in the most fragile situations have clearly played a role in this gradual abandonment of policies on fragile states. To be sure, state fragility is largely an abstract conceptualization that defies easy interpretation and compartmentalization and does not lend itself to simple analysis and policy prescription (Carment et al. 2010). Fragile states analysis is not an exact science, but the absence of a well-grounded, continuous assessment and functional networks for doing proper program evaluation and monitoring in the Canadian case have made policy prescription and implementation even more problematic.

Canadian Aid Allocation to Fragile States

To our knowledge, no one has systematically tracked the amount of Canadian aid allocated to fragile states and compared it to other donors' assistance. The Canadian case is in fact not unique in this respect. Even though many fragile and conflict-affected states (FCAS) are among the largest recipients of bilateral aid from the Development Assistance Committee of the Organisation for Economic Co-operation and Development (OECD/DAC) donors, the latter do not clearly report what proportion of their aid goes to FCAS. For example, we could not find any direct data from USAID on the proportion of its aid that goes to FCAS.

The International Network on Conflict and Fragility (INCAF), a subsidiary body of the OECD/DAC, has been monitoring financial flows from all DAC member countries to fragile states since 2006. In its 2012 report, INCAF uses a list of forty-seven countries classified as fragile, derived from the World Bank/African Development Bank/Asian Development Bank harmonized list of FCAS for 2012, and the Fund for Peace's 2011 Failed States Index. INCAF reports that ODA to fragile states by all DAC member countries was US$50 billion (or 38 percent) in 2010 (OECD 2012, 43).

Using the INCAF list, which covers the period 2000–10, we find that Canadian aid to these fragile states went from 18.2 percent in 2001 to 38.4 percent of Canada's aid budget in 2010.[2] If we also assume that this list is valid for 2011 and 2012, the proportions are 34.5 percent and 30.7 percent respectively.[3] We thus see a clear upward trend in Canadian aid allocated to fragile states over the decade, with a peak of 40.4 percent in 2006. Similar to findings for DAC donors as a group, Canadian aid to fragile states is also highly concentrated, indicating the presence of aid darlings and orphans. For instance, in 2010, the top five recipients of Canadian aid among the INCAF list of forty-seven fragile states (Haiti, Afghanistan, Ethiopia, Pakistan, and Sudan) received almost 55 percent of the funding allocated.

To check the robustness of these findings, we also examined aid allocation to the top forty and top fifty (to get a rough match with the INCAF list) fragile states, using the annual fragility ranking produced by the Country Indicators for Foreign Policy (CIFP) project.[4] CIFP uses a definition that captures the multi-faceted nature of fragility by bringing together the interrelated aspects of poverty, conflict, and fragility (Carment et al. 2010). The resulting CIFP fragility index provides an annual cross-country fragility ranking, as well as several subcomponents of fragility. As a result, the list varies from one year to the next, as the rankings of countries change over time.

Figure 1: Canadian Aid Allocation to Fragile States, 2001–2010

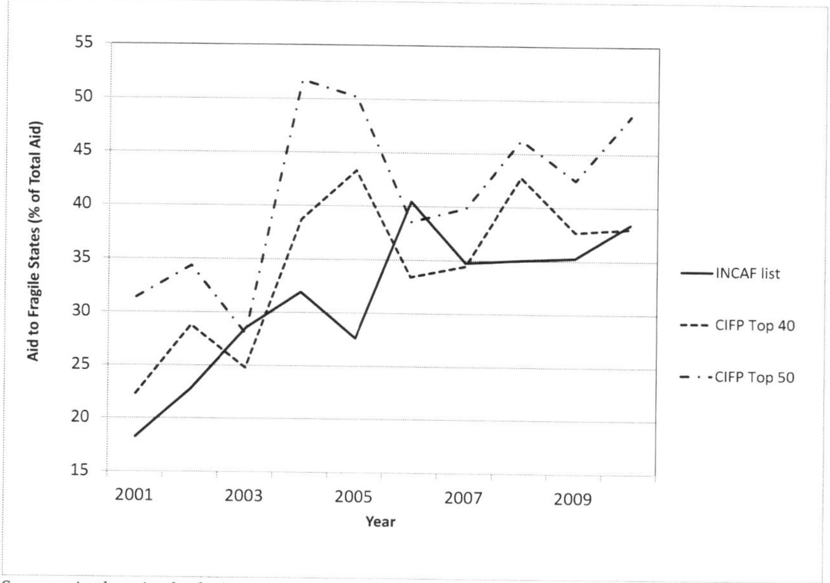

Source: Authors' calculations.

As we can see in Figure 1 above, using the ranking produced by CIFP yields a very similar trend to the one obtained when using the INCAF list. Canadian aid allocation to the top forty or top fifty fragile states (as a percentage of total Canadian aid) has increased over the period 2001–10 from 22.3 percent and 31.4 percent in 2001 to 38.0 and 48.5 percent in 2010, respectively. The year-on-year changes also indicate that volatility in aid allocation is a problem, again something that has been noted elsewhere for aid allocated by DAC member countries to fragile states (Carment et al. 2008).

In the next two sections, we discuss the reasons that have prevented Canadian aid from being effective in these fragile situations.

Conceptual and Organizational Challenges

The complexity of dealing with, and responding to, fragile situations is reflected in the way CIDA has generally allowed "a thousand flowers to bloom," to support partner organizations, academics, and NGOs that work on state fragility. Indeed, when it first appeared on the scene, as an idea in search of a policy, just around 9/11, the concept of state fragility brought with it a new and complex understanding of how donors and civil society interact and use analysis to support their policies. Given CIDA's prior investments in conflict analysis, peacebuilding, public policy, and consultations with civil society, it could be assumed that the agency would have been prepared to address these challenges. Such was not the case, for a couple of reasons.

First, if one examines the evolution of CIDA's fragile states analysis and policy, we see that initially at least the organization relied on a number of initiatives that emphasized transparency, collaboration, and value-based analysis. This is because, at the time, CIDA turned to the academic, humanitarian, and NGO community to build analytical support for its policy developments. The truth is that a lot of the momentum and investments made during this period were either squandered or forgotten as various donors, including CIDA, scrambled to shift their emphasis from support to civil society (1994–2002) to state building (2003–14) with the onset of the Iraq war following 9/11 (Carment et al. 2010).

A second conceptual problem is the way unstructured information reached the general public through modern technology, especially the Internet. State fragility as a concept is relatively abstract and mostly unclear in terms of cause and effect. However, its manifestations are more obvious. On the one hand, the unfiltered messaging through modern media of these symptoms worked to heighten public expectations for appropriate, effective, and timely responses to political crises, human rights violations, insurgency, complex emergencies, and natural disasters. On the other hand, media outlets typically picked up such events and retransmitted unstructured reporting, long before governments were able to construct the "situational awareness" necessary to develop a coherent and constructive policy.

The net result was a rather weak organizational response by the Department of Foreign Affairs and International Trade (DFAIT), which appeared to thrive on "situational ambiguity" and "institutional waffling." Faced with a raw and unstructured flow of information and lacking certainty about the causes of such events, the most expedient policy choice for Canada was to sit and wait until compelled to act by international mandate, public pressure, or political instruction. Bold, decisive, forward-looking action was in short supply. For all intents and purposes, DFAIT appeared perfectly happy to follow and not lead. This applied equally to the development and application of specific fragile states analytical tools and policies, and to operational response strategies. For its part, CIDA had already laid out a comprehensive plan to develop Country Development Planning Frameworks (CDPFs). CDPFs were supposed to align with nationally owned poverty reduction strategies. In most cases, however, fragile states did not have these policy strategies because they are typically incapable of developing them. However, DFAIT and CIDA seldom worked well together. Such planning was shown to be ineffective and rarely applied because coherence and integration were anathema to the DFAIT and CIDA work ethic.

Many noted a perceived need in the donor community for a greater degree of coordination among themselves, and Canada was no exception. In response, CIDA developed, among other things, a Post-Conflict Needs Assessment tool, in order to establish and align its policies with national priorities and to agree upon a division of labour that included the government and national civil society. However, CIDA used such an approach in only a few cases, and at the latest stages of conflict, such as Haiti and Sudan. Surprisingly, Afghanistan was not exposed to the same level of rigorous analysis and planning, despite the huge amounts invested there.

More generally, when one considers the ambitious plans CIDA (2008a) laid out in its core guidance document, it is quite clear that conceptual clarity and organizational robustness were primary goals in principle and rhetoric. Under Paul Martin, CIDA spoke of whole-of-government approaches and using new instruments such as the Global Peace and Security Fund (GPSF) to more effectively engage fragile states. CIDA recognized that there was a need to have a strong operational capacity to deliver aid in flexible and responsive ways, including through Program Support Units.

At the OECD/DAC level, with the exception of the INCAF working group (which is a forum for knowledge sharing and learning across various donors, and tracks resource flows to fragile states), none of the initiatives has been properly realized. The Conflict, Peace and Development Cooperation Network, which was meant to mainstream conflict prevention and peacebuilding in development cooperation, is now a portal for training, but has been usurped by INCAF as a shared analytical resource.

Similarly, the Harper government halted, within a year of being elected in 2006, the whole-of-government initiatives, including the engagement of civil society and support of knowledge networks. Canada Corps, an interdepartmental body based within CIDA to promote good governance, mutated into the Office for Democratic Governance for a brief period and was then abandoned in 2007. Neither CIDA's Policy Branch nor its geographical branches fully incorporated the available analytical tools and networks it had helped develop into its operational decision-making processes (CIFP 2006).

When we consider how much analytical capacity the Canadian government has abandoned since 2005, it is sobering and disappointing, to say the least. These include several tools such as the "Conflict and Peace Analysis and Response Manual" (FEWER 1999) and the Peace and Conflict Impact Assessment (PCIA), which were never fully operationalized and integrated into policy making. The potential impact on CIDA policy of its own Peacebuilding Unit, DFAIT's GPSF (abandoned in 2013), and CIFP, to name a few, were also never fully internalized. Indeed, prior to 2006, CIDA's fragility policy was informed by other related initiatives that it supported and funded, including all those enunciated in the International Policy Statement (Canada 2005)—namely the Responsibilities Agency, the Human Security Agenda, the GPSF, and START. Yet, despite previous attempts by CIDA, along with its domestic and international partners, to build continuity and consistency, the road travelled was uneven and inconsistent, occasionally heading off into dead ends and unending roundabouts.

The best example of this failure is the scandal-plagued PCIA initiative, also known as the Conflict Sensitivity Approach, which, had it been properly realized and managed, would have made CIDA a leader in the field of fragility analysis. The ingredients for success were there. Between 1997 and 2003, CIDA's Peacebuilding Unit, under the direction of Susan Brown, played a key role in advancing the role of analysis, assessment, and conflict-sensitive programming in conflict-plagued regions. Together with a number of international partners, a variety of NGOs, the Africa Peace Forum in Kenya, the Centre for Conflict Resolution in Uganda, and the Consortium of Humanitarian Agencies in Sri Lanka, CIDA pioneered the PCIA initiative. Domestic partners included the International Development Research Centre (IDRC) and DFAIT's Peacebuilding and Human Security Division.

The PCIA initiative sought to create a series of tools to aid in programming and policy decision making. Though not concerned with fragile states *per se*, the initiative's focus on early warning and early response, driven by objective analysis and risk assessment, clearly had much in common with recent efforts to enhance monitoring and assessment capability in fragile state environments. The PCIA initiative also sought to enhance research and policy networks in Canada, bringing together academics, policy makers, and members of the NGO community with expertise in monitoring and responding to conflict. Again, though the remit to monitor and assess fragile state environments went beyond issues of peace and conflict, the latter were nonetheless important pieces of the fragile state puzzle. Similarly, the Forum on Early Warning and Early Response (FEWER) methodology was built on the understanding that no single analytical approach, whether data- or judgment-based, was capable of adequately capturing the complexity of risk potential or of providing a sufficient foundation upon which to develop policy-relevant early warnings.[5] The key contribution of the FEWER network was making explicit the fact that early warning represents a proactive political process whereby networks of organizations conduct analysis together in a collective effort to prevent likely events from occurring.

Unfortunately, both the PCIA and the FEWER projects were never fully implemented, despite millions of dollars being spent through international and Canadian partners to support their rollout and development. The PCIA was modified so significantly that in the end it bore little resemblance to its original objective, which was to evaluate the impact of development assistance on conflict and fragility.[6] PCIA tools paid for by CIDA through the CIFP project were also never applied. They were not even taken up by CIDA's private sector and industrial relations units, where they could have played a role in strengthening multinational corporations and their corporate social responsibility obligations. DFATD has shown no interest in developing these tools, preferring to depend on foreign capacities such as those developed by Washington-based think tanks.

Political Challenges

At the same time as the above issues became more complex and difficult to apprehend, the ability of CIDA to respond in a timely and appropriate manner to emerging fragile states problems decreased. In retrospect, the political challenges that it faced were probably more acute than anything related to the conceptual and analytical problems outlined above. Rare is the example where CIDA ever made a straightforward and compelling case for immediate, swift, and directed action – in spite of over twenty-five years of investment in preventive strategies, legal doctrines, and tools and capabilities for prevention and early warning. Indeed, a more compelling case can be made for developing bureaucratic responses that tend to be biased towards addressing symptoms, while deeper structural and cultural factors and related power asymmetries were left to unfold more or less on their own. For CIDA, this result is partly a consequence of a default or "lowest common denominator" political strategy in which efforts were made to be the least offensive to the largest number of people and partner countries, regardless of what the evidence suggested.

Indeed, since 2008, CIDA has emphasized the need for more effective democratic systems, respect for human rights, and gender equality (CIDA 2008ab), but has very little to show for efforts in the most egregious cases of state fragility (such as the aforementioned Pakistan, Afghanistan, and South Sudan). This is mostly because the rhetoric rarely matched the reality, despite significant amounts of money being spent. The impact of such efforts, if any, was modest and the desire to pursue the least controversial policies was preferred over taking a hard, focused, and purposeful line (*National Post* 2012; *Toronto Star* 2013).

In brief, despite being handed an excellent opportunity to stake new ground on state fragility after 9/11, CIDA faced an existential identity crisis more serious than any other major bureaucracy in the Canadian government. It faced two problems in this regard. First, CIDA has always been an easy target for criticism. It has been expected to deliver stability, security, and economic development to vastly underdeveloped fragile states, while still being held accountable to both Canadian taxpayers and its political masters. However, CIDA's Policy Branch never really tried to make the case that its aid was having a meaningful impact. The fact that CIDA had within its own leadership circles those who wanted it to integrate fully with DFAIT was not helpful. It is difficult to strike a bold independent course when that process is being undermined internally.

This was certainly the case in Afghanistan, where CIDA was criticized for not meeting its objectives and DFAIT, despite having failed to deliver on its promises of regional stability, was not (Maloney 2008; *National Post* 2012). In particular, Pakistan's influence on Afghanistan was all but ignored by the Canadian government – even though that country's impact on Afghanistan would have been DFAIT's responsibility.[7] It is possible that Canada's representatives on the ground knew all along that Pakistan was undermining the Canadian mission, but their views apparently did not influence the policy process back in Ottawa (Carment 2011). In all aspects of policy making, from strategic analysis to public debate and intergovernmental cooperation, Canada appeared to have had no significant internal evaluation of or policy on Pakistan and the region until it introduced a rather undersized and somewhat superficial Canada Border Services Agency–led border training program in 2008, and initiated and supported the Dubai Peace process around the same time.

The second problem was the continuing lack of real and genuine interest within the donor community, but within CIDA in particular, in evidence-based decision making other than that which is narrowly focused on the state and state security. This major lack of interest characterized the Canadian government even before the election of the Conservatives in 2006, but has been acutely problematic since then. To recognize this as a genuine dilemma is, on one hand, to come to terms with the political nature of response (let alone effective response) by donor agencies. On the other hand, no self-respecting policy analyst at CIDA publicly decried the lack of space for decisions formed on the basis of good empirical evidence. That fact and the unwillingness at the political level to do things based on evidence unless it is expedient have been disconcerting. Canada's failure to heed the evidence may well come home to roost as the situation in the Middle East worsens.

Perhaps advocacy and the incredible force that thousands of blogs represent can generate change in fragile states, but they are clearly not enough to elicit behavioural and attitudinal change within the Harper government. It is a sad fact that the Harper government does not draw on structured and systematic analysis to generate policy (Carment and Samy 2010). Most frameworks are used for the purposes of lobbying and advocacy, but these should not be mistaken for operational response.

The reality for CIDA was that it invested in fire inspectors (and fire brigades for when the inspections fail or are ignored), but not enough in the political processes around how it helps build all kinds of different buildings (extending the fire analogy to states and other structures that are supposed to create security). To complicate this further, the response to violence, armed violent conflict, and fragility tends to be more controversial politically than responding to health pandemics or even a humanitarian crisis. CIDA did not even do *ex ante* assessments in order to "do no harm" where it was working.

Tackling the structural problems of fragility has been the biggest challenge for CIDA, in part because no politician will reap any political gain. Paradoxically, information about impending problems is always heard, but rarely heeded. As a result, the default policy and operational response is not so much to ignore these warnings as to limit the response to what is politically expedient, rather than to undertake the steps necessary to be able to respond at the level that would be needed over the long term to deal with deep-seated structural risks.

Conclusion

As aid flows increased since the early 2000s and larger funding envelopes became available for fragile states, donors were in a position to do immense good. However, they can also do harm if they fail to assess the impact of their actions. In fragile contexts, donors such as Canada have an even greater responsibility to ensure that aid is carefully monitored by applying impact assessment tools at every stage. This would help countries at the bottom of the fragility spectrum, including those that have signed up for the New Deal, improve their political, economic, and social indicators.[8]

As argued and explained above, CIDA, despite good intentions, faced several challenges in designing and implementing its fragile states policy. When it comes to realizing all the earlier work, conceptual development, and network building, its policy on state fragility was weakened to the point that by 2006 it could no longer claim leadership in the area. Evidence of this failure includes the failure to mainstream effective early warning and early response properly into the policy domains of government agencies; pockets of expertise are largely dwindling, and there remains limited synergy and sharing. Most of the support to the development of fragile states initiatives has been picked up by other donors. Canada has forfeited its leadership role in network development. The implications are significant for the inclusion of Southern perspectives into Northern decision-making processes, because the South has civil society networks to which Canada is no longer connected.

Ad hoc, unstructured, and unsystematic approaches to state fragility within the Canadian government persist. Failed and fragile state policies are usually not informed by regular situation analyses. Where such analyses are factored into programming, it is often a "one-off" exercise or an external analysis that does not reflect local perspectives. The impact of prevention activities has been reduced because of a lack of coordination and strategy emanating from the Harper government, which is not interested in public policy. Frequently, key actors (including NGOs, governments, multilateral organizations, and civil society groups) operate in isolation and do not properly coordinate activities across sectors. This often results from a lack of common analysis and the lack of multi-agency planning forums for the development of joint prevention strategies. An important step would thus be the creation of an independent research body to provide crucial evidence-based frameworks and benchmarks for evaluating aid effectiveness, as well as critical analysis tools in support of aid allocation decisions.

Notes

1. Baranyi and Khan, this volume, examine Canadian assistance to five specific conflict-affected and fragile states: Bangladesh, Ethiopia, Mali, Pakistan, and Palestine (West Bank and Gaza).
2. Canadian aid data was obtained from the North–South Institute (2013).
3. This is not an unfair assumption because countries tend to remain fragile for long periods of time and most are still classified as fragile by various organizations.
4. David Carment is principal investigator of this project and Yiagadeesen Samy senior research associate. The CIFP project has received funding from the Department of Foreign Affairs and International Trade, the Department of National Defence, and CIDA, among others.
5. FEWER's integrated approach has since become the basis for a number of methodological frameworks employed by the UN system and national governments.
6. Compare the original intent of PCIA (Bush 1998, 2013) with the final product (Conflict Sensitivity Consortium 2012).
7. DFAIT (whose contributions were historically focused on the regional, political, and diplomatic side of the ledger) and CIDA had complementary international mandates and significant programming and operational resources for crisis response and fragile states. DFAIT's START and GPSF were supposed to support important targeted responses to international crises, peacebuilding, conflict prevention, security-system reform, and associated democratization work, as well as coordinate whole-of-government responses to natural disasters and complex emergencies.
8. The so-called New Deal for international engagement in fragile states is an innovative model of partnership between FCAS and their DAC development partners. Signed by forty countries, including Canada, it sets out five peacebuilding and state-building goals that are based on principles of country leadership rather than the dictates of the donor community.

References

Bush, Kenneth. 1998. "A Measure of Peace: Peace and Conflict Impact Assessment (PCIA) of Development Projects in Conflict Zones." Ottawa: IDRC.

Bush, Kenneth. 2013. "A Genealogy of PCIA: Setting PCIA within the Context of its Constitutive Evaluative Practices." Internet, http://www. irisyorku.ca/wp-content/uploads/iris/2013/05/BUSH-Genealogy-of-PCIA-Powerpoint-Presn-and-Tables.pdf. Accessed November 16, 2013.

Canada. 2005. *Canada's International Policy Statement: A Role of Pride and Influence in the World. Development.* Gatineau, QC: CIDA.

Carment, David. 2011. "Afghanistan and the Regional Blindspot." *Embassy,* January 26.

Carment, David, and Yiagadeesen Samy. 2010. "Haiti without Tears: Getting Aid Right." *Policy Options,* April: 57–63.

Carment, David, and Yiagadeesen Samy. 2012. "Throwing Aid at Afghanistan is Not Working." *Embassy,* July 18.

Carment, David, Yiagadeesen Samy, and Stewart Prest. 2009. "State Fragility and Implications for Aid Allocation: An Empirical Analysis." *Conflict Management and Peace Science,* vol. 25, no. 4: 349–73.

Carment, David, Stewart Prest, and Yiagadeesen Samy. 2010. *Security, Development and the Fragile State: Bridging the Gap Between Theory and Policy.* London: Routledge.

CIDA. 2008a. "An Internal Guidance Document for Development Cooperation in Fragile States." Gatineau, QC: CIDA.

CIDA. 2008b. "Thought Leadership in Development: A Sampler of CIDA-Supported Knowledge Work and Innovations." Gatineau, QC: CIDA.

CIFP. 2006. "Failed and Fragile States: A Concept Paper for the Canadian Government." Internet, http://www4.carleton.ca/cifp/app/serve.php/1145.pdf. Accessed November 16, 2013.

Conflict Sensitivity Consortium. 2012. *How to Guide to Conflict Sensitivity.* Internet, http://www.conflictsensitivity.org/content/how-guide. Accessed November 16, 2013.

FEWER. 1999. "Conflict and Peace Analysis and Response Manual," 2nd ed. London: Forum on Early Warning and Early Response.

Maloney, Sean. 2008. "Time to Reassess Canada's Foreign Aid," *Policy Options.* September: 28–34.

National Post. 2012. "Canada's $1.5B Afghanistan Aid Effort Divorced from Reality according to Damning, Previously Unreleased Documents." October 12.

North–South Institute. 2013. *Canadian International Development Platform.* Internet, http://cidpnsi.ca. Accessed November 16, 2013.

OECD. 2012. *Fragile States 2013: Resource Flows and Trends in a Shifting World.* Paris: OECD.

Toronto Star. 2013. "Canada Spent $10 Million for Security at Afghan Dam Project." March 13.

CHAPTER XIV

Canada and Development in Other Fragile States: Moving beyond the "Afghanistan Model"

Stephen Baranyi and Themrise Khan

Introduction

Before 2013, Canadian government officials often cited Afghanistan as an example of successful whole-of-government engagement in fragile states. Official Ottawa lauded the Afghanistan taskforce system, with its extensive coordination of Canadian efforts from Ottawa down to the Provincial Reconstruction Team in Kandahar, as the gold standard for joined-up approaches (GOC 2012a). The peer review of Canada's development cooperation, carried out by the Development Assistance Committee of the Organisation for Economic Co-operation and Development (OECD/DAC), endorsed that view by praising Canada's "effective whole-of-government approach to disaster response and fragile states, particularly in Afghanistan and Haiti" (OECD 2012, 9). It recommended that Canada's "assistance to other partner countries would be more effective if it applied the relevant program considerations emerging from Afghanistan in those contexts" (OECD 2012, 12). Such considerations included ensuring high-level commitment from key departments, following the integrated approach down to the country level, injecting sufficient human and financial resources, and streamlining programming processes. Curiously, the DAC assessment focused almost entirely on "front-end" factors and did not refer to the considerable evidence of poor downstream results.

Non-governmental organizations (NGOs) and scholars have questioned that rosy reading of Canada's record in Afghanistan and other fragile and conflict-affected states (FCAS). Early on, the Canadian Council for International Co-operation suggested that joined-up approaches subordinated aid to security objectives and undermined poverty reduction in the poorest countries of the South (CCIC 2006). Banerjee (2008, 2010, 2013) grounded that critique in experience-based analyses of Canadian engagement in Afghanistan. Brown (2008) and Swiss (2012) suggested that the "securitization" of aid affected a wider swath of Canadian development policies. Together with Carment and Samy (2012), they also questioned the degree to which Canadian official development assistance (ODA) had been effective in high-profile FCAS – in terms of Canadian value-for-money or in terms of global aid effectiveness criteria rooted in the Paris Declaration.

However, based on a systematic comparison of Canadian involvement in Afghanistan, Haiti, and Sudan, Baranyi and Paducel (2012) argued that the effectiveness and securitization of aid varied significantly – from high securitization and very low effectiveness in Afghanistan, to lower securitization, greater conflict-sensitivity, and slightly higher effectiveness in the other two high-priority FCAS. This chapter extends that line of analysis to other contexts that the Canadian International Development Agency (CIDA) did not categorize as fragile. Historically, CIDA distinguished between programming in FCAS such as Afghanistan, where "programming objectives align closely with Canadian foreign policy objectives associated with regional and global security and stability," and in low-income countries (LICs), which "face pervasive poverty and limited institutional capacity, but have broadly stable governance and public security" (CIDA 2013, 17, 19).

That distinction may have been justified in the immediate post–9/11 era, when some CIDA officials sought to protect the agency's space from further incursion by central agencies or other government departments. Is the distinction still useful today, given the creation of an integrated Department of Foreign Affairs, Trade and Development (DFATD)? What do the sudden shifts from stability to fragility in LICs such as Mali, and the relative success of development cooperation in LICs such as Bangladesh, suggest about the possibilities for more two-way learning across the fragility-stability spectrum? Finally, to what extent has Canadian ODA been linked to commercial objectives in those countries, as suggested by some critics?

This chapter explores those issues by drawing lessons from five cases where Canadian involvement has been extensive but where state fragility has varied significantly. We call them "other" FCAS because, aside from the West Bank and Gaza, they have not historically been considered as such by the Canadian government, given that they have not recently suffered from the intensity of violent conflict or other forms of fragility found in Afghanistan, Haiti, and Sudan. However, as suggested by Table 1 and the fragility indices on which it is based, each of our five cases is affected in distinct ways by governance crises, weak state capacity, armed conflict, foreign military intervention, or vulnerability to natural disasters.

Table 1. Sampled Cases with ODA and FCAS Rankings

Country	Canadian ODA Rank (2012)	FCAS Rank (2012–13)
Ethiopia	1	19
Pakistan	8	13
Bangladesh	10	29
Mali	13	38
West Bank & Gaza	16	43

Sources: FCAS rankings are taken from Fund for Peace (2013), except the ranking for the West Bank and Gaza, which is taken from Carment and Samy (2012).
Canadian ODA rankings, by disbursement volume, are taken from CIDA (2012).

We selected these cases based on two criteria: inclusion in the top twenty Canadian ODA recipients and the top fifty FCAS on standard fragility indices. We excluded Afghanistan, Haiti, and Sudan because they have been analyzed elsewhere (Baranyi and Paducel 2012). We included the West Bank and Gaza (also known as the Occupied Palestinian Territories or Palestine) because that case has not been adequately analyzed from a Canadian development and security angle, even though CIDA classified it as a fragile state. There are no cases in the Americas, since Haiti is the only country in the region that ranks in the top twenty partners for Canadian cooperation by volume of disbursements. Other African FCAS, such as the Democratic Republic of Congo and Somalia, also fit our selection criteria, but we excluded them to keep the sample size manageable for a focused comparison.

In searching for answers to the questions noted above, we compared three aspects of Canadian whole-of-government engagement in the five contexts: (1) the extent to which Canada's ODA has been effective in developmental terms; (2) the degree to which Canadian aid has been securitized, as opposed to conflict-sensitive; (3) and the extent to which aid been commercialized. Our understanding of development effectiveness is rooted in the Paris Declaration and subsequent international norms, which assume that ODA will be more effective if it is nationally "owned," aligned with national priorities and systems, harmonized among donors, managed for development results, and based on the mutual accountability of partners. Despite their limitations, those standards are widely accepted, at least among Western donors, and have generated a significant body of comparable, longitudinal OECD/DAC data for most of our cases.

To analyze the connections between security and development programming, we used the standards codified in the OECD/DAC Principles for Good International Engagement in Fragile States and Situations (OECD 2007). That text called for the recognition of links between political, security, and development goals, yet it urged OECD governments to emphasize the prevention of violent conflicts (i.e., "conflict-sensitivity") through the coherent use of all policy instruments. It stressed the principles of taking context-specificities as the starting point for international engagement and the imperative of doing no harm – for example, when deciding in which sectors to use ODA, with which partners and to what ends. In the complementary OECD/DAC Guidelines for Security System Reform and Governance (OECD 2004), Western donors approved the use of ODA to support the development of state security institutions such as the police, but within clear parameters that excluded the use of ODA to support the repression of legitimate civilian opposition or directly strengthening the counterinsurgency capacities of Southern governments. The use of ODA to support such security-driven strategies is what we call the "securitization" of aid (Baranyi and Paducel 2012). Those standards enable us to situate Canadian ODA on a spectrum ranging from securitization to conflict-sensitive development.

With regard to the commercialization of development cooperation, international norms are less clear. As such, we take the extent to which ODA is tied to Canada's commercial goals and to specific trade or foreign investment promotion activities as a starting point to assess degrees of commercialization. This exploratory analysis is intended as a baseline for future studies on the consequences of Ottawa's aim of forging a *rapprochement* between Canada's aid efforts and its trade plus investment efforts.

This chapter makes four main arguments. First, we argue that the development effectiveness of Canadian cooperation varies across countries, from being quite low in the West Bank and Gaza, as well as in Pakistan, to somewhat better in Ethiopia and Mali, to fairly high in Bangladesh. Second, we suggest that the degree to which development cooperation is securitized, rather than conflict-sensitive, also varies: from high securitization in the West Bank and Gaza, to less securitization in Ethiopia, Mali, and Pakistan, to little securitization and considerable conflict-sensitivity in Bangladesh. Third, we argue that the commercialization of ODA is not a major concern in any of these cases. In Bangladesh, we suggest that there is complementarity between ODA and the trade relations. Finally, we build on those observations to conclude that it is time to rethink CIDA's traditional distinction between fragile states and low-income countries, and to foster more two-way learning across that spectrum, instead of assuming that the Afghanistan model is the appropriate template for all whole-of-government interventions in difficult contexts.

Our research is based mostly on publicly accessible primary documents and secondary literature. Given space limitations, it is not possible to provide deep background, though key characteristics of each case are noted. We do not analyze important aspects such as the institutional processes that undermined Canadian programming in FCAS because they are addressed by Carment and Samy (this volume).

Canadian Development Cooperation in FCAS

Size, Modalities, and Priorities
CIDA programming in this sample has reflected major trends in Canadian cooperation since 2001, notably its budget increases until 2011 and its concentration in a limited number of "countries of focus."[1] Beyond those general trends, ODA levels and modalities were influenced by events in each context, as suggested by the data in Table 2.

Table 2. Canadian ODA to Sample Cases, 2007–2013 (in C$ millions)

Country	2007–08	2008–09	2009–10	2010–11	2011–12	2012–13
Ethiopia	118	146	176	211	177	208
Pakistan	75	103	75	130	167	107
Bangladesh	98	110	120	121	96	96
Mali	78	96	131	129	125	80
West Bank & Gaza	42	46	68	67	78	65

Source: NSI (2013).

Ethiopia has consistently been the largest recipient of ODA in our sample – and was the largest CIDA country program in the world in 2011–12. However, in 2006, Canada cut bilateral aid to Ethiopia, following the government's alleged fraud and violence during the 2005 national elections, redirecting ODA through multi-donor trust funds and NGOs (OECD 2012, 110). Mali received less but still considerable ODA during the 2001–11 decade, most of it channelled through general budget support. After the military *coup* in April 2012, Ottawa also suspended government-to-government cooperation to Mali.

Pakistan and Bangladesh have also received significant levels of development assistance. In Pakistan, Canada channelled most of its ODA through multilateral and civil society organizations. In Bangladesh, those modalities have also been important, though considerable cooperation has also been channelled through government programs. The West Bank and Gaza received the lowest level of ODA in our sample, mostly as humanitarian aid channelled through multilateral agencies and Canadian NGOs.

According to CIDA country strategy documents, between 2007 and 2009, priorities in these countries ranged from private sector development and democratic governance to basic education, natural resource management, and gender equality (CIDA 2009abc). Country priorities became somewhat more focused in 2009, in line with CIDA's revised aid effectiveness strategy.

Effectiveness

The country reports of the 2011 Paris Declaration (PD) Survey suggest that the effectiveness of Canadian ODA has varied across the five cases, at least on certain indicators (OECD 2011abcd).[2] It has been most aligned with government priorities and systems in Bangladesh. In Ethiopia and Mali, Canadian cooperation has aligned with government priorities, but it largely disengaged from government systems after the 2005 governance crisis in Ethiopia and the 2012 *coup* in Mali. Canada–Pakistan cooperation is the least aligned with government systems.

Although CIDA has reported on development results in all cases since 2007, it is difficult to match those reports with host country results data. This seems partly attributable to weak development evaluation systems in those countries. It also reflects the problematic performance of CIDA and its host country partners with regard to the PD principle of mutual accountability. That pattern seems to apply across the board, even in relatively enabling contexts such as Bangladesh.

CIDA also suggests that its aid has been fairly effective in the West Bank and Gaza, where Canadian assistance priorities have been aligned with priorities codified in key documents, including the 2008–2011 Palestinian Reform and Development Plan (GOC 2013). Canada can also credibly claim that it coordinates with Western donors and with the Palestinian Authority in the West Bank via key sector working groups, such as the security and justice working groups. However, Ottawa's claims about development results should be treated with caution, given the compelling questions that have been posed about the effectiveness of aid in the context of protracted occupation (Ibrahim and Beaudet 2012; Abu-Zahra and Kay 2012).

The evolution of CIDA's engagement in Ethiopia illustrates the challenges of remaining engaged in LICs when they drift towards authoritarian governance. The last evaluation of CIDA's Ethiopia program suggested that after the 2005 electoral crisis, CIDA managed to balance support for the poverty reduction agenda of the government with a consistent message on human rights and democratic governance (CIDA 2010, x). However, the report acknowledged that CIDA missed an historic opportunity to significantly scale up its support to Ethiopian civil society and thereby foster the social base for longer term democratization (CIDA 2010, 16).

The Ethiopian experience is not unique. The difficulties of adapting cooperation with LICs when apparently good governance degenerates into major crises raise profound questions about simple distinctions between LICs and FCAS. As we will demonstrate in the next section, the cases of Ethiopia and Mali also underscore the importance of building conflict sensitivity into programming in such contexts, despite their image of stability.

From Securitization to Conflict Sensitivity

As explained in the introduction, the distinction between securitization and conflict sensitivity enables us to situate our cases on a spectrum ranging from the Palestinian Territories, where Canadian ODA has become quite securitized, through Pakistan, Mali, and Ethiopia, where traces of securitization are present, to cases such as Bangladesh, where development-security linkages appear more conducive to conflict prevention.

Canada's engagement in the West Bank and Gaza has been transformed by the Harper government. From 1948 to 2006, Ottawa maintained an even-handed approach to the Israeli-Palestinian conflict, supporting peacekeeping through the United Nations and maintaining a small ODA program focused on relief, social development, and dialogue on Palestinian refugees' rights (Bell et al. 2007; Funk 2007). After the violent fragmentation of the Palestinian territories in 2006, Ottawa doubled its assistance and developed new projects aiming to "establish a safe environment in the West Bank conducive to Israel's security priorities" (DFATD 2012, 1). Those projects included counterterrorism capacity building for the Palestinian Authority, and support for Joint Operations Centres with the Israeli Defence Force, linked to the deployment of Canadian security personnel embedded in the US and European Union security assistance missions. They also included using ODA to support justice sector projects such as strengthening the Palestinian Authority Prosecution Services and building new courthouses. Ottawa has justified those projects in terms that echo OECD/DAC norms on security-development linkages. Yet critics seem correct in viewing Canadian and broader Western assistance since 2006 as driven largely by the aim of modernizing the Palestinian Authority in the West Bank, while keeping it subservient to Israeli security interests and isolating Hamas (which Ottawa lists as a terrorist organization) in the Gaza Strip (Brynen 2007; Ibrahim and Beaudet 2012).

Canadian cooperation with Pakistan, Mali, and Ethiopia differs significantly from that approach. In Pakistan, post–9/11 concerns about Islamic terrorism also affected the rationale of Canadian programming, particularly in education and in the conflict-affected province of Balochistan, which borders on Afghanistan (Lee 2013). However, Ottawa did not establish a security assistance program and does not appear to have aligned other elements of the CIDA program on security objectives. CIDA programming does not appear to have been particularly conflict-sensitive either, notably in Balochistan, and instead focused on socio-economic development "to support Canadian interests in Afghanistan" (CIDA 2009b, 3).

There is more historical evidence of conflict-sensitivity in Mali, where CIDA programming was framed by the goals of democratic development and peacebuilding in the early 1990s. That sensitivity dwindled after 9/11, with the abandonment of substantial CIDA support to decentralization in the North (McGregor 2013). With the rise of Al-Qaeda in the Islamic Maghreb and the kidnapping of two former Canadian diplomats, Canadian policy took on a harder edge. That shift was reflected in Canadian counter-terror assistance to the Malian Army in 2011–12 (Pugliese 2011, 2012). As mentioned above, Canada cut government-to-government assistance after the *coup*, but the retrenchment of ODA programming to southern Mali suggests that Ottawa is not yet addressing the factors underlying the renewed North–South conflict (McGregor 2013).

In Ethiopia, Canada displayed more consistent conflict-sensitivity when it cut government-to-government cooperation after the ruling party and security forces committed grave violations of human rights during the 2005 elections (OECD 2012, 110). Despite Ethiopia's importance for the West in the Horn of Africa, Canada did not establish a security assistance program and does not appear to have overtly aligned its ODA with Western regional security goals. Nonetheless, the spectacular growth of the Ethiopia program as the largest Canadian ODA partnership in 2011–12, despite the authoritarian record of the regime in Addis Ababa, suggests that geopolitics can influence development cooperation more subtly.

In Bangladesh, there has been no drift towards the securitization of aid and more progress towards conflict-sensitive policy coherence. The Bangladeshi Army has long benefited from Canada's Military Training Assistance Program. Most of that training seems to be linked to the country's participation in UN peacekeeping operations. Indeed, Ottawa frames its relations with Bangladesh as part of a broader partnership that includes converging positions on regional and global security issues, notably on international peacekeeping (GOC 2014).

The distance between Canada's support for counter-terror operations in Palestine or even Mali, and its approach in Bangladesh, highlights both the risks of securitization in certain FCAS and the potential of conflict-sensitive policy coherence in others. It also validates the idea of situating Canada's involvement in different FCAS along a spectrum of development-security relationships that runs from complete securitization at one end to consistent conflict-sensitivity at the other, a point to which we will return in the last section of this chapter.

Commercialization

What is the relationship between Canadian trade and development cooperation in these cases? As suggested in Table 3, there is no simple correlation between volumes of Canadian trade and development cooperation with these countries. Canada trades little with Ethiopia, its largest ODA partner. It trades much more with Bangladesh and Pakistan, but very little with Mali, and apparently little with the Palestinian Territories.[3]

Table 3. Sampled Cases with ODA Rankings and Trade Volumes

Country	Canadian ODA Rank (2012)	Two-Way Trade in C$ Millions (2012)
Ethiopia	1	141.3
Pakistan	8	558.9
Bangladesh	10	1,654.7
Mali	13	17.2
West Bank & Gaza	16	N/A

Sources: ODA rankings are taken from CIDA (2012) and trade statistics from DFATD (2013a).

Due to lack of data on Canadian foreign direct investment (FDI) for our sample, it is also difficult to establish clear links between Canadian FDI and ODA. However, anecdotal evidence suggests that Canadian investments are significant in some contexts. For instance, in Ethiopia, thirteen Canadian companies have signed contracts for the exploration of potash and precious and base metals, with a registered capital of C$6.5 million (GOC 2012b). Canadian mining firms are active in Mali (Cousineau and Mackrael 2013). Yet there does not appear to be a direct relationship between the content of Canadian development cooperation and business involvement in these countries. For example, in Ethiopia, despite Canadian firms' growing interests in mining, ODA remains focused on food security, health, and strengthening democratic institutions.

Canada's growing trade relations with Bangladesh illustrate the indirect synergies that can be nurtured between trade and ODA. Indeed, Bangladesh is one of the countries that has benefited from the reduction of Canadian tariff barriers on garment manufactures and other imports from least developed countries in 2003 (Weston 2003). Ottawa's decision to provide assistance to improve health and safety practices in the Bangladeshi garment industry, in the wake of an industrial catastrophe in Dhaka (DFATD 2013d), suggests that the linkages between trade and ODA might grow tighter. That could be positive, but it seems wise for scholars to monitor that scenario in Bangladesh, as well as in FCAS such as Ethiopia and Mali, to understand if Ottawa's renewed drive to promote Canadian commerce might undermine conflict-sensitive and sustainable development.

Conclusions and Options

Our study of Canadian development engagement in a range of fragile states other than the high-profile cases of Afghanistan, Haiti, and Sudan, enables us to extend Baranyi and Paducel's (2012) analysis to other contexts. It suggests that the effectiveness and securitization of aid in lower-profile cases has varied significantly – from questionable effectiveness and high securitization in West Bank and Gaza, to lower securitization yet diminishing effectiveness in Ethiopia, Mali, and Pakistan, to more conflict-sensitivity and effectiveness in Bangladesh. The shifts from stability to fragility in LICs such as Ethiopia and Mali, and the relative success of development cooperation in LICs such as Bangladesh, suggest that it would be useful to draw (context-appropriate) lessons from the latter, rather than assuming that the "Afghanistan model" should be applied to all FCAS. The cases of Ethiopia and Mali certainly highlight the importance of building conflict sensitivity into programming in such contexts, despite their historic image of stability. The 2013 evaluation of the Mali country program pointed towards the need for "additional resources and tools to more thoroughly analyse risk scenarios, and make relevant plans and adaptation measures" (DFATD 2013c). It also noted that this approach would be useful "for the Mali Program as well as other CIDA Country Programs operating in countries in conflict" (DFATD 2013c).

The differences between Canada's counter-terror capacity building in Palestine and Mali, and Ottawa's approach in Bangladesh, clearly underscore the risks of securitization in *certain* FCAS and the potential of conflict-sensitive policy coherence in others. Together, these cases suggest that it is useful to look beyond the one-way application of considerations lessons from whole-of-government involvement in Afghanistan, to more two-way learning across a wider range of cases on the fragility-stability spectrum.

Some of these lessons appear to have been drawn in official Ottawa. In 2012, Canada scaled down its aid program in Afghanistan, in line with the reduction of Western forces on the ground (GOC 2012). In January 2013, it announced a freeze on new Canadian aid to Haiti, pending a review of the apparently slim development results on the ground (Fantino 2013). Around the same time, Minister of Foreign Affairs John Baird declared that Canada would not be dragged into "another Afghanistan" in Mali (Murray 2013). Development programming in Pakistan and Sudan, as well as the West Bank and Gaza, were also placed under review. As a result of those reviews, in July 2014 Pakistan was moved from being a country of focus to becoming a "development partner" with a more modest ODA program (DFATD 2014). So despite earlier claims about the success of Canadian whole-of-government programming in Afghanistan, the "Afghan model" seems unlikely to become the template for Canadian engagement in other FCAS.

Nonetheless, our comparative analysis suggests that while Canada may continue to scale down assistance to FCAS where results fall dramatically short of Western expectations, it will continue to provide assistance to most countries. In cases with relatively stable governance such as Bangladesh, government-to-government cooperation and support to civil society may remain the preferred modalities, partly because they have demonstrated fairly satisfactory results. Despite its concerns about democratic governance and poor development results in Ethiopia, Mali, and Pakistan, Ottawa will stay involved because of their regional importance. In the West Bank and Gaza, where policies and their outcomes are more profoundly contested at the national and international levels, Ottawa will probably be more cautious and channel relatively low levels of funding through international and civil society organizations. Humanitarian assistance is likely to endure as a major component of cooperation programs there and in other FCAS, with predictably negative consequences for national ownership and development sustainability.

The chapter also suggests that development-security linkages will vary considerably in different FCAS. The degree of securitization that emerged in Afghanistan is unlikely to be replicated in other contexts. Nonetheless, a significant security assistance portfolio linked to justice sector programming will probably endure in the West Bank and Gaza, due to its connections with Western and Israeli geopolitical interests. Ottawa may be tempted to take a similar approach in Mali, given the latter's increasing regional importance, though Prime Minister Harper's reaction to calls for Canadian military intervention in early 2013 suggests that caution may also prevail there. At the other end of the spectrum, there should be opportunities to cultivate more positive development-security linkages in Bangladesh, where a multi-dimensional development partnership fits well with conflict-sensitive capacity building for UN-mandated peacekeeping.

Our preliminary exploration of links between Canada's commercial and ODA relations suggests that there is only modest cause for concern about the commercialization of ODA in these contexts. In Bangladesh, commercial ties may keep expanding in ways that complement ODA-based cooperation. In countries such as Ethiopia, Mali, and Pakistan, where commercial activity is more risky due to state fragility or armed conflict, Ottawa will likely use ODA to nurture an environment for future investment and trade. Given the announcement in 2014 of new ODA programs in Benin, Burkina Faso, the Democratic Republic of the Congo, Mongolia, and Myanmar, where Canadian commercial interests could converge with problematic governance to generate high risks for many stakeholders, and given the government's aim of fostering synergies between FDI and ODA, this dimension of our study clearly requires further examination.

Finally, our analysis calls into question CIDA's traditional distinction between FCAS and LICs. As we have seen in the cases of Ethiopia, Mali, and Pakistan, the distinction between FCAS and states with "broadly stable governance and public security" is sometimes based more on wishful thinking about stability rather than on a rigorous understanding of conditions in these societies. Viewing such partners as moving along a spectrum of fragility over time may enable Canada to adapt its cooperation more wisely in fluid contexts. It may also enable DFATD to draw on relevant lessons from less fragile states such as Bangladesh to inform policy in more fragile contexts, rather than trying to apply a problematic "Afghanistan model."

There is considerable convergence between the lessons one can draw from these contexts and the learning codified in the New Deal for Engagement in Fragile States, a document signed by OECD donors and nineteen self-designated FCAS in 2011 (IDPS 2013). The New Deal's core principles — letting FCAS lead their own development processes; prioritizing legitimate politics, peoples' security, and employment; and remaining engaged in partnerships over the long run — echo the norms that have governed cooperation in contexts such as Bangladesh. The New Deal and its follow-up processes embody other lessons learned in FCAS over the past decade, including the need to help partner countries conduct their own fragility assessments and the importance of using common assessments to orient external assistance. DFATD might be in a better position to practice such conflict-sensitive programming, as envisaged by Carment and Samy (this volume). The merger might even enable the department to provide coherent advice about the risks of unduly commercializing ODA in contexts of fragile governance, particularly in the extractive sector.

While that advice may not always be heeded by the Harper government, it could be picked up in the future. The next government in Ottawa could certainly rethink Canada's narrowly partisan approach in the West Bank and Gaza, by bringing Ottawa back into line with international norms, including the New Deal. Scholars could contribute to that scenario through nuanced analyses of how the development dimension of Canada's whole-of-government engagement evolves in different FCAS. In that connection, it is essential to complement research on (decreasingly) high-profile cases such as Afghanistan and Haiti with more grounded research on Canadian involvement in "other" FCAS, such as those examined herein. It also seems important to extend that analysis in particular to the Democratic Republic of the Congo and Myanmar, since their "new deals" have attracted Canadian attention across the ODA-commerce spectrum — despite enduring governance and human rights concerns.

Notes

1. In 2005, the Martin government identified twenty-five countries in which it sought to concentrate its bilateral aid. The Harper government issued a new list of twenty "countries of focus" in 2009. In July 2014, it increased the number to twenty-five, dropping two countries and adding seven.
2. The OECD did not conduct a survey for the West Bank and Gaza.
3. Canada's trade with West Bank and Gaza is included in the data on its significant trade relationship with Israel (C$1.4 billion in 2012), facilitated by the 1997 Canada–Israel Free Trade Agreement (DFATD 2013b).

References

Abu-Zahra, Nadia, and Adah Kay. 2012. *Unfree in Palestine: Registration, Documentation and Movement Restriction*. London: Pluto Press.

Banerjee, Nipa. 2008. "Ineffective Aid Hobbles Afghan Transition." *Policy Options*. June: 24–27.

Banerjee, Nipa. 2010. "Aid Development for a Secure Afghanistan." *Policy Options*. November: 48–52.

Banerjee, Nipa. 2013. "How Canadian Branding Trumped Results in Afghanistan." *Ottawa Citizen*, August 27.

Baranyi, Stephen, and Anca Paducel. 2012. "Whither Development in Canada's Approach towards Fragile States?" In Stephen Brown, ed. *Struggling for Effectiveness: CIDA and Canadian Foreign Aid*. Montreal and Kingston: McGill–Queen's University Press: 108–34.

Bell, Michael, Michael Molloy, David Sultan, and Sallama Shaker. 2007. "Practitioners' Perspectives on Canada-Middle East Relations." In Paul Heinbecker and Bessma Momani, eds. *Canada and the Middle East: In Theory and Practice*. Waterloo, ON: CIGI and Wilfrid Laurier University Press: 7–24.

Brown, Stephen. 2008. "CIDA Under the Gun." In Jean Daudelin and Daniel Schwanen, eds. *Canada Among Nations 2007. What Room for Manoeuvre?* Montreal and Kingston: McGill–Queen's University Press: 91–107.

Brynen, Rex. 2007. "Canada's Role in the Israeli-Palestine Peace Process." Paul Heinbecker and Bessma Momani, eds. *Canada and the Middle East: In Theory and Practice*. Waterloo, ON: CIGI and Wilfrid Laurier University Press: 73–90.

CCIC. 2006. "Failures of the 'Failed States' Framework." Ottawa: Canadian Council for International Co-operation.

CCIC. 2012. "CCIC Comments on the Report of the Standing Committee on Foreign Affairs and International Development." Ottawa: CCIC.

Carment, David, and Yiagadeesen Samy. 2012. "Assessing State Fragility: A Country Indicators for Foreign Policy Report." Ottawa: Carleton University.

CIDA. 2009a. "Bangladesh Country Strategy (Effective as of 2009)." Gatineau, QC: CIDA.

CIDA. 2009b. "Pakistan Country Strategy (Effective as of 2009)." Gatineau, QC: CIDA.

CIDA. 2009c. *Ethiopia: CIDA Report*. Gatineau, QC: CIDA.

CIDA. 2009d. "Country Development Programming Framework (CPDF). Pakistan Program." Gatineau, QC: CIDA.

CIDA. 2010. "Ethiopia Country Program Evaluation 2003–2004 and 2008–2009. Synthesis Report." Gatineau, QC: CIDA.

CIDA. 2012. *Statistical Report on International Assistance. Fiscal Year 2011–2012*. Gatineau, QC: CIDA.

CIDA. 2013. *Canadian International Development Agency 2013–2014. Report on Plans and Priorities*. Gatineau, QC: CIDA.

Cousineau, Sophie and Kim Mackrael. 2013. "Mali and the Quebec Connection." *Globe and Mail*. February 9: F1 and F5.

DFATD. 2012. "START and the Middle East Peace Process." Internet, http://www.international.gc.ca/start-gtsr/middle_east-moyen_orient.aspx. Accessed July 27, 2013.

DFATD. 2013a. "International Commerce by Country." Internet, http://w03.international.gc.ca/Commerce_International/Commerce.aspx?lang=eng. Accessed August 24, 2013.

DFATD. 2013b. "Israel." Internet, http://www.canadainternational.gc.ca/ci-ci/assets/pdfs/fact_sheet-fiche_documentaire/Israel-FS-en.pdf. Accessed July 27, 2013.

DFATD. 2013c. "Mali Country Program Evaluation 2006–2007 – 2010–2011 – Synthesis Report." Internet, http://www.international.gc.ca/development-developpement/evaluation-mali.aspx?lang=eng. Accessed July 12, 2014.

DFATD. 2013d. "Canada Backs Initiative to Improve Working Conditions in Bangladesh." Internet, http://news.gc.ca/web/article-en.do?mthd=advSrch&crtr.mnthndVl=7&crtr.mnthStrtVl=1&crtr.page=1&nid=801449&crtr.yrndVl=2014&crtr.kw=Bangladesh&crtr.yrStrtVl=2002&crtr.dyStrtVl=1&crtr.dyndVl=21. Accessed May 26, 2014.

DFATD. 2014. "Where We Work in International Development." Internet, http://www.international.gc.ca/development-developpement/countries-pays/index.aspx?lang=eng#. Accessed July 1, 2014.

Fantino, Julian. 2013. "Development in Haiti." January 8. Internet, http://www.acdi-cida.gc.ca/acdi-cida/acdi-cida.nsf/eng/NAT-18123021-NJJ. Accessed November 2, 2013.

Fund for Peace. 2013. "Failed States Index 2013." http://ffp.statesindex.org/rankings. Accessed August 10, 2013.

Funk, Nathan. 2007. "Applying Canadian Principles to Peace and Conflict Resolution in the Middle East." In Paul Heinbecker and Bessma Momani, eds. *Canada and the Middle East: In Theory and Practice.* Waterloo, ON: CIGI and Wilfrid Laurier University Press: 25–44.

Government of Canada. 2012a. *Canada's Engagement in Afghanistan, Fourteenth and Final Report to Parliament.* Ottawa: GOC.

Government of Canada. 2012b. "Canada-Ethiopia Relations." Internet, http://www.canadainternational.gc.ca/ethiopia-ethiopie/bilateral_relations_bilaterales/canada_ethiopia-ethiopie.aspx?menu_id=7&view=d. Accessed August 5, 2013.

Government of Canada. 2013. "Canada-West Bank/Gaza Strip Relations." Internet, http://www.canadainternational.gc.ca/west_bank_gaza-cisjordanie_bande_de_gaza/bilateral_relations_bilaterales/canada-wbg-cg.aspx?lang=eng&menu_id=7. Accessed July 27, 2013.

Government of Canada. 2014. "Canada-Bangladesh Relations." Internet, http://www.canadainternational.gc.ca/bangladesh/bilateral_relations_bilaterales/index.aspx?lang=eng&menu_id=19. Accessed July 21, 2014.

Ibrahim, Nassar, and Pierre Beaudet. 2012. "Effective Aid in to Occupied Palestinian Territories?" *Conflict, Security & Development*, vol. 12, no. 5: 481–500.

International Dialogue on Peacebuilding and Statebuilding. 2013. "New Deal Snapshot." Internet, http://www.newdeal4peace.org/new-deal-snapshot/. Accessed August 21, 2013.

Lee, Allison. 2013. "Canadian Aid, Education and (In)Security in Pakistan." Unpublished manuscript.

McGregor, Katherine. 2013. "Canadian Engagement in Fragile States: Conflict and Democracy in Mali." Unpublished manuscript.

Murray, Robert. 2013. "Why Mali is Not Another Afghanistan." Troy Media, February 19. Internet, http://www.troymedia.com/2013/02/19/why-mali-is-not-another-afghanistan/. Accessed November 2, 2013.

North–South Institute. 2013. "Canadian International Development Platform." Internet, http://cidpnsi.ca/. Accessed on August 24, 2013.

OECD. 2004. *OECD Development Assistance Committee Guidelines for Security System Reform and Governance.* Paris: OECD.

OECD. 2007. *DAC Principles for Good International Engagement in Fragile States and Situations.* Paris: OECD.

OECD. 2008. *Paris Declaration and Accra Agenda for Action.* Internet, http://www.oecd.org/dac/effectiveness/parisdeclarationandaccraagendaforaction.htm. Accessed August 5, 2013.

OECD. 2011a. "OECD; Aid Effectiveness 2011: Progress in Implementing the Paris Declaration – Volume II Country Chapters – Bangladesh." Paris: OECD.

OECD. 2011b. "OECD; Aid Effectiveness 2011: Progress in Implementing the Paris Declaration – Volume II Country Chapters – Ethiopia." Paris: OECD.

OECD. 2011c. "OECD; Aid Effectiveness 2011: Progress in Implementing the Paris Declaration – Volume II Country Chapters – Pakistan." Paris: OECD.

OECD. 2011d. "OECD; Aid Effectiveness 2011: Progress in Implementing the Paris Declaration – Volume II Country Chapters – Mali (French). Paris: OECD.

OECD. 2012. *Canada. Development Assistance Committee (DAC) Peer Review 2012.* Paris: OECD.

Pugliese, David. 2011. "Canadian Special Forces Mentors Mali's Military." Postmedia News, December 3.

Pugliese, David. 2012. "Uprising in Mali Postpones Canadian Military Training Mission." *Ottawa Citizen*, February 28.

Swiss, Liam. 2012. "Gender, Security, and Instrumentalism: Canada's Foreign Aid in Support of National Interest?" In Stephen Brown, ed. *Struggling for Effectiveness: CIDA and Canadian Foreign Aid.* Montreal and Kingston: McGill–Queen's University Press: 135–58.

Weston, Ann. 2003. "Bangladesh's Access to the Canadian Market: Implications of the New Canadian LDC Initiative and Prospects for Export Diversification." Dhaka: Center for Policy Dialogue.

CHAPTER XV

Charity Begins at Home: The Extractive Sector as an Illustration of Changes and Continuities in the New De Facto Canadian Aid Policy

Gabriel C. Goyette

Development aid must be rooted in the expression of Canadian values and granted according to the strategic interests of Canada, as defined in an integrated foreign policy.

(Conservative Party 2011)

The Harper government has made its mark on Canadian development assistance through numerous and profound changes to practices, the institutional set-up, and the instruments used to provide aid. While some of these changes may have gone unnoticed by the Canadian public, others have attracted more attention, especially the merger of the Canadian International Development Agency (CIDA) with the Department of Foreign Affairs and International Trade to create the Department of Foreign Affairs, Trade and Development (DFATD). These changes not only affect public institutions and programs, they also impact the private and associative spheres, with significant changes experienced by the NGO community, including the growth in the proportion of funds going to religious and especially proselytizing organizations, as well as NGOs based in western Canada (Audet et al. 2013).[1] These changes, however, have not been the subject of an explicit and systematic policy statement, nor indeed has Canadian foreign policy, for that matter. In fact, since the Conservatives came to power, defence strategy is the only component of foreign affairs that has been the subject of a policy statement, along with white papers on the Arctic in 2009 and 2010 and on cybersecurity in 2010.

Of the many changes that have occurred, two stand out in the literature on Canadian aid for their importance. First, the government has placed programmatic emphasis on aid effectiveness, which has led to an overly technical conception of practices. Second, it has instrumentalized aid policy and made it subservient to broader foreign policy, notably through changes in CIDA's countries of focus and the criteria for selecting them, the emergence of priority themes with a strong impact on disbursements, a religious and security turn in aid delivery, an emphasis on humanitarian assistance, the marginalization of gender issues, and the growth of the role of the private sector, both in policy making and in practice. This last tendency is particularly clear in the extractive sector, which emerges as an implicit government priority (Brown 2012; Campbell 2013; Goyette 2011).

These changes have not been formalized in a policy statement are thus in a new *de jure* aid policy. I argue that the systematic nature of the reforms implemented while Bev Oda was Minister of International Cooperation (Goyette 2011), their continuous implementation in Canadian aid practices, and the adaptation of governance structures to serve them demonstrate the existence a new *de facto* Canadian aid policy — one in which aid loses its autonomy and becomes a mere tool of foreign policy. I do not wish to overstate the coherence of Canadian aid practices. Nonetheless, the changes mentioned above are clearly not just a series of decisions made independently. They are a manifestation of the Harper government's integrated foreign policy, which places domestic interests at the core of all activities, including development assistance. I support my argument with an analysis of *Building the Canadian Advantage: A Corporate Social Responsibility (CSR) Strategy for the Canadian International Extractive Sector*. After briefly introducing this initiative and its implementation modalities, I show how it abides by the principles, and is in fact emblematic, of this new *de facto* policy. In doing so, I wish to pull together the different strands of this new *de facto aid policy*, to identify the contours of the changes, and to highlight the magnitude of these changes. I also want to identify the risks this approach poses, notably in terms of development effectiveness.

The initiative, *Building the Canadian Advantage*, rests on four pillars: the creation of a CSR centre of excellence; the appointment of an Extractive Sector CSR Counsellor; encouraging Canadian companies to adopt high-quality CSR standards; and strengthening the capacity of developing countries to manage the exploitation of the extractive sector and use its benefits to reduce poverty (CIDA 2011b). The government assigned the responsibility for implementing the fourth pillar to CIDA, notably because 50 percent of its countries of focus were rich in natural resources.

The recent emphasis by CIDA, and now DFATD, on the extractive sector for the realization of the fourth pillar has led to interventions in Canada and at the multilateral and bilateral levels, as well as in specific projects. First, at the multilateral level, the government seeks to promote the strengthening of international standards, mainly through the World Bank's Extractive Industries Transparency Initiative (EITI), to which DFATD will contribute $10 million between 2012 and 2016 (CIDA 2012a). At the bilateral level, the department's commitment is embodied in the Andean Regional Initiative, which aims to strengthen local governments' and communities' capacity to implement projects and manage their relationship with the private sector, as well as royalties. The bilateral level and the strengthening of local capacities are both official DFATD priorities for CSR (Singleton 2011), and the department is providing $20 million for these purposes over a period of five years. At the local level, DFATD is funding three CSR projects in collaboration with Canadian mining companies and NGOs in Ghana, Burkina Faso, and Peru (CIDA 2011b; see Brown, this volume). Finally, at the national level, the strategy has resulted in the creation of the Canadian International Institute for Extractive Industries and Development, based at the University of British Columbia.[2] Its objectives are "improving and strengthening resource-extraction governance; increasing capacity building in policy, legislation, regulatory development and implementation; and educating skilled workers, providing technical training and assistance" (UBC 2013).

I chose this example to illustrate the contemporary transformations of Canadian aid mainly because of its novelty. As an initiative exclusively designed and implemented by the Harper government, it best illustrates the trends that are specific to that government, whereas an analysis of recent reforms would highlight instead its ability to alter existing practices. Although qualitatively significant, it is important to note that this policy is quantitatively marginal, insofar as it currently only involves annual commitments of approximately $5 million out of a total official development assistance (ODA) budget of $5.68 billion in 2012 (OECD 2013).

Physician, Heal Thyself

Because they all work towards the promotion of the same fundamental interests, different components of Canada's foreign policy have had a certain consistency under any government. Nevertheless, trade, defence, foreign affairs, and international development all interpreted these core interests differently in their specific areas of responsibility and translated them into their own policy priorities. What sets apart the Harper government's vision of an integrated foreign policy is its strong unity and prioritization of objectives. It is based on the principles of the Conservative Party as defined in successive party platform statements since 2004. Foreign policy is integrated in that its various components – defence, trade, diplomacy, and aid – all have the same objectives, "to defend the economic interests of the country, while respecting human rights and individual freedom" (Conservative Party 2011). These components are prioritized, with trade and national defence policies at the top of the list. Together, these priority policies define foreign policy, which must therefore help meet their objectives. Aid is perceived as an instrument of foreign policy, rather than an independent, or even semi-autonomous, sector with its own goals. In fact, the first words of the Conservative platform's section on foreign aid are, "The Conservative Party believes in the inherent benefits of development assistance to Canadians and the world" (Conservative Party 2011). This statement, adopted in 2011 and slightly modified in 2013 to include references to democracy, is clear about who the primary beneficiaries of Canadian aid are: Canadians and Canadian businesses. It is not "the poor," as specified of the Official Development Assistance Accountability Act, unanimously adopted by Parliament in 2008. Section 4 reads:

> Official development assistance may be provided only if the competent minister is of the opinion that it: *a*) contributes to poverty reduction; *b*) takes into account the perspectives of the poor; and *c*) is consistent with international human rights standards. (Parliament of Canada 2008, 3)

As such, it is therefore not trivial to see the emergence of a focus on the extractive sector, a key sector for the Canadian economy, which is itself the priority of the Conservatives, as they frequently remind voters. In 2011, the mining sector contributed more than $35 billion to the Canadian economy. It represented nearly 23 percent of Canada's exports and brought in $9 billion in taxes and royalties (Mining Association of Canada 2011).

The negotiation of free trade agreements, launched in 2007, with two key continental players in the extractive sector, Peru and Colombia, fits especially well in this strategy. So does the government's response to the report of the *National Roundtables on Corporate Social Responsibility and the Canadian Extractive Industry* tabled in 2007. Rather than seeking to regulate the industry, as would have been the case with the adoption of Bill C-300 (An Act respecting Corporate Accountability for the Activities of Mining, Oil or Gas in Developing Countries), the government provided instead a series of opportunities for the industry: funding for their CSR strategies and to improve their business environments through DFATD, and the chance to improve their corporate image through a Centre of Excellence, which "help[s] Canadian companies doing business around the world" (CSR Centre 2011).

Effectiveness and Public Policy

Aid effectiveness has been a central concern of donors and international aid agencies since the mid-1990s. The Organisation for Economic Co-operation and Development's (OECD) 1996 report, *Shaping the 21st Century: The Contribution of Development Co-operation*, and the World Bank's report, *Assessing Aid: What Works, What Doesn't, and Why* (World Bank 1998), marked the public emergence of this debate. However, it is the adoption of the Paris Declaration on Aid Effectiveness in 2005 that established this concern at the heart of the development, implementation, and evaluation of aid policies and practices for Western donors.

Canada is often sensitive to international trends in aid policy, programs, and aid management and delivery mechanisms (Goyette 2008). The Harper government was quick to adopt the effectiveness narrative as the *leitmotif* for the reshaping of its aid policy. However, its conceptualization of effectiveness is essentially self-referential, rather than centred on recipient country ownership, as prescribed

by the Paris Declaration. It focuses on internal, administrative procedural efficiency, rather than development outcomes, and is designed
with Canadian taxpayers in mind, instead of the actual beneficiaries
of aid in recipient countries (Brown 2012). As such, it illustrates the
tendency to conceptualize Canadian aid in technical terms, particularly through the widespread use of results-based management and
its administrative incarnation, the logical framework.

This approach to effectiveness translates into public policies
and government practices that seek short-term, clearly defined, easily
quantifiable and measurable, small-scale, low-impact, results. CIDA's
CSR projects in the extractive sector fit well within this framework,
funding, for instance, worker training, well digging, and micro-credit
(see Brown, this volume, for more on these projects). Although these
projects are not likely to have a significant developmental impact,
and therefore rate poorly from a development effectiveness perspective, they are coherent with the government's aid effectiveness perspective and thus epitomize Canada's new *de facto* aid policy.

Focus

The aid effectiveness paradigm has increased donors' concern for
greater geographic concentration, thought to improve efficiency.
The OECD has praised the Harper government on this issue. Since
1998, the OECD had been highlighting the excessive dispersal of
Canadian aid and recommended limiting the number of countries to
which Canada provided ODA (OECD 1998, 29). Although the Martin
government initiated the trend of focusing on fewer countries, the
Harper Conservatives made significant steps towards greater country focus. As a result, the OECD commended Canada in 2007 for its
intention to increase the concentration of its assistance and urged it
to continue do so (OECD 2007, 10) and later, in 2012, congratulated
Canada for its greater geographic focus (OECD 2012, 50). In fiscal
year 2010–11, Canada spent 88 percent of its bilateral aid in its twenty
priority countries (CIDA 2012b). In 2014, the Harper government
announced it was adding seven new countries (and removing two,
for a total increase of five) to the list of countries of focus, but would
also further increase the target proportion of bilateral aid going to
these from 80 percent to 90 percent. Nonetheless, it is worth recalling
that no comprehensive study has substantiated the notion that aid
concentration is a major contributor to development effectiveness.

In fact, some sectorial studies of Canadian aid show that greater focus, whether it is geographical or sectoral, does not increase the effectiveness of aid (Essex 2012).

The changes to CIDA's countries of focus in 2009 shifted emphasis from Africa to the Americas. The addition of Latin American countries with abundant extractive resources and the removal of seven of the fourteen African countries from the previous list (CCCI 2009) is consistent with Canadian trade policy. The two South American countries added, Peru and Colombia, are performing well economically, with past, current, and projected growth at or above the continental average (IMF 2013), suggesting that, although they could benefit from Canadian development assistance, they did not have the most urgent needs. However, they are both countries with a large extractive sector and had each signed a free trade agreement with Canada the previous year, making them national strategic trade priorities. The 2014 addition of seven new countries also fit the trend of alignment with trade interests, notably those of the extractive sector, with the addition of Burkina Faso (an important gold producer) and the Democratic Republic of the Congo (a country rich in extractive resources), both in Africa.[3] Observers noted that "more than half of the countries that were added to the list are considered priority markets under Canada's Global Markets Action Plan" (Mackrael 2014).

CIDA's thematic focus on sustainable economic growth is particularly well suited to support extractive industries. Its three areas of privileged intervention are "building economic foundations, growing business and investing in people" (CIDA 2011a). These areas favourably align with the requirements of the extractive sector, in terms of institutional conditions of operation, labour needs or, as is the case in Peru, managing externalities of mining activities (see Brown, this volume). Moreover, the maintenance of priorities over a number of years breaks with a history of significant volatility in Canadian aid priorities, as highlighted in 2009 by the Auditor General of Canada (Auditor General 2009).

In sum, the Canadian government's choice of countries of focus and priority themes demonstrates a desire to ensure that aid will contribute to Canada's trade policy priorities and benefit Canada's own economic interests, rather than those of developing countries. These new aid policies illustrate the practical implications of the integrated foreign policy mentioned above. This does not mean Canada's aid will have no development result on the ground. However, it illustrates how decisions are made not for the sake of development efficiency or maximal impact of Canadian ODA, but for their foreign policy impact and benefits to Canadians.

The Role of the Private Sector in Canadian Aid

The role of the private sector in Canada's international development policies and endeavours goes beyond the mere implementation of projects, such as the repair and upgrade of the Dahla Dam irrigation system in Afghanistan by SNC-Lavalin. Rather, its influence can be found across the whole range of aid policy, from the development model on which aid relies to the policy-making process, in governmental management strategies, and in the implementation of aid activities in the field. The extractive sector offers a sound illustration of this trend, which is not unique to Canada (Kindornay and Reilly-King 2013), but rather, quite common among OECD donors, particularly since the International Conference on Financing for Development, held in Monterrey, Mexico in 2002.

Canada's aid policy explicitly puts the private sector at the centre of development dynamics, as exemplified by statements made by Bev Oda in 2011 and her successor Julian Fantino in 2013, as well as by the report of the House of Commons Standing Committee on Foreign Affairs and International Development, *Boosting Inclusive Economic Growth: The Role of the Private Sector in International Development,* chaired by Conservative MP Dean Allison and released in November 2012.[4] From the government's perspective, Canadian aid's role is to maximize the developmental impact of investments and the management of externalities, which are precisely the goals of DFATD involvement in the extractive sector. The Andean Regional Initiative and government's support for the EITI both seek to achieve the first objective. The same is true for the projects designed to increase the local communities' involvement in mining activities by providing them with training. For example, the project in Burkina Faso, "implemented by Plan Canada and co-financed by IAMGOLD, will help develop Burkina Faso's human capital. Girls and boys of Burkina Faso, aged from 13 to 18, will receive job skills training linked to labour market needs in the mining sector and its sub-sectors" (CIDA 2011b). The DFATD–NGO–mining company partnerships also help manage externalities. For instance, one project will provide micro-credit to populations affected by a Canadian mining project in Peru to develop income-generating activities (CIDA 2011b). While that may help affected families, it raises the question: Should the population affected by a mining project in a developing country be helped by the company profiting from the investment, as they do in Canada, or by Canadian ODA, particularly at a time where aid budgets are shrinking?

The influence of the Canadian extractive industry in the aid decision-making process is increasingly noticeable, while at the same time a growing number of voices in the NGO community condemn their own loss of influence, exemplified by CIDA's de-funding of the Canadian Council for International Co-operation, an umbrella group of development NGOs. The presence of private companies in the decision-making process was particularly visible in 2009 and 2010: As CIDA was deciding how to implement its national CSR strategy, it held several meetings with extractive companies (CIDA 2011b). Some NGO coalitions, such VOICES and its Quebec-based counterpart *Pas de démocratie sans droits,* argue that the government has deliberately silenced NGOs, citing as evidence the de-funding of KAIROS and the closure of Rights & Democracy.

The lack of civil society input can also be observed CIDA's public consultation processes. For instance, CIDA held public consultations on the establishment of the Canadian International Institute for Extractive Industries and Development and the determination of its exact mandate, in which more than 160 organizations were invited to participate (Gailloux 2013). An independent review of the process concluded that the adopted vision, "that is to say, the vision presented by the government and approved by the industry – just dominates and buries the other perspectives and proposals." It noted that the NGOs consulted qualified the process as being a "too fast and superficial" and that the mandate originally proposed had not been altered or enhanced significantly by this public consultation process, one that some participants described as a smokescreen (Gailloux 2013). This episode illustrates the marked difference in the government's treatment of input from the business community and from NGOs. DFATD subsequently hosted an electronic consultation on its *Proposed Approach to Effective Development Cooperation with Civil Society* during June and July 2014.[5]

Finally, the proportion of Canadian aid projects that involve a private company as an implementing partner has grown significantly, especially those in the extractive sector. Excluding multilateral undertakings over which Canada has no direct control, most of the CSR activities are carried out in partnership with private companies. These public-private partnerships also tend to confine NGO partners to an implementing role, rather than recognizing their full agency. This practice contradicts internationally recognized principles of aid effectiveness, as defined by the *Paris Declaration on Aid Effectiveness* and its complementary documents, in particular the *Busan Partnership for Effective Development Co-operation*, in which the partner states, including Canada, have committed to "implement fully our respective commitments to enable CSOs [civil society organizations] to exercise their roles as independent development actors, with a particular focus on an enabling environment, consistent with agreed international rights, that maximizes the contributions of CSOs to development" (OECD 2011).

In sum, there has been both a quantitative increase the scale and scope of private sector involvement in Canadian international assistance and a qualitative growth of its influence on the policy-making process.

Conclusion

Ultimately, even without a new official Canadian aid policy, one can conclude from the great consistency found in government discourse and practices and the changes made to aid management structures that a new *de facto* aid policy is emerging. It is part of a process of redefinition of Canadian foreign policy, one that is integrated and prioritized and where aid is a tool for strategic and commercial priorities, such as the expansion of Canadian companies abroad. These tendencies are best illustrated by the extractive industry CSR policy. Although such instrumentalization of aid is worrisome in itself, it is particularly so in the context of the declining Canadian aid budgets. In 2012, the government announced that it intended to cut $800 million from the aid budget between 2012 and 2015 (Canada 2012). In addition, CIDA underspent in fiscal years 2011 and 2012, which further reduced the amount of money available for development assistance.

While one can lament this instrumentalization of aid policy for the promotion of Canadian commercial interests, it is important to emphasize that, if the means are new, they do not mark a complete break with historical aid patterns. While the previous Canadian aid policies were given altruistic titles, such as *Canada Making a Difference in the World,* they still provided significant benefits to Canada. For decades, Canada has tied a substantial proportion of its aid, almost always at a rate higher than the OECD average (see Figure 1). This figure also suggests that after a decline in the proportion of tied aid under the Progressive Conservative government of Brian Mulroney (1984–93), this proportion began to expand again under the Liberal rule. The Harper government has abandoned this practice, due to OECD pressure, growing difficulties in its implementation, and the significant additional costs to aid programs (Goyette 2008). The same is true of Canadian food aid from the 1950s to the 1980s, which served domestic price stabilization purposes (Côté and Caouette 2012). Thus, while the new *de facto* aid policy is introducing new mechanisms to ensure that Canadian aid benefits Canadians, the underlying objective is not as new as some might claim.

Figure 1. Proportion of Tied Aid in Total ODA from 1979 to 2011 (Canada and DAC total)

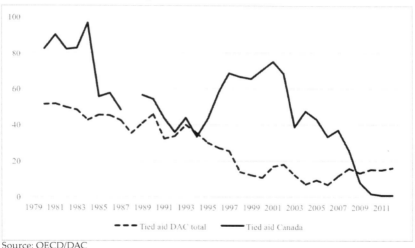

Source: OECD/DAC

Beyond the content of this policy, the manner in which it was adopted and implemented is problematic, and undermines its effectiveness in three ways. First, the absence of an explicit policy guiding government aid programs threatens public policy coherence between departments and within them, even in a unified ministry such as the DFATD. The civil servants and government officials do not have an explicit policy to refer to, neither in Ottawa/Gatineau nor on the field. By way of contrast, the UK has demonstrated the effectiveness of an explicit and comprehensive approach that ensures coherence by defining approaches and strategies for both policy and management with its *Blue Book: The Essential Guide to Working at DFID* (Goyette 2009).

Moreover, by making such important and fundamental changes to Canadian aid in the absence of a *de jure* policy debated and adopted by Parliament, the government's reforms suffer from a lack of legitimacy. By failing to produce a genuine policy document detailing the logic and strategy behind the policies and actions it promotes, the government makes it difficult to assess their merits and potential for effectiveness. In addition, by not going through the official channels and associated debates, the government denies itself the support and improvements that Parliament and its specialized committees could have provided. This may be representative of the Harper government's governance model (Wells, 2013), but it is nonetheless likely to reduce the effectiveness of Canadian aid, even from a procedural, results-based management perspective. An example of the consequence of that policy process on the quality of the *de facto* aid policy is the approach to CSR it promotes. The nature of the activities undertaken in the DFATD CSR strategy is essentially defensive, or compliance-oriented. While the literature shows that these types of CSR can help in terms of risk and corporate image management (Porter and Kramer 2006, 2011), they fail to provide the full value, long-term stability, proper orientation of innovation, and first-mover opportunities attainable by a strategic or "civil" approach to CSR (Zadek 2004, 2006). Although qualitative progress on CSR can bring value to company shareholders and society alike, it is a complex, and often long and costly process. By promoting a simplistic and primary approach to CSR, the government has missed an opportunity to help Canadian companies in this process. An open policy process would presumably have helped identify and resolve this weakness in the government's approach, thus maximizing the benefits of the expenses incurred.

Finally, the method by which the government adopted this *de facto* policy also poses a significant risk for development effectiveness. Indeed, it is now widely accepted that the predictability of aid flows is an important contributor to development effectiveness, particularly for aid-dependent countries. Developing countries frequently call for increased predictability, for instance, in the context of the Accra High-Level Forum on Aid Effectiveness in 2008. Historically, Canadian aid has been particularly volatile, as highlighted in both the report of the Auditor General mentioned above (2009) and the 2012 OECD peer review of Canada (OECD 2012). An open debate could potentially create a consensus, even a minimal one, on Canadian aid policy, its objectives, and preferred means, as was the case with the unanimous adoption of the Official Development Assistance Accountability Act in 2008. In turn, such an agreement would have been likely to ensure greater consistency in the Canadian practices in the medium term and perhaps even in case of a change of government. With the current approach, such continuity is highly unlikely, given the harsh criticism it has attracted from the two main opposition parties. Conversely, the Harper government's covert and unilateral approach contradicts a central goal of its aid policy, as stated on many occasions by the Harper government itself and the ministers responsible for aid, that is to say, effectiveness, as well as the principle of transparency. Paradoxically, although effectiveness was the primary objective of the *de facto* aid policy, it could ultimately be defeated by a lack of transparency, a value at the heart of Conservative political project since the creation of the party.

Acknowledgments

I want to thank Stephen Brown, Tony Porter, two anonymous reviewers, and the participants of the Mapping the Global Dimensions of Policy conference for their useful comments on earlier versions of this chapter. The views expressed are my own.

Notes

1. The importance of the growth has been disputed by Ray Vander Zaag of the Canadian Mennonite University in a 2013 article, in which he nonetheless mentions that "faith-based NGOs constituted about one-quarter of all NGOs receiving CIDA funding, and received about one-third (about C$100 million per year) of CIDA program and project funding to Canadian NGOs," which illustrates the overrepresentation of these organizations (Vander Zaag 2013, 321).

2. The creation of the institute was the subject of a certain level of controversy, which I address below, fuelled by the declaration of then

International Development Minister Julian Fantino, who told the mining industry that it "will be your biggest and best ambassador" (MiningWatch Canada 2014, 1).

3. Though newly added Benin does not fit that pattern, Mongolia and Burma do.

4. Oda: "The Canadian extractive industries – particularly mining industries – are the largest in the world, working in many developing countries that have an abundance of natural resources. Working in partnership with the private sector, these resources can contribute to poverty reduction in many of these countries and improve the standard of living for their populations ... CIDA is supporting Canada's Corporate Social Responsibility (CSR) Strategy for the Canadian International Extractive Sector with initiatives that will contribute to sustainable economic growth, create jobs and long-term poverty reduction" (CIDA 2011b).

5. Fantino: "The new investment that Canada realizes today demonstrates that it continues to be a leader to build on the strengths, resources and innovations in the private sector for the benefit of the most vulnerable people ... The participation of the private sector leads to better job opportunities and more investment and resources to improve productivity and increase well-being in the world" (CIDA 2013).

6. At the time of finalizing this chapter, the results of the consultation were not yet available.

References

Audet, François, Francis Paquette, and Stéfanie Bergeron. 2013. "Religious Nongovernmental Organisations and Canadian International Aid, 2001–2010: A Preliminary Study." *Canadian Journal of Development Studies*, vol. 34, no. 2: 291–320.

Auditor General of Canada. 2009. "Chapitre 8 – L'amélioration de l'efficacité de l'aide – Agence canadienne de développement international." In *Rapport de la vérificatrice générale du Canada*. Ottawa: Travaux publics et des Services gouvernementaux du Canada.

Brown, Stephen, ed. 2012. *Struggling for Effectiveness: CIDA and Canadian Foreign Aid*. Montreal and Kingston: McGill–Queen's University Press.

Campbell, Bonnie. 2012. "Activités minières et enjeux de développement: Mise en contexte pour une discussion sur le rôle des différents acteurs." Conférence prononcé au séminaire *Perspectives sur la collaboration entre OCI et compagnies minières* de l'AQOCI, Montréal.

Canada. 2012. *Emplois, croissance à long terme et prospérité : Plan d'action économique de 2012*. Ottawa: Travaux publics et Services gouvernementaux du Canada.

CCIC. 2009. "Examen de la liste des pays prioritaires émise par l'ACDI." *Note d'information du CCCI*, February 2009.

Centre for Excellence in Corporate Social Responsibility. 2011. *2011 Progress Report and 2012 Priorities*. Internet, http://web.cim.org/csr/documents/Block118_Doc169.pdf. Accessed November 15, 2013.

CIDA. 2011a. *Stimulating Sustainable Economic Growth: CIDA's Sustainable Economic Growth Strategy*. Internet, http://www.acdi-cida.gc.ca/acdi-cida/ACDI-CIDA.nsf/eng/NAD-9241625-RHC. Accessed November 15, 2013.

CIDA. 2011b. "Minister Oda Announces Initiatives to Increase the Benefits of Natural Resource Management for People in Africa and South America." September 29. Internet, http://www.acdi-cida.gc.ca/acdi-cida/acdi-cida.nsf/eng/CAR-929105317-KGD. Accessed November 15, 2013.

CIDA. 2012a. "Project Profile: Extractive Industries Transparency Initiative." Internet, http://www.acdi-cida.gc.ca/cidaweb/cpo.nsf/vLUWebProjEn/5513583B67EE77D5852579CA0035B46C. Accessed November 15, 2013.

CIDA. 2012b. *Rapport statistique sur l'aide internationale 2010–2011*. Gatineau: CIDA.

CIDA. 2013. "Canada Promotes Private-Sector-Led Development to Help the World's Most Vulnerable People." Internet, http://www.acdi-cida.gc.ca/acdi-cida/acdi-cida.nsf/eng/ANN-61112024-LSB. Accessed November 15, 2013.

Conservative Party of Canada. 2011. "Policy Statement, as Modified by Delegates at the National Convention on June 11, 2011." Internet, http://www.conservative.ca/media/2012/07/ 20120705-CPC-PolicyDec-F.pdf. Accessed July 1, 2012.

Côté, Denis, and Dominique Caouette. 2012. "CIDA's Land and Food-Security Policies: A Critical Review." In Stephen Brown, ed. *Struggling for Effectiveness: CIDA and Canadian Foreign Aid*. Montreal and Kingston: McGill–Queen's University Press: 159–85.

Essex, Jamey. 2012. "The Politics of Effectiveness in Canada's International Development Assistance." *Canadian Journal of Development Studies*, vol. 33, no. 3: 338–55.

Gailloux, Chantal. 2013. "Évaluation du processus de consultation pour consultation pour l'Institut canadien international pour les industries extractives et le développement par l'Agence canadienne de développement international." *Les cahiers du CIRDIS*, no. 2013-05. Montreal: Université du Québec à Montréal.

Goyette, Gabriel C. 2008. "Le déliement de l'aide au développement canadienne." *Les cahiers de la Chaire C.-A. Poissant*, no. 2008-01. Montreal: Université du Québec à Montréal.

Goyette, Gabriel C. 2009. "La mise en œuvre de la Loi C-293 : Quelques pistes de réflexion." *Les cahiers de la Chaire C.-A. Poissant*, no. 2009-01. Montreal: Université du Québec à Montréal.

Goyette, Gabriel C. 2011. "Les transformations de l'aide canadienne : Quelle efficacité pour quel développement?" *Techniques Financières et Développement*, no. 105: 71–85.

IMF. 2013. *World Economic Outlook: Hopes, Realities and Risks*. Washington, DC: IMF.

Kindornay, Shannon, and Fraser Reilly-King. 2013. *Investing in the Business of Development: Bilateral Donor Approaches to Engaging the Private Sector*. Ottawa: North–South Institute and Canadian Council for International Development.

Mackreal, Kim. 2014. "Ottawa Expands List of Countries to Receive Foreign Aid Priority." *Globe and Mail*, June 27.

Mining Association of Canada. 2011. "How Mining Contributes to the Canadian Economy." Internet, http://www.mining.ca/site/index.php/en/mining-in-canada/economic-impact.html. Accessed November 16, 2013.

MiningWatch Canada. 2014. "Brief: The Canadian International Institute for Extractive Industries and Development (CIIEID)," March. Internet, http://www.miningwatch.ca/sites/www.miningwatch.ca/files/ciieid_overview_march2014.pdf. Accessed July 17, 2014.

OECD. 1998. *Development Co-operation Review Series: Canada*. Paris: OECD.

OECD. 2007. *Canada: Development Assistance Committee Peer Review*. Paris: OECD.

OECD. 2011. *Partenariat de Busan pour une coopération efficace au service du développement*. Document final du Quatrième Forum de Haut Niveau sur l'Efficacité de l'Aide, République de Corée, November 29 to December 1, 2011.

OECD. 2012. *Canada: Development Assistance Committee Peer Review 2012*. Paris: OECD.

OECD. 2013. *OECD.StatExtracts*. Paris: OECD. Internet, http://stats.oecd.org. Accessed October 1, 2013.

Parliament of Canada. 2008. *Official Development Assistance Accountability Act*. Internet, http://laws-lois.justice.gc.ca/PDF/O-2.8.pdf. Accessed June 26, 2013.

Porter, Michael E., and Mark R. Kramer. 2006. "Strategy and Society: The Link Between Competitive Advantage and Corporate Social Responsibility." *Harvard Business Review*, December.

Porter, Michael E., and Mark R. Kramer. 2011. "Creating Shared Value." *Harvard Business Review*, January.

Singleton, Bill. 2011. "Explaining CIDA's Programmes for African Mining Sector Support." Presentation at the International Forum on Mining Investment and Development in Africa, Montreal, April 29, 2011.

University of British Columbia. 2013. *The Canadian International Institute for Extractive Industries and Development*. Internet, http://apsc.ubc.ca/apsc-eng/giving/faculty-priority-projects/ciieid. Accessed October 1, 2013.

Vander Zaag, Ray. 2013. "Canadian Faith-Based Development NGOs and CIDA Funding." *Canadian Journal of Development Studies*, vol. 34, no. 2: 321–47.

Wells, Paul. 2013. *The Longer I'm Prime Minister: Stephen Harper and Canada*. Toronto: Random House Canada.

World Bank. 1998. *Assessing Aid – What Works, What Doesn't, and Why*. Oxford: Oxford University Press.

Zadek, Simon. 2004. "The Path to Corporate Responsibility." *Harvard Business Review*, December: 36–44.

Zadek, Simon. 2006. *The Civil Corporation*. London: Routledge.

CHAPTER XVI

Undermining Foreign Aid: The Extractive Sector and the Recommercialization of Canadian Development Assistance

Stephen Brown

In 2011, the Canadian International Development Agency (CIDA) announced three new development projects in conjunction with Canadian NGOs and mining companies.[1] The total amount of CIDA funding committed was not especially high, nor was it the first time that the CIDA had supported such projects. Nonetheless, the partnerships attracted considerable media attention, much of it critical. Claims and counterclaims about whether CIDA was subsidizing mining companies multiplied in the press, on the radio, and in the blogosphere, as the various parties involved struggled to establish a clear and consistent narrative on the concrete nature of the partnerships and their underlying rationales.

This chapter argues that the new initiative was emblematic of a new turn in Canadian development assistance – namely, the explicit recommercialization of aid. Canadian trade interests have always underpinned Canadian aid to a certain extent (Morrison 1998). However, a clear trend in the 2000s, under Jean Chrétien, Paul Martin, and the Stephen Harper minority government, had been to move away from commercial self-interest. The progressive elimination of the requirement that be aid funds be tied to procurement in Canada, first in the area of food aid and then for goods and services more generally, epitomized that trend. The new partnerships thus represent a shift in the "first principles" of foreign aid, openly reintroducing and celebrating benefits to Canadians – or, more accurately, shareholders of Canadian companies – as a motive for the renewed commercialization of Canadian aid, with an emphasis on Canadian foreign investment, rather than on the Canadian farming and manufacturing sectors, which had been the main rationale of tied aid.

The package that CIDA announced in 2011 represents a stark public declaration of the Harper government's intention to reorient official development assistance (ODA) towards the interests of private Canadian companies, particularly those in the extractive sector. The government's use of aid funds to support the mining sector is impelled primarily by a top-down desire to rehabilitate the image of the Canadian mining sector and increase its investment opportunities – and hence its profits – overseas. Though undoubtedly some benefits will accrue to poor people in developing countries, the emphasis on extractives is an ineffective and potentially illegal use of ODA funds that will benefit wealthy mining companies more. This use of ODA resources for non-development purposes is facilitated by nebulous discourse in two areas: (1) the role of the private sector in development, which conflates small and medium-sized businesses in developing countries with large Canadian multinational extractive firms, and (2) corporate social responsibility (CSR).

Below, I first introduce the projects mentioned above. Second, I consider whether the CIDA funding constitutes a subsidy or not, a significant bone of contention. Third, I explore the competing rationales invoked to justify the projects, most of which are contradictory and implausible. Fourth, I assess the potential benefits to the various parties involved in the partnerships, as well as the risks. Finally, I conclude by contextualizing these initiatives within Canadian foreign aid and government policy, and in relation to the extractive industry and commercial self-interest.

The Three "Pilot Projects"

The CIDA announcement, made by Minister of International Cooperation Bev Oda on September 29, 2011, comprised three "pilot projects" with well-established Canadian NGOs and mining companies (total budget $9.5 million, of which $6.7 million were CIDA funds), presented as a package (CIDA 2011b). Of the three projects, the one that received the most attention was a $7.6 million youth training program in Burkina Faso, to which CIDA contributed 75 percent and the mining company IAMGOLD only 13 percent, while the implementing NGO, Plan Canada, provided the remaining 12 percent. The second project, implemented by World University Service of Canada (WUSC) and co-financed by Rio Tinto Alcan, provides assistance to residents of the mining communities of Bibiani-Anhwiaso Bekwai district in Ghana, notably via education and improved access to water (CIDA 2011b, 2013). CIDA allocated $500,000 to the project, over half of the total cost of $928,000. By the time CIDA announced the project, Rio Tinto Alcan had sold its mine to a Chinese company and no longer operated in Ghana. CIDA also contributed $500,000 (50 percent) to the third project, implemented by World Vision Canada and co-funded by Canadian giant Barrick Gold. It provides socio-economic assistance to residents of the Quiruvilca district of Peru, where Barrick operates a mine.

The total value of Canadian development assistance to these three pilot projects is $6.7 million, to be provided over five and a half years (CIDA 2011b).[2] This represents a very small proportion of Canadian ODA, barely 0.1 percent of annual disbursements. It was also not the first time CIDA had partnered with NGOs and Canadian mining companies. For instance, CIDA provided almost $500,000 to a reforestation project near a Barrick Gold mine site in Peru, run by Quebec-based NGO SOCODEVI, to which the mining company contributed $150,000 (Blackwood and Stewart 2012, 229). However, since the government presented the partnership arrangements as "pilot projects" and otherwise suggested they would be replicated in the future (Mackrael 2012b), they merit closer analysis as indicators of future trends.

Subsidies or Not?

Following the announcement, critics decried the use of public funds to subsidize highly profitable private mining companies (Leblanc 2012). Part of the confusion around subsidies related directly to the largest project, in Burkina Faso. Especially controversial was CIDA's claim that the project "will receive job skills training linked to labour market needs in the mining sector and its sub-sectors" (CIDA 2011b). Further suggesting that IAMGOLD would benefit from the training, the *Globe and Mail* cited a Burkinabé government official statement that, "A number of graduates are expected to go directly into jobs at the mining company." It also reported that the project would "provide at least 500 internships" with the mining company (York 2012), a claim that Plan officials subsequently and vehemently denied.[3]

The government responded to accusations of subsidization by emphasizing that no funds were being transferred to the mining companies themselves (e.g., Fantino 2012a), which was technically accurate but sidestepped two key critiques. First, CIDA was indeed subsidizing the companies' CSR *programs*, even if not the companies directly (MiningWatch Canada 2012). In a sense, this is not very different from how CIDA funds NGO projects, which are only called subsidies by critics. However, a key difference is the profit-making nature of the private corporations carrying out the CSR projects.

Second, CIDA funds were being directed specifically to communities affected by Canadian mining companies, providing them with benefits that they would not otherwise have received. This will have a positive impact on the companies' reputation and also make it easier to obtain and maintain a "social licence to operate," that is to say, the consent of mining communities. In short, the message to sceptical local communities is that if they accept Canadian mining projects, the Canadian government will provide them with extra assistance. Some refer to this as a "pacification program" (Arnold 2012).

Pierre Gratton, the president of the Mining Association of Canada, initially argued in an interview with the *Globe and Mail*, that such endeavours "make it easier for mining firms to sell their sometimes controversial projects to local populations" (Leblanc 2012). Gratton, a key lobbyist for the industry, later stated that "the mining industry does not need nor want subsidies from CIDA" (Gratton 2012b, 8), echoing CIDA minister Bev Oda's claim that, "In no way are public funds being used to increase the profitability (of these companies)" (quoted in Payne 2012). These denials were contradicted by Oda's successor, Julian Fantino, who declared that "CIDA's work with mining companies would help them compete on the international stage" (Mackrael 2012a). If this is indeed the case, it is hard to deny that CIDA is providing a public subsidy to private businesses.

Confused Rationales

CIDA announced the three-project package as part of "Canada's Corporate Social Responsibility (CSR) Strategy for the Canadian International Extractive Sector" (CIDA 2011b). The Canadian government conceptualizes its broader support for CSR as a means to "improve the competitive advantage of Canadian international extractive sector companies by enhancing their ability to manage social and environmental risks" – also implying a subsidy to increased profitability by enhancing international competitiveness. The strategy's title, "Building the Canadian Advantage," also suggests that Canadian companies are the desired beneficiaries (FATDC 2013a; see also Goyette, this volume). The CSR rationale created an oxymoron: public funds being used for private CSR. This was especially contradictory for the Burkina Faso project, where CIDA was providing three-quarters of the project's financing and the private corporation only 13 percent. For that reason, NGO and mining company officials have expressed discomfort with the government's decision to apply the CSR label to the partnerships.[4]

The Mining Association's Pierre Gratton (2012a) also argued that the public-private partnerships helped companies access NGO expertise, ignoring the fact that mining companies could enter into agreements with NGOs or hire experts without CIDA funding, which in fact many already had. He further stated that CIDA funding would help ensure that the mining companies would be held accountable for their development projects (Gratton 2012b), inadvertently suggesting that they otherwise were not – and that this was a problem, implying that the Canadian government would be justified to enact mandatory accountability regulations for their activities. A senior representative from one of the three NGOs involved, however, has argued that there will be little benefit to the mining companies or the extractive industry more broadly, and that they are acting purely philanthropically.[5] This contradicts public statements on the CIDA website and others by two CIDA ministers, as well as the presidents of World Vision Canada, IAMGOLD, and the Mining Association of Canada.

CIDA and other Canadian government officials have also justified the partnership on the grounds that they provide better development assistance. Bev Oda, for instance, stated, "It's another way of improving the effectiveness of CIDA's work" (quoted in Payne 2012). There are two separate and somewhat contradictory strands to the effectiveness argument. One is that the private sector does things better than the public sector (such as job creation or achieving concrete results). The other is that the main advantage is resource mobilization for CIDA's work. Neither of these arguments is convincing.

Those invoking the first strand (see, for instance, Conservative MP Bob Dechert's comments in SCFAID [2012b]) ignore the fact that the mining companies are not implementing the projects, but rather the NGOs are. As mining industry lobbyist Gratton admitted, "We're miners, we're not in the business of social and community development that the NGOs are experts at" (quoted in Mackrael 2012c). The mining companies' inputs are mainly financial and the projects themselves do not differ substantively from traditional aid projects. Second, if the main concern is leveraging funds (Mackrael 2012c), why seek funds from specifically Canadian companies and why only companies in the extractive sector and not, say, RBC or Tim Horton's? When I asked a CIDA official those questions, he replied that it was because CIDA already had contacts with the Canadian mining sector, failing to mention that CIDA had actively sought out those contacts.[6] Moreover, the actual contributions of the mining companies to the three projects range from $300,000 to $1 million, meagre sums by CIDA standards (not to mention mining company budgets). If CIDA is doing it for the money, it sure is cheap.

Other reasons invoked by the projects' supporters include the fact that other donor countries, such as the US and the UK, are already funding similar partnerships, that it is "the way of the future," or that public-private partnerships are inherently more efficient (CBC 2012; Dade 2012, 7; Fantino 2012b). Deploying huge, vague, and highly debatably generalizations, they fail to address the specific merits of the projects themselves, or show how corporate involvement actually makes a difference.

The origins of the partnerships could shed some light on the underlying motivations. IAMGOLD president Steve Letwin stated in a radio interview that CIDA "came to see us" (CBC 2012), a claim contradicted by the other parties. According to a senior CIDA official, Plan and IAMGOLD developed the project on their own and then applied for CIDA funding that would "probably" have been approved even without mining company participation.[7] Such claims are disingenuous because CIDA actively encouraged the mining–NGO partnerships and had in fact let it be known that special funds had been set aside to fund them, at a time when it was cutting the foreign aid budget, including support to Canadian NGOs.[8]

The reasons CIDA has promoted these partnerships are unclear. Is it subsidizing or promoting the mining industry or not? Does it constitute CSR or not? Will Canada mining companies benefit or not?

Clearly, there is insufficient coordination among the various parties in explaining the initiative's nature and rationale to the Canadian public. Many actors involved may also lack an understanding of the issues, or even lack competence in public relations. It could also be that different actors are trying to sell different messages to distinct audiences, hoping other people will not notice discrepancies and contradictions.

The Benefits and Risks of Involvement

The lack of coherent narrative does not prevent the various parties from having their own reasons to participate in such partnerships. For NGOs, participation allows them to access additional funds and scale up their operations (McCarney on CBC 2012), even if they assert that it is "not about money," but rather that – as stated by the heads of the three NGOS – "our goal is to see that maximum benefits accrue to the communities where we work, while also working diligently to mitigate and prevent harm" (Eaton et al. 2012). Claims by the executive director of WUSC (quoted in Schulman and Nieto 2011) and others that working with mining companies will help the latter improve their corporate practices can be considered magical thinking, as the projects contain no provisions for NGO input on actual mining activities.

Moreover, by focusing on mining companies' "philanthropic" side activities, the partnerships actually deflect attention away from accountability for Canadian corporate malpractice in the extractive sector (Denault et al. 2008) and the significant problems associated with mining-led development (Coumans 2012). Public relations "greenwashing," if anything, can make it easier for environmental and human rights abuses to continue (Hamann and Kapelus 2004).[9] In that sense, to use John Cameron's terminology, the projects may "do good," but they fail to support the more fundamental imperative of "do no harm" and may even facilitate harm (see Cameron, this volume).

Rosemary McCarney, president of Plan Canada, stated that accepting money from IAMGOLD would not prevent her organization from criticizing it: "No partnership ... would keep us from speaking out when we see abuses or bad practices," adding, "Shame on us if that would silence us in any way" (CBC 2012). Other NGO actors, such as Samantha Nutt, are more sceptical of any NGO's willingness to "[bite] the hand that feeds" (quoted in Westhead 2013; see also Nutt 2012). In fact, Plan Canada's official project documentation suggests that Plan would refrain from commenting publicly on any allegations regarding IAMGOLD's mining practices and foresees helping the company manage public relations problems in case of public outcry.[10]

For mining companies, CIDA funding allows them to scale up their CSR programs. The partnerships allow them to claim credit and get positive publicity for development projects towards which they contribute as little as 13 percent of total costs. These partnerships also help them refashion their image. CIDA-funded projects help extractive companies, generally seen as highly problematic actors,[11] reinvent themselves as philanthropic development actors and dodge demands for accountability for their actual operations – though mining companies have done very little to advertise in Canada their involvement in these partnerships. They, along with some NGO officials, were in fact unpleasantly surprised when CIDA publicized their projects as of a broader strategy, which brought unwanted Canadian public attention to them.[12] Still, as mentioned above, the partnerships can help convince local communities to welcome mining operations, and specifically Canadian ones, with the promise that the Canadian government and Canadian NGOs will provide some sweeteners. Moreover, by mobilizing additional Canadian government resources, the companies help protect themselves from tax and royalty increases or even expropriation in the host countries (Dawson 2013; see also Schulman and Nieto 2011).

For CIDA, DFATD, and the Canadian government more broadly, the reasons for initiating and supporting the partnerships appear to be mainly commercial and ideological; they produce a non-critical, pro-business stance across various areas of activity – not just in foreign aid – often in favour of the widely criticized extractive sector. In early 2011, the Harper government started to develop a new strategy to increase the involvement of the Canadian private sector in Canadian aid programs, which included having a parliamentary committee study the issue (Foster 2013). The report of the committee, which was dominated by Conservative MPs, recommended setting aside funds for public-private partnerships, among other measures (SCFAID 2012a). It portrayed the private sector as the motor of economic growth worldwide (see also Fantino 2012a), but repeatedly confused growth with development and conflated local small and medium-sized enterprises with Canadian multinationals. Moreover, the committee ignored CIDA's very poor history of directly funding the Canadian private sector (see CIDA 2007). I do not mean to imply that the private sector should play no role in development assistance; rather, the government has overstated its case and poorly justified its rationale for using aid funds to work with Canadian multinational corporations.

During this period, successive CIDA ministers defended both the record of Canadian companies and the idea that they should benefit from Canadian aid. For instance, Oda said in April 2012, "There's nothing wrong with private sector, and particularly our Canadian private sector. They're responsible. They're good" (quoted in Shane 2012, 5).[13] In November 2012, Fantino echoed that perspective, stating, "Canadian companies have shown themselves to be socially responsible," adding, "most importantly: this has contributed to [their] bottom line" and that, "building on [Canada's free-trade agreement with Peru], CIDA has focused its work in areas of benefit to Canadian interests" (Fantino 2012a). The following month, Fantino further developed the centrality of self-interest in Canadian foreign aid when he stated, "we have a duty and a responsibility to ensure that Canadian interests are promoted" and that "Canadians are entitled to derive a benefit" (quoted in Mackrael 2012b). In 2013, Fantino told the board of directors of the Mining Association of Canada, "we want to help you succeed" (quoted in Mackrael 2013). This framing of aid is compatible with Cranford Pratt's "dominant class perspective" (see discussion in Black, this volume).

The partnerships also pose risks for all parties involved, but unequally. The NGOs' reputations have already been somewhat compromised by their partnerships with mining companies whose operations are seen by many as unethical. Both WUSC and Plan Canada have lost private donors as a result. McCarney initially defended Plan Canada's partnership with IAMGOLD, stating that they knew the risks and did "an extraordinary amount of due diligence ... on the ethical standards of that company" (CBC 2012; see also York 2012). However, her subsequent comments suggest Plan Canada might be regretting its involvement: "Would we try it again? Probably not ... It's upsetting to donors. People are mad. The reality is that working with any mining company is going to be a problem. There are going to be (employee) strikes and spills. Is it worth the headache? Probably not" (quoted in Westhead 2013).

Risks can extend to NGOs who do not work with mining companies. Some NGO officials feel that the sector as a whole has been discredited as development actors in their own right and will be increasingly viewed by beneficiaries as handmaidens of the mining companies or, in the words of Samantha Nutt (2012), "bagmen, advancing Canadian mining interests with taxpayer funding by appeasing local communities with gifts of health care and education," instead of advocates for the poor. Moreover, these partnerships have proven highly divisive in the NGO community, in effect driving a wedge between those that prioritize access to funding and those that are more interested in playing an advocacy role.

Like the NGOs, CIDA/DFATD will also suffer a reputational risk if a scandal erupts concerning any of the three mining companies. A Swiss business intelligence firm considers two of them – Rio Tinto and Barrick – to be among the world's ten most controversial mining companies because of their "negative impacts on communities and the environment" (RepRisk 2012, 1). An American NGO has placed Barrick Gold on its "Top 10 Corporate Criminals List" – covering all industries, not just mining – for "contaminating waterways in Latin America and failing to uphold safety promises to nearby residents" (Global Exchange 2013; see also Arnold 2012). For the mining companies, however, there are few risks, unless the NGO-run projects prove disastrous, which is highly unlikely, or if the partnerships bring extra attention to their transgressions linked to their extractive activities, as they have begun to do (which might help to explain why the mining companies have done little to publicize the partnerships in Canada). Meanwhile, the companies stand to gain financially from association with development actors.

Conclusion: The Bigger Picture

Though ODA grants to date for CIDA–NGO–mining company partnerships are relatively small, they are likely a harbinger of things to come, as the Canadian government has reiterated on several occasions its intent to expand the three "pilot projects," even though using aid funds to support for the Canadian extractive sector lacks a justifiable rationale. The three projects will surely, as their proponents assert, provide assistance to thousands of people, but that is not the key issue. The World Vision/Barrick Gold project in Peru, the WUSC/Rio Tinto project in Ghana (though not the Plan/IAMGOLD one in Burkina Faso), as well as the $20 million Andean Regional Initiative for Promoting Effective Corporate Social Responsibility, all focus on mining-affected communities. Though poor people in such communities are worthy of assistance, the same can be said about all poor people – certainly not just those living in communities affected by Canadian mining companies specifically.[14] Moreover, such activities use ODA funds to provide public subsidies to private corporations, even if only indirectly, which is highly problematic and poses reputational risks to the Canadian government and especially NGOs. The partnerships do nothing to actually improve the practices of extractive companies; they merely encourage adding on charitable side projects.[15]

The central question is why the Canadian government is setting aside resources and allocating them to these projects, particularly at a time when it is reducing its overall aid budget and cutting back on funding to NGO projects that do not include mining company involvement. Explanations based on the mobilization of additional resources or expertise are not convincing, since the amounts the mining companies are contributing are relatively small and those companies do not actually have development expertise. Nor do the projects include components that monitor or help improve the practices of the companies. Indeed, the greatest beneficiaries of the projects are the mining companies themselves: public funds enhance their ability to operate in mining-affected communities and their competitiveness on the global scene, while reducing their risks. In short, through at least two of the three "pilot projects," foreign aid is, in fact, subsidizing the bottom line of Canadian companies, which contradicts the provisions of Canada's Official Development Assistance Accountability Act (which mandates a central focus on poverty reduction) and may therefore be illegal (Blackwood and Stewart 2012).

The use of foreign aid to bolster the Canadian mining industry constitutes a significant shift in the renewed commercialization of Canadian development assistance and the latter's "first principles." Though self-interested goals and altruistic objectives can be compatible in some "win-win" situations, the growing emphasis on aid's benefits to Canada led other Western donors to remind the government that "there should be no confusion between development objectives and the promotion of commercial interests" (OECD 2012, 11). Canada's concerted efforts to promote its own mining sector as a tool of development abroad also contradicts the principles of the Paris Declaration on Aid Effectiveness, endorsed by Canada, which emphasises the importance of donors aligning their policies with recipient countries' priorities, rather than selecting their own.

Under the guise of support to CSR and emphasis on the private sector as the driver of growth, the Canadian government's aid discourse is increasingly shifting from altruistic humanitarian principles to explicit claims of "mutual benefit" (Fantino 2012a; Mackrael 2012b). These claims echo the Chinese government's justification of its use of aid to promote Chinese commercial and investment interests, as well as some of the discourse of African elites who seek to move away from a charity-based approach.

For decades, commercial self-interest characterized much Western foreign aid, but this decreased as Canada and most other donors progressively eliminated aid tied to procurement in the donor country. However, commercial interests are now resurging under a new form. At least in the Canadian case, aid is promoting Canadian companies' foreign investment and overseas operations far more than the export of Canadian products. Benefits will therefore accrue to shareholders and not support the job-creating manufacturing industries and agricultural production in Canada. The benefits of the recommercialization of aid are thus likely to be more concentrated among wealthy Canadians, along with foreign shareholders, than was previously the case.

CIDA's activities in support of the mining sector are not limited to those discussed here. It also funds NGOs set up by the extractive industry, such as the Lundin Foundation, to which it granted $4.5 million in 2011, with an additional $2.8 million in 2012, for its work in conjunction with Engineers without Borders (CIDA 2011a, 2013).[16] CIDA/DFATD is also contributing $25 million to create the Canadian International Institute for Extractive Industries and Development, housed at the University of British Columbia (discussed in Goyette, this volume). In 2014, Minister of International Development Christian Paradis announced a new DFATD-managed fund "to support large-scale development projects in the extractive sector in Africa" with an annual budget of $25 million (FATDC 2014). For a fuller picture, future research should consider those and other government-supported projects involving the mining sector.

Another promising path for future research is the concept of conflict of interest, invoked by Helleiner (2013, 296) and Payne (2013a), which applies when a country such as Canada that has powerful mining interests not only advocates foreign investment in mining as a path to development, but uses ODA funds – legally committed to fighting poverty in developing countries – in ways that benefit its own industry. For instance, CIDA funds have helped rewrite the Colombian mining code in ways that favour Canadian companies, including by reducing the royalty rates that foreign companies have to pay (Blackwood and Stewart 2012). In Peru, Canada will help "streamline" the environmental impact assessments that proposed mining projects must undergo (Berthiaume 2013). CIDA's absorption into DFATD is likely to increase pressure for the use of ODA funds for commercial purposes, which warrants close monitoring. The chief executive officer of Rio Tinto Alcan is one of five members of an external advisory group on the merger-related restructuring (Payne 2013b). DFATD's first post-merger policy blueprint mentions the government's intention to "leverage development programming to advance Canada's trade interests" (FATDC 2013b, 14).

This chapter has limited its discussion to CIDA and ODA funds, but the Canadian government is in fact deploying a "whole-of-government approach" in favour of the extractive sector that extends far beyond the use of foreign aid, including the erstwhile Department of Foreign Affairs and International Trade (DFAIT), as well as Export Development Canada (Blackwood and Stewart 2012). DFAIT, for instance, contributed $564,000 directly to Quebec-based Société d'exploitation minière–Afrique de l'Ouest (SEMAFO), whose president, Benoît La Salle, used to chair Plan Canada's Board of Directors (FATDC 2012).[17] In future research, more attention should be paid not only to such grants from different government actors, but also to the formal and informal connections between government, NGOs, and mining interests, which could shed more light on the recommercialization of Canadian aid.

Notes

1. Though CIDA was absorbed into the newly renamed Department of Foreign Affairs, Trade and Development (DFTAD) in 2013, I still refer to it in this chapter by the name it had at the time.
2. The announcement also included the mining-related Andean Regional Initiative for Promoting Effective Corporate Social Responsibility, with a CIDA contribution of $20 million, to cover Colombia, Peru, and Bolivia,

but provided little detail. In the DFATD international development project browser, one can find an entry under the initiative for each of the countries. They all list WUSC as the executing agency and mention partnerships with other Canadian NGOs, including CARE, CECI, and SOCODEVI.

3. Unattributable author conversation with Plan Canada officials.
4. Schulman and Nieto (2011); unattributable interviews with NGO and mining company officials.
5. Unattributable interview with an NGO official.
6. This exchange took place at a public event under the Chatham House rule. I cannot therefore provide additional information on his identity.
7. The CIDA official was speaking at a public event under the Chatham House rule and therefore cannot be identified here by name.
8. Unattributable interview with NGO officials.
9. On the limits of CSR, the failure of court cases to date against mining companies, and the need for Canadian government regulation, see Campbell (2008) and North and Young (2013).
10. The project's implementation plan recognizes that allegations of malpractice against IAMGOLD and other mining companies operating in Burkina Faso are "probable" and that this poses a reputational risk to Plan and the project. The document anticipates that Plan and IAMGOLD will develop a crisis management strategy that could best be described as public relations damage control, in case the media generate negative publicity (in other words, the joint strategy would try to counter media criticisms and not address any actual malpractice). The document also strongly suggests that Plan Canada and its local counterpart Plan Burkina would not share information critical of IAMGOLD with the public or in any way act contrary to the company's interests. In particular, it specifies that Plan should not address any allegations concerning IAMGOLD's mining operations and would limit its public comments to matters directly related to the project itself (Plan Canada 2011, 26, 32–33).
11. A study commissioned by the Prospectors and Developers Association of Canada in 2009 but never officially released found that "Canadian mining companies are far and away the worst offenders in environmental, human rights, and other abuses around the world," as well as "more likely to be engaged in community conflict, environmental and unethical behaviour" than companies based in other countries (Whittington 2010).
12. Unattributable interviews with NGO and mining company officials. Had the government not specifically used ODA funds to support these three projects or had CIDA not prominently announced them as a package, the partnerships might have escaped public attention in Canada.

13. Oda's assertions fly in the face of well-documented record of abuses by numerous Canadian mining companies, as recognized by the industry's internal report cited by Whittington (2010). They were also swiftly contradicted by multiple corruption scandals at construction and engineering giant SNC-Lavalin. The company had held numerous CIDA contracts, including for the Dahla Dam in Afghanistan, and was subsequently banned from bidding on CIDA and World Bank projects for a ten-year period.
14. That Rio Tinto Alcan ceased operating in Ghana after the project with WUSC was initiated does not obviate the fact that they would have similarly benefited had it stayed.
15. Mining is often destructive, but nonetheless a necessary economic activity. Some degree of public-private interaction is therefore essential to try to mitigate the damage to communities and the environment. For a discussion of positive measures the Canadian government and its industry partners could undertake in the extractive sector, see McLeod Group (2012).
16. The Lundin Foundation, initially named Lundin for Africa, was established by the Lundin Group of Companies, which includes Lundin Petroleum, accused of complicity with war crimes and crimes against humanity in Sudan (Sunderland 2010).
17. It was a SEMAFO mine in Niger that Robert Fowler and Louis Guay had just visited when they were kidnapped in 2008 (Engler 2009).

References

Arnold, Rick. 2012. "Mining, CIDA Partnership in Peru is Pacification Program, Not Development." *Embassy*, March 7, 7.

Berthiaume, Lee. 2013. "Questions Raised as Canada Moves to Help Peru Streamline Environmental Assessments for Mining Projects." *Postmedia News*, May 22. Internet, http://www.canada.com/business/Questions+raised+Canada+moves+help+Peru+streamline+environmental+assessments+mining/8419215/story.html. Accessed August 22, 2013.

Blackwood, Elizabeth, and Veronika Stewart. 2012. "CIDA and the Mining Sector: Extractive Industries as an Overseas Development Strategy." In Stephen Brown, ed. *Struggling for Effectiveness: CIDA and Canadian Foreign Aid*. Montreal and Kingston: McGill–Queen's University Press, 217–45.

Campbell, Bonnie. 2008. "Regulation and Legitimacy in the Mining Industry in Africa: Where Does Canada Stand?" *Review of African Political Economy*, vol. 35, no. 117: 367–85.

CBC. 2012. "CIDA Partnerships." *The Current*, January 26. Internet, http://www.cbc.ca/thecurrent/episode/2012/01/26/cida-partnerships/. Accessed August 20, 2013.

CIDA. 2007. "Executive Report on the Evaluation of the CIDA Industrial Cooperation (CIDA-INC) Program." Gatineau, QC: CIDA Evaluation Division.

CIDA. 2011a. "Minister Oda Announces Canadian Partnerships in International Development." December 23. Internet, http://www.acdi-cida.gc.ca/acdi-cida/ACDI-CIDA.nsf/eng/NAT-1222104721-LJ6. Accessed August 22, 2013.

CIDA. 2011b. "Minister Oda Announces Initiatives to Increase the Benefits of Natural Resource Management for People in Africa and South America." September 29. Internet, http://www.acdi-cida.gc.ca/acdi-cida/acdi-cida.nsf/eng/CAR-929105317-KGD. Accessed August 20, 2013.

CIDA. 2013. *Project Browser*. Internet, http://www.acdi-cida.gc.ca/project-browser. Accessed August 20, 2013.

Coumans, Catherine. 2012. "CIDA's Partnership with Mining Companies Fails to Acknowledge and Address the Role of Mining in the Creation of Development Deficits." Brief prepared for the House of Commons Standing Committee on Foreign Affairs and International Development's Study on the Role of the Private Sector in Achieving Canada's International Development Interests. Ottawa: MiningWatch Canada.

Dade, Carlo. 2012. "Public-Private Controversy Only in Canada." *Embassy*, February 22, p. 7.

Dawson, Grant. 2013. "Player, Partner and Friend: Canada's Africa Policy since 1945." *International Politics*, vol. 50, no. 3 (May): 412–34.

Deneault, Alain, Delphine Abadie, and William Sacher. 2008. *Noir Canada : Pillage, corruption et criminalité en Afrique*. Montreal: Écosociété.

Eaton, Chris, Rosemary McCarney, and Dave Toycen. 2012. "NGOs Are Part of the Mining Conversation." *Globe and Mail*, January 31. Internet, http://www.theglobeandmail.com/commentary/ngos-are-part-of-the-mining-conversation/article1360219/#dashboard/follows/. Accessed August 22, 2013.

Engler, Yves. 2009. "An Abduction in Niger: Canada, the UN and Canadian Mining." *Canadian Dimension*, January 31. Internet, http://canadiandimension.com/articles/2170/. Accessed August 22, 2013.

Fantino, Julian. 2012a. "Minister Fantino's Keynote Address to the Economic Club of Canada Titled 'Reducing Poverty – Building Tomorrow's Markets'." Toronto, November 23. Internet, http://www.acdi-cida.gc.ca/acdi-cida/acdi-cida.nsf/eng/NAT-1123135713-Q8T. Accessed August 22, 2013.

Fantino, Julian. 2012b. "The Status Quo of Foreign Aid is Not an Option." *Globe and Mail*, December 10. Internet, http://www.theglobeandmail. com/news/politics/julian-fantino-the-status-quo-of-foreign-aid-is-not-an-option/article6149440/#dashboard/follows/. Accessed August 22, 2013.

FATDC. 2012. "Disclosure of Grant and Contribution Awards over $25,000: DFAIT – International Trade: SEMAFO Inc." Internet, http://w03.inter national.gc.ca/dg-do/index.aspx?dept=2&lang=eng&p=4&r=33&c=6457. Accessed August 22, 2013.

FATDC. 2013a. *Building the Canadian Advantage: A Corporate Social Responsibility (CSR) Strategy for the Canadian International Extractive Sector* (March 2009). Internet, http://www.international.gc.ca/trade-agreements-accords-commerciaux/topics-domaines/other-autre/csr-strat-rse.aspx?lang=eng. Accessed August 21, 2013.

FATDC. 2013b. *Global Markets Action Plan*. Internet, http://international. gc.ca/global-markets-marches-mondiaux/assets/pdfs/plan-eng.pdf. Accessed July 10, 2014.

FATDC. 2014. "Minister Paradis Concludes a Constructive Visit to South Africa." Internet, http://www.international.gc.ca/media/dev/news-communiques/2014/02/3a.aspx?lang=eng. Accessed July 20, 2014.

Foster, Ally. 2013. "Private Sector Focus on Aid: A Long Time Coming." *Embassy*, July 24, 1, 10.

Global Exchange. 2013. "Top 10 Corporate Criminals List." Internet, http:// www.globalexchange.org/corporateHRviolators. Accessed August 26, 2013.

Gratton, Pierre. 2012a. "CIDA Changes Long Overdue." *Ottawa Citizen*, January 25.

Gratton, Pierre. 2012b. "Mining Partnerships the Right Thing to Do." *Embassy*, February 15, 8.

Hamann, Ralph, and Paul Kapelus. 2004. "Corporate Social Responsibility in Mining in Southern Africa: Fair Accountability or Just Greenwash?" *Development*, vol. 47, no. 3 (September): 85–92.

Helleiner, Gerald. 2013. "Conclusion." In Rohinton Medhora and Yiagadeesen Samy, eds. *Canada Among Nations 2013. Canada-African Relations: Looking Back, Looking Ahead*. Waterloo, ON: Centre for International Governance Innovation, 291–300.

Leblanc, Daniel. 2012. "CIDA Funds Seen to Be Subsidizing Mining Firms." *Globe and Mail*, January 29. Internet, http://www.theglobeandmail. com/news/politics/cida-funds-seen-to-be-subsidizing-mining-firms/ article1360059. Accessed August 20, 2013.

Mackrael, Kim. 2012a. "Canada's Foreign Aid Doesn't Exist to Keep NGOs Afloat, Fantino Says." *Globe and Mail*, November 28. Internet, http://www.theglobeandmail.com/news/politics/canadas-

foreign-aid-doesnt-exist-to-keep-ngos-afloat-fantino-says/article
5751774/. Accessed August 22, 2013.

Mackrael, Kim. 2012b. "Fantino Defends CIDA's Corporate Shift." *Globe and Mail*, December 3. Internet, http://www.theglobeandmail.com/news/
politics/fantino-defends-cidas-corporate-shift/article5950443/. Accessed
August 20, 2013.

Mackrael, Kim. 2012c. "Ottawa Signals Shift in Foreign-Aid Policy toward
Private Sector." *Globe and Mail*, November 23. Internet, http://www.
theglobeandmail.com/news/politics/ottawa-signals-radical-shift-in-
foreign-aid-policy/article5582948/. Accessed August 22, 2013.

Mackrael, Kim. 2013. "'Huge Opportunities' for Canadian Mining Industry
to Work in Developing Countries." *Globe and Mail*, June 19. Internet,
http://www.theglobeandmail.com/news/politics/huge-opportuni-
ties-for-canadian-mining-industry-to-work-in-developing-countries/
article12670581/. Accessed August 26, 2013.

McLeod Group. 2012. "Of Mines and Minefields: Canada, the Extractive
Sector and Development." Ottawa: McLeod Group. Internet, http://
www.mcleodgroup.ca/wp-content/uploads/2013/02/Extractives-Paper-
July-2012-PDF.pdf. Accessed August 22, 2013.

MiningWatch Canada. 2012. "CIDA Subsidizes Mining's Social Responsibility Projects." Ottawa: MiningWatch Canada. Internet, http://www.
miningwatch.ca/news/cida-subsidizes-mining-s-social-responsibility-
projects. Accessed August 20, 2013.

Morrison, David R. 1998. *Aid and Ebb Tide: A History of CIDA and Canadian
Development Assistance*. Waterloo, ON: Wilfrid Laurier University Press.

North, Liisa L., and Laura Young. 2013. "Generating Rights for Communities Harmed by Mining: Legal and Other Action." *Canadian Journal of
Development Studies*, vol. 34, no. 1: 96–110.

Nutt, Samantha. 2012. "Should NGOs Take the Corporate Bait?" *Globe
and Mail*, January 25. Internet, http://www.theglobeandmail.com/
commentary/should-ngos-take-the-corporate-bait/article1359759/
#dashboard/follows/. Accessed August 22, 2013.

OECD. 2012. *Canada: Development Assistance Committee (DAC) Peer Review
2012*. Paris: OECD.

Payne, Elizabeth. 2012. "Foreign Aid Gets Down to Business." *Ottawa Citizen*,
January 27. Internet, http://www2.canada.com/news/foreign+gets+
down+business/6058794/story.html?id=6058794&p=1. Accessed August
21, 2013.

Payne, Elizabeth. 2013a. "Canada's Peruvian Conflict of Interest." *Ottawa
Citizen Blog*, May 24. Internet, http://blogs.ottawacitizen.com/2013/05/
24/canadas-peruvian-conflict-of-interest/. Accessed August 22, 2013.

Payne, Elizabeth. 2013b. "Foreign Affairs/CIDA Restructuring Panel Includes
CEO of Rio Tinto Alcan." *Ottawa Citizen*, October 21. Internet, http://

www.ottawacitizen.com/business/CIDA+restructuring+panel+ includes+mining/9063512/story.html. Accessed November 2, 2013.

Plan Canada. 2011. "Développer les capacités des jeunes pour faire croître l'économie : Un partenariat public-privé canadien pour la RSE an [sic] Burkina Faso – Plan de mise en œuvre du projet et Premier Plan Annuel de Travail," December 5. Toronto: Plan Canada.

RepRisk. 2012. *Most Controversial Mining Companies of 2011.* Zurich: RepRisk.

Schulman, Gwendolyn, and Roberto Nieto. 2011. "Foreign Aid to Mining Firms." *The Dominion,* December 19. Internet, http://www.dominion-paper.ca/articles/4300. Accessed July 10, 2014.

Shane, Kristen. 2012. "Budget to Be Balanced on Backs of Poor, Say Critics." *Embassy,* April 4, 1, 5.

Standing Committee on Foreign Affairs and International Development. 2012a. *Driving Inclusive Economic Growth: The Role of the Private Sector in International Development.* Ottawa: House of Commons.

Standing Committee on Foreign Affairs and International Development. 2012b. *Evidence.* May 7. Ottawa: House of Commons. Internet, http://www.parl.gc.ca/HousePublications/Publication.aspx?DocId=5559228 &Language=E&Mode=1. Accessed August 20, 2013.

Sunderland, Ruth. 2010. "Oil Companies Accused of Helping to Fuel Sudan War Crimes." *Guardian,* June 13. Internet, http://www.theguardian.com/world/2010/jun/13/oil-fuelled-sudan-war-crimes. Accessed August 26, 2013.

Westhead, Rick. 2013. "Donors Closing Wallets to Canadian Charities Who Work with CIDA, Mining Companies." *Toronto Star,* January 31. Internet, http://www.thestar.com/news/world/2013/01/31/donors_closing_wallets_to_canadian_charities_who_work_with_cida_mining_companies.html. Aaccessed August 21, 2013.

Whittington, Lee. 2010. "Canadian Mining Firms Worst for Environment, Rights: Report." *Toronto Star,* October 19. Internet, http://www.thestar.com/news/canada/2010/10/19/canadian_mining_firms_worst_for_environment_rights_report.html. Accessed August 21, 2013.

York, Geoffrey. 2012. "In West Africa, a Canadian Mining Company Pioneers 'the New Humanitarianism'." *Globe and Mail,* March 20. Internet, http://www.theglobeandmail.com/news/world/in-west-africa-a-canadian-mining-company-pioneers-the-new-humanitarianism/article535009/. Accessed August 20, 2013.

Conclusion: Rethinking Canadian Development Cooperation—Towards Renewed Partnerships?

David R. Black, Stephen Brown and Molly den Heyer

Taken together, the chapters in this collection paint a picture of a Canadian aid policy marked by varied and ambiguous purposes, unstable thematic and geographic focus, and insecure institutional modalities. Although many contributors place particular emphasis on the changing contours of aid policy under the Harper government, others (e.g., Black, Massie and Roussel, Swiss, Tiessen) explicitly track these characteristics over a period of decades. In short, as suggested in this volume's Introduction, the need to "rethink" Canadian aid extends far beyond technical and institutional reforms or contemporary controversies over particular shifts in thematic emphasis, as salient as these may be. It must also involve an explicit emphasis on situating the study and practice of Canadian aid in relation to the diverse means through which Canadians engage with the people and countries of the global South.

In this Conclusion, we use the theme of "partnership" to sketch the multiple ways in which Canadian aid policies should be recast as policies of and for development cooperation. More specifically, we identify four domains of partnership that the various contributions in this collection point towards, explicitly or implicitly. These are: foundations of development partnerships, partnerships within the changing international aid regime, partnerships with key "stakeholders" in Canadian society, and intra-governmental partnerships. The dynamics within these four overlapping domains serve both as descriptive frames for analyzing Canadian development cooperation as it is or has been, and as prescriptive frames for thinking about Canadian development policies as they could or should be. They also highlight the changing *structures* – material, ideational, and institutional – within which Canadian development efforts are situated and the diversifying *agents* that undertake those efforts. While the reflections that follow can be no more than suggestive, they serve to highlight key directions for future research.

Rethinking Development Partnerships

The idea of partnership has long been ubiquitous, dynamic, and contested in development cooperation, both within Canada and internationally (Black and Tiessen 2007; Fowler 1997; Macdonald 1995; Pearson 1969). Development scholars sharply critiqued the term in the 1990s and 2000s for the degree to which its benign image of equality and reciprocity masked deeply inequitable structures of power. However, the partnership motif has resurged and deepened in recent development praxis. There are several closely related explanations for this. First, it has been a core theme in several milestones within the international aid regime, beginning with its incorporation as the eighth Millennium Development Goal (MDG) in 2000 ("Develop a Global Partnership for Development") and culminating in the adoption by the Busan High Level Forum on Aid Effectiveness in 2011 of a new "Global Partnership for Effective Development Cooperation" (see respectively United Nations 2013; OECD 2013). Second, it captures both the inevitability and the necessity of complex collaborative relationships in the pursuit of development – and the costs of failure to achieve them. Third, it brings attention to a variety of relatively novel actors and relationships that have become crucial features of contemporary development cooperation, as highlighted in Busan. These include: "emerging economy aid providers" (e.g., Brazil, China, India, Turkey, and South–South cooperation; private sector actors and public-private partnerships; the "new philanthropists" associated with wealthy and highly focused foundations, such as the Bill and Melinda Gates Foundation (Bishop and Green 2011; Brown 2012b; Kharas 2012; Quadir 2013; Ramdas 2011); and civil society organizations, now recognized as "independent development actors in their own right" (*Accra Agenda for Action* 2008). These trends have increasingly challenged and complicated the work of traditional bilateral and multilateral development agencies. They have also provided a key rationale for various institutional reorganizations – notably the incorporation of the Canadian International Development Agency (CIDA) into the newly integrated Department of Foreign Affairs, Trade and Development (DFATD).

A focus on the main dimensions of development partnership as they relate to the evolving dynamics of Canadian development cooperation is particularly apt, for two reasons. First, it is critical that the new architecture of the integrated DFATD, and specifically its role in development cooperation, be informed by these trends. Second, Canadian non-state development actors, both old and new, face unprecedented challenges requiring fresh and sustained analyses, particularly in the context of a new post-MDG development framework that will emerge in 2015. The chapters in this collection serve to highlight some of the questions, issues, and relationships that need to be (re)considered.

Foundations of Development Partnerships

In a policy domain centrally concerned with reducing global poverty and deprivation, it is hardly surprising that several chapters in this collection highlight the need to revisit the ethical foundations of Canadian aid, moving it from simplistic and often paternalistic underpinnings to more just and equitable ones (Black, Cameron, den Heyer). In particular, cosmopolitan ethics and narrative frames can be used as a means of interrogating traditional motifs such as enlightened self-interest, charity, generosity, and North–South dichotomies, or the newer emphasis on mutual benefit that emerging economy aid providers and South–South cooperation have brought to the fore. In doing so, these frames expose the contested normative underpinnings that guide, or should guide, Canada's engagement with the developing world. They also highlight the relationship between the positive duty to "do good" through the provision of aid and the relatively neglected but arguably more significant negative duty to "do no harm" in the various other ways Canadians engage people and countries in the global South (e.g., through trade, investment, immigration, environment, security, and defence – see Cameron, this volume).

Other contributors, however, are sceptical about the need for an explicitly ethical foundation for Canadian aid. Indeed, Chapnick argues that a sufficiently long-term and "enlightened" notion of self-interest derived from the realist tradition is not only sufficient, but also far more likely to persuade policy and political elites that are pivotal to policy renewal in view of the relative indifference of Canadian public opinion to development aid (see also Silvio, this volume). Smillie, while not directly engaging the logic of cosmopolitan or "humane internationalist" ethics, has made the case for "self-interest, properly understood" as the most persuasive foundation for Canadian aid. In his contribution to this collection, he stresses the many more basic and pragmatic ways in which Canadian aid policy could be reformed to produce improved development results in the field (and far from the tarmac), along with a more mature and sensible policy debate.

Flowing from this discussion of ethical foundations is a critical analysis of "donor–recipient" or "North–South" development partnerships. As Brown (2012a; also Lalonde 2009) has emphasized, "aid effectiveness" became a pervasive theme in Canadian and international development policy and practice during the first decade of the new century, epitomized by the Paris Declaration on Aid Effectiveness (OECD 2005) to which Canada remains committed. A question posed (implicitly or explicitly) by several authors is whether the Conservative government, in stressing its own conception of effectiveness and the need to place aid policy at the service of Canadians, has engineered a *de facto* policy shift that sharply diverges from Canada's international commitments to aid effectiveness (Audet and Navarro-Flores, Brown, Goyette, Macdonald, and Ruckert).

Assuming their continued salience, the Paris principles of aid effectiveness highlight the linked objectives of "harmonization" among donors and "alignment" with "recipient-owned" development objectives. The emphasis on recipient ownership could anchor a more genuine partnership with recipient governments and societies; yet, in practice, it has been compromised by the intense and power-laden politics of inter-donor harmonization. Moreover, because donor–recipient partnerships are principally with developing country *governments*, their responsiveness to the needs and aspirations of relatively poor and marginalized communities and people, or even elected officials, is often doubtful (den Heyer). This makes the perspectives of scholars and "partners" from developing countries vitally important. The relative absence of these perspectives is a key limitation of this collection. In future research, it will be necessary to probe the choice and character of relationships with key Canadian "countries of focus" and the meaning and prospects of more substantial recipient country ownership.

Partnerships within the International Aid Regime

To what extent has Canada's approach to foreign aid and development cooperation been shaped by transnational norms and dynamics, aggregated within what has been termed the international aid regime? Several contributors (Carment and Samy, Clark-Kazak, den Heyer, Swiss) consider the impact of the increasingly complex array of old and new actors in this regime on where and how Canada can both follow and lead – and the continuing relevance of the aid regime itself in the wider context of development cooperation. Historically, Canada has been relatively responsive to the changing thematic and administrative priorities/fashions of the aid regime, as orchestrated largely through the Development Assistance Committee of the Organisation for Economic Co-operation and Development (OECD/DAC) and other multilateral venues (Black, Thérien, and Clark 1996). Occasionally, Canada has provided a significant measure of leadership on key themes such as gender equality (Swiss 2012; Tiessen, this volume). In other cases, such as Fragile and Conflict Affected States, promising opportunities for leadership have arguably been squandered (Carment and Samy; see also Baranyi and Khan). Meanwhile, the process of and opportunities to exercise influence within the regime have become increasingly complex as the regime itself has mutated to encompass a range of significant new players. One prospective focus for future research, therefore, is how "traditional" OECD donors, Canada among them, can and should adjust to their diminished centrality in the aid regime, and what opportunities persist for thematic leadership, especially in multilateral settings and in such key areas as climate change and food security. A second focus is how we understand the roles and influence of emerging economy aid providers and South–South cooperation – both individually and collectively (Bilal 2012; Schoeman 2011). To what extent, for example, should Canada attempt to resurrect its traditional (if intermittent) role as interlocutor, in this case between DAC and non-DAC aid providers?

Finally, what is the record of Canadian collaboration with the "new philanthropists" and other private actors in the international context? What is the balance of risk and opportunity in these novel partnerships? How do partnerships at this level affect the prospects for southern "ownership" of their own development agendas? And what role will the newly recast DFATD play in relation to the emerging, multi-dimensional "Global Partnership for Effective Development Cooperation" launched at Busan (Kharas 2012; Kindornay and Samy 2012) and the post-2015/post-MDG agenda? How will the new Canadian international policy architecture affect the propensity and capacity of Canadian representatives to play an influential role in this new context?

In general, these forward-looking issues receive less attention in this collection than they warrant. To be sure, Tiessen's discussion of the government's new approach to maternal and child health issues through its Muskoka Initiative, which she regards as a backwards step in Canada's approach to gender issues, indirectly highlights the relevance of partnerships with the Gates Foundation and other non-traditional philanthropic and multilateral agencies. However, as bilateral aid budgets tighten and as these novel actors further refine their already formidable agenda-setting capabilities, greater attention needs to be paid to their roles in relation to Canadian development cooperation.

Partnerships with Key Canadian Stakeholders

Historically, the best-known Canadian development partnerships – for which CIDA had a long-standing dedicated branch – were with Canadian civil society and non-governmental organizations (CSOs/ NGOs). Indeed, CIDA was long regarded as a leader in responsive partnerships with this vibrant sector of Canadian society (Morrison 1998, 21), which was in turn closely connected with CSO partners in developing countries. Beginning in the mid-1990s, however, and accelerating under the Conservative government, Canada's community of development-oriented CSOs has faced a series of unprecedented challenges, including growing intra-sectoral divisions and estrangement from the government of the day (Plewes and Tomlinson 2013; Smillie 2012). At the same time, the civil society landscape has become more diverse as diaspora groups from developing countries become an increasingly important locus of partnerships, offering new opportunities and challenges through such connections as remittances, lobbying, and inter-community relationships (Brinkerhof 2008; Carment et al. 2013). In this context, it is particularly timely and important to take stock of the sector's achievements and capacities and to begin to map the changes required for renewed partnerships with both Canadian and transnational non-governmental partners.

More recently, in parallel with the international aid regime as a whole, much attention has been focused on partnerships with the private sector, including a wide array of actors and issues that often fall under the broad rubric of corporate social responsibility (CSR) (Felsen and Besada 2013; Kindornay and Reilly-King 2013; SCFAID 2012). In fact, the Canadian government has prioritized the role of the private sector in development cooperation policies since the early 2000s, albeit under several different labels. However, since the election of a majority Conservative government in 2011, this emphasis has become more forthright and strategic – as reflected in the government's controversial decision to initiate several collaborative projects involving Canadian mining companies and leading NGOs (Besada and Martin 2013; Blackwood and Stewart 2012). This trend presents important new challenges to all partners, notably (though not only) in the context of the extractive sector, where Canada is a world leader and the activities of its "corporate citizens" have important – and controversial – developmental and societal repercussions.

These shifting societal and state–society dynamics are an important recurring theme in this collection. Several contributors analyze the increasing emphasis of the Harper government on partnerships with the private sector – particularly extractive companies – and how this is shaping country and regional as well as project priorities (Brown, Goyette, Macdonald, and Ruckert). They discuss how these and other shifts are affecting relationships with and among civil society actors, leading to divisions between those (often large and multinational) NGOs that are prepared to collaborate with extractive companies and the government on specially funded projects that, among other things, burnish the image of Canadian extractives in their host communities, and those NGOs that are sharply critical of these initiatives and the record of the extractive sector more generally. Others note the controversial way that the Conservative government appears to have favoured some, particularly religious and "proselytizing" NGOs, over other, secular and/or "progressive" ones in its funding decisions, with dubious implications for its oft-invoked priority of effectiveness (Audet and Navarro-Flores). Yet other authors counsel caution in overstating the significance and durability of these trends, given limited evidence of "commercialization" and the continued salience of more ethical, poverty-focused priorities in the policy practices of the Harper government (Baranyi and Khan, Swiss). Clearly, these are important dynamics and debates, requiring ongoing scrutiny in the medium and long term.

Intra-Governmental Partnerships

Finally, the question of how Canadian governmental institutions can and should concert their efforts to maximize development effectiveness has become a major preoccupation of both practitioners and analysts (e.g., Kindornay 2011). Most immediately, and to the surprise of many, the Canadian government announced in its March 2013 budget the merger of Canada's main aid agency, CIDA, with the Department of Foreign Affairs and International Trade. This new intra-departmental "partnership" (or "forced marriage" – Swiss 2013; see also Foster 2013) could enhance the coherence of Canadian engagement with development issues, but could also lead to the subordination of development concerns and aid resources to Canadian commercial and security priorities. In an important sense, this debate circles back to the changes occurring in the international aid regime, with many pro-business commentators arguing that Canada and other traditional OECD donors are losing out to emerging economy aid providers, such as Brazil, China, India, and Turkey, that are less constrained in linking aid to commercial objectives. On the other hand, others argue that Canada's "comparative advantage" in the global South is best advanced by a reputation for generosity and responsiveness in its development cooperation policies. Tracking how the new administrative arrangements of the merged department navigate these crosscurrents, and at the same time informing the policy thinking of those responsible for development issues within DFATD, will be a key priority for Canadian development researchers.

For most authors in this collection, it is far too soon to tell what the consequences of the merger will be – though several have ventured informed commentaries on what to expect (Brown 2013; McLeod Group 2013). Early indicators include a workforce adjustment that saw the elimination of over 300 CIDA positions (Duggal 2014) and the discarding of CIDA hiring pools (Foster 2014), exacerbating concerns about the privileging of commercial and diplomatic expertise over development knowledge and priorities. While many contributors remain critical of the merger decision and concerned that it will strongly reinforce the trend towards commercialization, others see it as "a significant opportunity to effect real political change" towards a better performing aid program, whatever that might entail (Chapnick). Regardless, the creation of this new institutional structure and the bureaucratic partnership it internalizes clearly represents an important conjuncture that will have lasting effects on the future trajectory of Canadian development cooperation. Close attention will have to be paid to a range of novel dynamics, including the new balance of bureaucratic interests that will be brought to bear on development policy making and the personnel policies and career paths within DFATD. They could play an important medium-term role in shaping the extent to which Canada's development cooperation adopts a truly developmental perspective *versus* one shaped by diplomatic or commercial imperatives.

Beyond DFATD, however, there has been a longer standing concern with the need to "de-centre" aid within development policy, and enhance "policy coherence for development" (Bülles and Kindornay 2013). Much of this concern arose in the context of post-9/11 efforts to foster "whole-of-government" collaboration in key fragile and conflict-affected states, notably Afghanistan, Haiti, and Sudan (Baranyi and Paducel 2012; Carment and Samy, this volume). Though efforts to understand and respond to the critical interplay of development and security dynamics have intensified since 9/11, the more or less explicit pursuit of "complementarity" between development and security policies – and bureaucracies – has been on the agenda of Canadian governments for several decades, as Massie and Roussel show. Moreover, Baranyi and Khan argue for the need to take closer account of the security-development relationship and to pursue conflict-sensitive development policies in a much wider array of Southern partners than the focus on the more extreme cases of state fragility has heretofore contemplated. This, in turn, challenges an array of both security- and development-oriented government agencies to explore the potential, risks, and limits of more systematic collaboration.

The imperative of intra-governmental partnership is much broader, however, than the "security-development nexus," encompassing the need to promote coherence (or at least mitigate contradictions) between trade, investment, environment, immigration, health, agriculture, and natural resource policies towards the developing world, to cite some of the more obvious examples. This suggests a requirement for greater collaboration between the relevant departments and agencies – an exceptionally challenging task that the newly integrated DFATD might or might not enable. Moreover, in the Canadian context, policy coherence for development requires attentiveness to the important responsibilities of provincial governments, including their various engagements with developing countries. For instance, the Quebec government, under the Parti Québécois, announced plans to create its own international development agency (Salvet 2013). Studying the challenges and prospects for intra-governmental partnerships in development cooperation must therefore be a key focus of Canadian development researchers in the years ahead. Moreover, the imperative to "do no harm" (or at least minimize it) – whether understood as a consequence of cosmopolitan ethical imperatives or simply as prudent policy in pursuit of a more secure and prosperous international system – is a good place from which to launch this inquiry.

The Canadian government's technical solutions (notably the whole-of-government approach and CIDA's absorption into DFATD) could fit within the cosmopolitan ethical framework, but appear to lack a commitment to cosmopolitan values and the political will to carry through with the "do no harm" imperative. DFATD's sole policy paper to date, the *Global Markets Action Plan*, makes no mention of poverty reduction or a development perspective; its only reference to foreign aid expresses a desire to "leverage development programming to advance Canada's trade interests" (FATDC 2013, 14). To the extent that the plan promotes policy coherence, it is not for development, but rather to ensure that "all diplomatic assets of the Government of Canada will be marshalled on behalf of the private sector" (FATDC 2013, 11). Thus, while some authors (e.g., Chapnick) would argue that a more coherent policy process guided by "enlightened realist" thinking could yield significant advances for development policy, others argue that intra-governmental policy coherence may actually be "a bad thing" for development (Brown 2014).

Conclusion

We have entered a new era of fluidity and uncertainty in development cooperation and in Canadian development cooperation policies in particular. Yet many of the challenges that foreign aid has aspired to address – poverty, inequality, marginalization, and (in the critical theoretical tradition) the quest for greater human solidarity and emancipation – remain stubbornly entrenched or elusive. Similarly, while aid has clearly diminished in significance relative to other forms of exchange with the developing world (e.g., trade, investment, migration, remittances), it nevertheless remains an important component of the wider politics of global development, with a historical record of both beneficial and retrograde repercussions. In this fluid and contingent context, the chapters in this collection should be understood as stimulants to a more open, expansive, and constructive conversation about Canada's changing role in development cooperation and how it can be strengthened.

There is no easy solution to the problems that bedevil Canadian foreign aid or the challenges that lie ahead. This chapter's use of a "partnership" lens focuses on four specific dimensions of development cooperation that warrant further attention: the foundations of development partnerships, partnerships within the changing international aid regime, partnerships with key "stakeholders" in Canadian society, and intra-governmental partnerships. Only through solid empirical research, analysis, debate, and renewal in all four areas will it be possible to do justice to the challenge of rethinking not only Canadian aid, but also Canada's broader role in development cooperation.

References

Accra Agenda for Action. 2008. Adopted by the 3rd High-Level Forum on Aid Effectiveness, Accra, Ghana, September 2–4. Internet, http://siteresources.worldbank.org/ACCRAEXT/Resources/4700790 -1217425866038/AAA-4-SEPTEMBER-FINAL-16h00.pdf. Accessed December 13, 2013.

Baranyi, Stephen, and Anca Paducel. 2012. "Whither Development in CIDA's Approach toward Fragile States?" In Stephen Brown, ed. *Struggling for Effectiveness: CIDA and Canadian Foreign Aid*. Montreal and Kingston: McGill–Queen's University Press: 108–34.

Besada, Hany, and Philip Martin. 2013. "Mining Codes in Africa: Challenges and Canada's Position." In Rohinton Medhora and Yiagadeesen Samy, eds. *Canada Among Nations 2103: Canada-Africa Relations – Looking Back, Looking Ahead*. Waterloo, ON: Centre for International Governance Innovation: 153–67.

Bilal, San. 2012. "The Rise of South–South Relations: Development Partnerships Reconsidered." Brussels: European Centre for Development Policy Management.

Bishop, Matthew, and Michael Green. 2011. "Counterpoint: False Dichotomies." Blog entry. *Stanford Social Innovation Review*, December 15. Internet, http://www.ssireview.org/point_counterpoint/ philanthrocapitalism. Accessed December 13, 2013.

Black, David R., and Rebecca Tiessen. 2007. "The Canadian International Development Agency: New Policies, Old Problems." *Canadian Journal of Development Studies*, vol. 28, no. 2: 191–212.

Black, David, and Jean-Philippe Thérien with Andrew Clark. 1996. "Moving with the Crowd." *International Journal*, vol. 51, no. 2: 259–86.

Blackwood, Elizabeth, and Veronika Stewart. 2012. "CIDA and the Mining Sector: Extractive Industries as an Overseas Development Strategy." In Stephen Brown, ed. *Struggling for Effectiveness: CIDA and Canadian Foreign Aid*. Montreal and Kingston: McGill–Queen's University Press: 217–45.

Brinkerhoff, Jennifer. 2008. *Diasporas and Development: Exploring the Potential*. Boulder, CO: Lynne Rienner.

Brown, Stephen. 2012a. "Aid Effectiveness and the Framing of New Canadian Aid Initiatives." In Stephen Brown, ed. *Struggling for Effectiveness: CIDA and Canadian Foreign Aid*. Montreal and Kingston: McGill–Queen's University Press: 79–107.

Brown, Stephen. 2012b. "Introduction: Canadian Aid Enters the 21st Century." In Stephen Brown, ed. *Struggling for Effectiveness: CIDA and Canadian Foreign Aid*. Montreal and Kingston: McGill–Queen's University Press: 3–23.

Brown, Stephen. 2013. "Killing CIDA: The Wrong Solution to Real Problems." Blog entry, Centre for International Policy Studies, University of Ottawa, March 25. Internet, http://cips.uottawa.ca/killing-cida-the-wrong-solution-to-real-problems/. Accessed December 13, 2013.

Brown, Stephen. 2014. "When Policy Coherence is a Bad Thing." Blog entry, Centre for International Policy Studies, University of Ottawa, February 3. Internet, http://cips.uottawa.ca/when-policy-coherence-is-a-bad-thing. Accessed July 10, 2014.

Bülles, Anni-Claudine, and Shannon Kindornay. 2013. "Beyond Aid: A Plan for Canada's International Cooperation." Ottawa: North–South Institute.

Carment, David, Milana Nikolko, and Dacia Douhaibi. 2013. "Canadian Foreign Policy and Africa's Diaspora: Slippery Slope or Opportunity Unrealized?" In Rohinton Medhora and Yiagadeesen Samy, eds. *Canada Among Nations 2013: Canada-Africa Relations – Looking Back, Looking Ahead*. Waterloo, ON: Centre for International Governance Innovation: 61–78.

den Heyer, Molly. 2012. "Untangling Canadian Aid Policy: International Agreements, CIDA's Policies, and Micro-Policy Negotiations in

Tanzania." In Stephen Brown, ed. *Struggling for Effectiveness: CIDA and Canadian Foreign Aid.* Montreal and Kingston: McGill–Queen's University Press: 186–216.

Duggal, Sneh. 2014. "Budget 2012 Saw over 300 CIDA Positions Cut: Docs." *Embassy*, April 2.

FATDC. 2013. *Global Markets Action Plan.* Internet, http://international.gc.ca/global-markets-marches-mondiaux/assets/pdfs/plan-eng.pdf. Accessed July 10, 2014.

Felsen, David, and Hany Besada. 2013. "The Role of the Third Sector as Partners in the Development Aid System." In Hany Besada and Shannon Kindornay, eds. *Multilateral Development Cooperation in a Changing Global Order.* New York: Palgrave Macmillan: 138–57.

Foster, Ally. 2013. "'Unassuming New Foreign Affairs DM to Tackle Merger." *Embassy*, October 30.

Foster, Ally. 2014. "Foreign Affairs Ignores Former CIDA Hiring Pools: Internal Memo." *Embassy*, January 29.

Fowler, Alan. 1997. "Introduction: Beyond Partnership – Getting Real about NGO Relationships in the Aid System." *IDS Bulletin*, vol. 31, no. 3: 1–13.

Kharas, Homi. 2012. "The Global Partnership for Effective Development Cooperation." Washington: Brookings Institution.

Kindornay, Shannon. 2011. "From Aid to Development Effectiveness." Ottawa: North–South Institute. Internet, http://www.nsi-ins.ca/wp-content/uploads/2012/10/2011-From-aid-to-development-effectiveness.pdf. Accessed December 13, 2013.

Kindornay, Shannon, and Yiagadeesen Samy. 2012. "Establishing a Legitimate Development Co-operation Architecture in the Post-Busan Era." Ottawa: North–South Institute. Internet, http://www.nsi-ins.ca/wp-content/uploads/2012/10/2012-Establishing-a-Legitimate-Development-Co-operation-Architecture-in-the-Post-Busan-Era.pdf. Accessed December 13, 2013.

Kindornay, Shannon, and Fraser Reilly-King. 2013. *Investing in the Business of Development – Bilateral Donors' Approaches to Engaging the Private Sector.* Ottawa: Canadian Council for International Co-operation.

Lalonde, Jennifer. 2009. "Harmony and Discord: International Aid Harmonization and Donor State Influence: The Case of Canada and the Canadian International Development Agency." PhD diss., Johns Hopkins University, Baltimore.

Macdonald, Laura. 1995. "Unequal Partnerships: The Politics of Canada's Relations with the Third World." *Studies in Political Economy*, vol. 41: 111–41.

McLeod Group. 2013. "CIDA's Dead-end Merger." Blog entry, May 18. Internet, http://www.mcleodgroup.ca/2013/05/18/cidas-dead-end-merger/. Accessed December 13, 2013.

Morrison, David R. 1998. *Aid and Ebb Tide: A History of CIDA and Canadian Development Assistance.* Waterloo, ON: Wilfrid Laurier University Press.

OECD. 2005. "The Paris Declaration on Aid Effectiveness." Internet, http://www.oecd.org/dac/effectiveness/parisdeclarationandaccraagendaforaction.htm#Paris. Accessed November 30, 2013.

OECD. 2013. "Fourth High Level Forum on Aid Effectiveness." Internet, http://www.oecd.org/dac/effectiveness/fourthhighlevelforumonaideffectiveness.htm. Accessed November 30, 2013.

Pearson, Lester B. 1969. *Partners in Development: A Report of the Commission on International Development.* London: Pall Mall.

Plewes, Betty, and Brian Tomlinson. 2013. "Canadian CSOs and Africa: The End of an Era?" In Rohinton Medhora and Yiagadeesen Samy, eds. *Canada Among Nations 2013: Canada-Africa Relations — Looking Back, Looking Ahead.* Waterloo, ON: Centre for International Governance Innovation: 213–26.

Quadir, Fahimul. 2013. "Rising Donors and the New Narrative of 'South–South' Cooperation: What Prospects for Changing the Landscape of Development Assistance Programmes." *Third World Quarterly,* vol. 34, no. 2: 321–38.

Ramdas, Kavita, "Point: Philanthrocapitalism Is Not Social Change Philanthropy." Blog entry. *Stanford Social Innovation Review,* December 15. Internet, http://www.ssireview.org/point_counterpoint/philanthrocapitalism. Accessed December 13, 2013.

Salvet, Jean-Marc. 2013. "Jean-François Lisée veut une ACDI québécoise." *Le Soleil,* September 26. Internet, http://www.lapresse.ca/le-soleil/actualites/politique/201309/25/01-4693265-jean-francois-lisee-veut-une-acdi-quebecoise.php. Accessed December 13, 2013.

Schoeman, Maxi. 2011. "Of BRICS and Mortar: The Growing Relations between Africa and the Global South." *International Spectator,* vol. 46, no. 1: 33–51.

Smillie, Ian. 2012. "Tying up the Cow: CIDA, Advocacy, and Public Engagement." In Stephen Brown, ed. *Struggling for Effectiveness: CIDA and Canadian Foreign Aid.* Montreal and Kingston: McGill–Queen's University Press: 269–86.

Standing Committee on Foreign Affairs and International Development. 2012. *Driving Inclusive Economic Growth: The Role of the Private Sector in International Development.* Ottawa: House of Commons.

Swiss, Liam. 2012. "Gender, Security, and Instrumentalism: Canada's Foreign Aid in Support of National Interest?" In Stephen Brown, ed. *Struggling for Effectiveness: CIDA and Canadian Foreign Aid.* Montreal and Kingston: McGill–Queen's University Press: 135–58.

Swiss, Liam. 2013. "A Forced Marriage: DFAIT and CIDA for Better or for W=orse." Blog entry. *Ottawa Citizen,* October 31. Internet, http://blogs.

ottawacitizen.com/2013/10/31/a-forced-marriage-dfait-and-cida-for-better-or-for-worse/. Accessed December 13, 2013.

United Nations. 2013. "Millennium Development Goals and Beyond 2015." Internet, http://www.un.org/millenniumgoals/. Accessed November 30, 2013.

Contributors

François Audet is Professor at the School of Management, Université du Québec à Montréal, and the Scientific Director of the Canadian Research Institute on Humanitarian Crisis and Aid (OCCAH). He holds a PhD in Public Administration at ÉNAP for his research on local capacity building and decision-making processes of humanitarian organizations. He has been a visiting scholar at Harvard University's Program on Humanitarian Policy and Conflict Research. He also has over fifteen years' experience in humanitarian action. He was previously Head of the Regional Delegation of East Africa and the Indian Ocean for the Canadian Red Cross, and also served as Program Director for CARE Canada. He worked for several years in Latin America and Southeast Asia on behalf of the Canadian Centre for International Study and Cooperation, where he served as chief of humanitarian aid projects in Honduras and Vietnam.

Stephen Baranyi is Associate Professor at the School of International Development and Global Studies at the University of Ottawa. He currently works at the nexus of development and security, on the challenges of reforming state security agencies, development cooperation, and gender equality in fragile states, particularly in Haiti. Prior to joining the University of Ottawa in 2008, he worked as a principal researcher at the North–South Institute, a grant manager at the International Development Research Centre, a policy adviser to Canadian government agencies, and a human rights advocate for various NGOs in Europe. He has lived in Central America, the Caribbean, and Europe, and has conducted field missions to numerous countries in Africa, the Americas, and Asia. He has published widely on issues of peacekeeping, peacebuilding, security sector reform, and gender in fragile and conflict-affected states, as well as on Canadian policy in these areas.

David R. Black is the Lester B. Pearson Professor of International Development Studies and Professor of Political Science at Dalhousie University in Halifax. His research has focused on Canada's role in Sub-Saharan Africa, with an emphasis on development assistance, human security, multilateral diplomacy, and extractive industry investment; post-apartheid South Africa in Africa; and sport in world politics and development. He is the author or editor of numerous articles, chapters, and collections on these subjects.

Stephen Brown is Professor of Political Science at the University of Ottawa. He is the author of numerous publications on foreign aid, and editor of *Struggling for Effectiveness: CIDA and Canadian Foreign Aid* (2012). He has published widely on democratization and political violence in Sub-Saharan Africa, and is currently working on issues relating to aid effectiveness and policy coherence.

John D. Cameron is Associate Professor and Chair of the Department of International Development Studies at Dalhousie University. His current research, funded by SSHRC and IDRC, analyzes processes of indigenous self-governance in Bolivia, as well as global citizenship and representations of poverty and development by international humanitarian agencies.

David Carment is Professor of International Affairs at Carleton University and has over eighteen years' experience in policy relevant research on fragile states, conflict prevention, mainstreaming risk analysis, and aid allocation. He led a CIDA-funded initiative on mainstreaming research on failed and fragile states into policy making over the 2005–08 period. He also served on the OECD/DAC's working group on fragile states. He has developed risk analysis training workshops for NGOs in Africa, Asia, and Europe. He is the editor of *Canadian Foreign Policy Journal*.

Adam Chapnick is the Deputy Director of Education at the Canadian Forces College, and an Associate Professor of Defence Studies at the Royal Military College of Canada. He is the author or editor of five books and over thirty refereed articles and book chapters on Canada's international policy.

Christina Clark-Kazak is Associate Professor at York University's bilingual Glendon College. Her research interests include age main-streaming, political participation of young people, methodology in interdisciplinary contexts, and international development policy and programming, particularly in contexts of conflict and migration. She teaches undergraduate, graduate, and professional development courses related to research methodology, migration, international development, peace and security, child rights, and gender. Since 1999, she has also worked as a development practitioner and consultant for the Canadian government, non-governmental organizations, and the United Nations. Christina is currently serving as editor-in-chief of *Refuge: Canada's Journal on Refugees*.

Molly den Heyer is Senior Program Analyst with the Coady International Institute at St. Francis Xavier University, and Research Fellow with the Centre for Foreign Policy Studies at Dalhousie University. Her areas of expertise include critical approaches to aid administration, planning, monitoring and evaluation, aid policy, research methods, participation, and development theory. Molly holds a PhD in Interdisciplinary Studies from Dalhousie University and an MSc in Rural Planning and Development from the University of Guelph.

Gabriel C. Goyette is coordinator of the Centre d'études de l'Asie de l'Est and a PhD student at the Université de Montréal. He specializes in public policy analysis in the field of development assistance, and particularly on linkages between international norms and national practices, as well as the role of the private sector in Canadian aid. He is an international correspondent for the French journal *Techniques financières et développement* and acts as a trainer and consultant for many Canadian NGOs and associations. He is the author of the article "Les transformations de l'aide canadienne: Quelle efficacité pour quel développement?" (2011).

Themrise Khan has almost twenty years of experience in South Asia as a research, evaluation, and communication professional, working with a range of bilateral and multilateral agencies and non-profits. Originally from Pakistan, Themrise has worked across sectors ranging from gender and marginalized groups to aid effectiveness, local governance, and civil society initiatives. She has worked closely as a consultant with major donors such as CIDA, DFID, various UN agencies, and the World Bank. She is currently based in Ottawa as an independent researcher and policy analyst. Themrise has a bachelor's degree in Environmental Studies from York University and an MSc in Development Management from the London School of Economics as a British Council Chevening Scholar.

Laura Macdonald is Professor in the Department of Political Science, and the Director of the Institute of Political Economy at Carleton University. She has published books and articles on North American relations, civil society, development and democratization, Canadian foreign policy toward Latin America, and Mexican social policy.

Justin Massie is Professor of Political Science at the Université du Québec à Montréal, and Research Fellow at the Centre interuniversitaire de recherche sur les relations internationales du Canada et du Québec (ÉNAP). His current research focuses on Canada's strategic cultures and transatlantic burden-sharing in contemporary peace operations. He is the author of numerous papers on Canadian foreign and defence policy, including his latest book, *Francosphère: L'importance de la France dans la culture stratégique du Canada* (Montreal: Presses de l'Université du Québec, 2013).

Olga Navarro-Flores has a bachelor's degree in Economics and Administration and a master's degree in International Cooperation from the Université de Sherbrooke, as well as a PhD in administration from the Université du Québec à Montreal. Her dissertation, titled "Les relations de partenariat Nord-Sud : Du paradoxe au compromis. Une étude institutionnaliste des relations entre ONG dans le secteur de la coopération internationale," was published by the Presses de l'Université du Québec in 2009. She received the prestigious Best Thesis Award from the Institut de recherche en économie contemporaine in 2007. Before undertaking her doctoral studies, Ms. Navarro-Flores worked for more than ten years as a consultant in management and development for cooperatives, community development groups, and NGOs. She also worked as a consultant in development project and program evaluation, including policy design and development for both funding and implementing agencies. She has worked in a diversity of contexts such as Latin America, Africa, and Asia, as well as across Canada. Ms. Navarro-Flores is particularly interested in development NGOs and their relationships with the private sector, government, and other NGOs from institutional and organizational perspectives. She is also interested in project management and evaluation, gender and development issues, and inter-sector partnerships and their intrinsic power relations.

Stéphane Roussel is Professor of Political Science at the École nationale d'administration publique (ÉNAP). From 2002 to 2012, he was Professor at the Université du Québec à Montréal (UQÀM), where he held the Canada Research Chair in Canadian Foreign and Defence Policy. His research interests relate to Canadian foreign and defence policy, with particular emphasis on relations with the United States and European countries. He currently directs three research programs: "Competing Views of Emerging Challenges in the Arctic," "The (Neo)Continentalist Approach in Canadian Foreign Policy," and "Quebec's Public Opinion Attitude toward International Security."

Arne Ruckert is Research Associate at the University of Ottawa's Institute of Population Health, researching health equity in the Globalization and Health Equity research unit. His principal areas of research include the international financial institutions, the international aid architecture, the financial crisis and health equity, and global health governance and diplomacy. He is co-author of *Globalization and the Health of Indigenous Peoples* (Routledge, 2015) and co-editor of *Post-Neoliberalism in the Americas* (Palgrave, 2009), and has published widely in academic journals in the area of global development and health.

Yiagadeesen (Teddy) Samy is Associate Professor at the Norman Paterson School of International Affairs, Carleton University. He is also a Distinguished Research Associate with the North–South Institute in Ottawa. Samy holds a PhD in Economics and his fields of specialization are international trade and development economics. His current research focuses on aid and state fragility, aid and taxation, and income inequality. He recently co-edited (with Rohinton Medhora) the 2013 issue of the *Canada among Nations* series, which was on Canada–Africa Relations.

Dominic H. Silvio is a doctoral candidate in the Interdisciplinary PhD program at Dalhousie University. His area of research is focused on the relationship between public opinion and foreign aid policy in Canada. Dominic is also a Reference and Instruction Librarian and the subject specialist for political science, international development studies, black Canadian studies, sociology and social anthropology, gender and women's studies, and sustainability, based in Dalhousie's Killam Library.

Ian Smillie has delivered telephone books in Montreal, carried bags at the Banff Springs Hotel, and taught high school students in West Africa and university students at Tulane University in New Orleans. He has lived in Sierra Leone, Nigeria, Bangladesh, and Britain. He co-founded Inter Pares and was Executive Director of CUSO. Since 1983, he has worked widely as a development consultant and writer. He has written nine books, edited five, and has produced chapters for twenty-seven more. He is a leader in the campaign to end "blood diamonds," helping to create the 80-government Kimberley Process Certification Scheme for rough diamonds. He chairs the Board of the Diamond Development Initiative and is a founder-member of the McLeod Group. His latest book, *Diamonds*, was published in 2014. Smillie was inducted into the Order of Canada in 2003.

Liam Swiss is Assistant Professor of Sociology at Memorial University. His research examines foreign aid, international development, globalization, and gender and has appeared in journals such as *American Sociological Review, International Sociology,* and *Social Forces.* His current research project examines the global foreign aid network and aid's role in the diffusion of global norms and policy models. He is a past President of the Canadian Association for the Study of International Development (CASID) and worked previously at the Canadian International Development Agency on Canada's aid program to Pakistan.

Rebecca Tiessen is Associate Professor at the School of International Development and Global Studies, University of Ottawa. Her research focuses on Canada and Canadians in the world, with a specific emphasis on gender equality, youth abroad, and development assistance. Her research includes a study on the impact of Canadians volunteering in international development, as well as research with civil society actors and non-governmental organizations in the global South to understand the perceptions of contributions made by Canadians and Canadian aid "on the ground."

Index

tension with national interest, 20,
    35–36, 103, 127, 288
Americas
    Canadian aid to, 111–112, 125,
        128–131, 138, 139n2, *182*, 265
    free trade with, 129–130, 136, 263, 265
Americas Strategy, 125, 129, 137
Andean Regional Initiative for
    Promoting Effective Corporate
    Social Responsibility, 133, 261, 266,
    289n2
Asia: Canadian aid to, 129, 130, *131*,
    139n2, 146
Australia
    aid allocation network, *108*
    as aid donor, 86, 95n3
    aid focus on results, 83
    children in development policy, 211
Austria: aid allocation network, *108*
Axworthy, Lloyd, 152

Baird, John, *183*, 184, 252
Bangladesh
    aid effectiveness, 247–248, 251
    Canadian aid projections, 252–253
    Canadian aid to, 245–246, *246*
    conflict sensitivity and aid, 248,
        249–250, 251, 252
    and fragility-stability spectrum, 242,
        243, 254
    trade and aid, 250–251, *250*
banking in developing countries, 136
Barrick Gold (company), 131, 132, 279,
    286
Belgium: aid allocation network, *108*
Benin: Canadian aid to, 253, 272n3
Bill and Melinda Gates Foundation, 298
Bolivia
    Canadian aid to, 128, 139n2
    Canadian mining interests, 133,
        289n2
Boosting Economic Growth (SCFAID),
    266
Bosnia: Canadian military
    participation, 152
Brazil

as aid provider, 2, 298, 304
as emerging economy, 79
Breakwater Resources (company), 136
BRICs (Brazil, Russia, India, China), 79
Britain *see* United Kingdom
Brown, Susan, 233
Building the Canadian Advantage
    (DFTAD), 260–261, 281
bureaucrats *see* political class
Burkina Faso
    Canadian aid to, 253
    Canadian mining interests, 261, 265,
        266, 278–281
Burma *see* Myanmar
Busan High Level Forum, 268, 298

Canada *see also* economy, Canadian
    aid focus on results, 88–90
    comparisons with other donors,
        101–102
    foreign policies in relation to aid
        policies, 3
    as international do-gooder in
        saviour–victim narratives, 76–77
    as peacekeeper, 147, 148
    recognizes Lobo as Honduran
        president, 137
    risk avoidance, 90–91
    role in aid effectiveness framework,
        70–71
    role in world, 2–3
    tied aid, 87, *269*
Canada Committed to Protecting and
    Promoting Religious Freedom, *183*
Canada Corps, 232
Canada Making a Difference in the World
    (CIDA), 70
Canadian aid *see also* aid debate; aid
    policies
    allocation patterns, 102–103, *104*, *105*,
        106, 107, *108–109*, 110–111
    as complement to military action,
        150–155
    complexity of motivations, 134–136
    criteria, 111–113, *114*
    criteria compared with other
        countries, 113, *114*, 115–116

Studies in International Development and Globalization

Edited by Charmain Levy

The *Studies in International Development and Globalization* collection presents new perspectives on a range of topics in development and globalization studies—including indigenous peoples, women, social movements, labour issues, agriculture, governance, and migration—revealing the tensions and conflicts that occur in the wake of development and highlighting the quest for social justice in global contexts.

Previous titles in this collection

Pierre Beaudet et Paul A Haslam (dir.), *Enjeux et défis du développement international*, 2014.

Andrea Martinez, Pierre Beaudet et Stephen Baranyi (dir.), *Haïti aujourd'hui, Haïti demain. Regards croisés*, 2011.

Daniel C. Bach et Mamoudou Gazibo (dir.), *L'État néopatrimonial. Genèse et trajectoires contemporaines*, 2011.

Jacques Fisette et Marc Raffinot (dir.), *Gouvernance et appropriation locale du développement. Au-delà des modèles importés*, 2010.

Pierre Beaudet, Jessica Schafer et Paul Haslam (dir.), *Introduction au développement international. Approches, acteurs et enjeux*, 2008.

Isabelle Beaulieu, *L'État rentier. Le cas de la Malaysia*, 2008.

Saturnino M. Borras, *Pro-Poor Land Reform. A Critique*, 2007.